WHY HITLER CAME
INTO POWER

WHY HITLER CAME INTO POWER

THEODORE ABEL

HARVARD UNIVERSITY PRESS
CAMBRIDGE, MASSACHUSETTS,
AND LONDON, ENGLAND

Copyright © 1938 by Prentice-Hall, Inc.
Copyright renewed © 1966 by Theodore Abel
Foreword copyright © 1986 by the President and Fellows of
Harvard College
All rights reserved
Printed in the United States of America
10 9 8 7 6 5

This Harvard University Press paperback is published
by arrangement with Prentice-Hall, Inc.

LIBRARY OF CONGRESS CATALOGING-IN-
PUBLICATION DATA

Abel, Theodore Fred, 1896–
    Why Hitler came into power.

    Reprint. Originally published: New York:
Prentice-Hall, 1938. With new foreword.
    Includes index.
    1. Hitler, Adolf, 1889–1945.
    2. Nationalsozialistische Deutsche Arbeiter-Partei—
History. 3. National socialists—Biography. 4. Germany—
Politics and government—1933–1945.
    I. Title.
DD247.H5A75 1986   943.086   86-11998
ISBN 0-674-95200-6 (pbk.)

TO

Elsie Cleveland Mead

AND

Robert Gillespie Mead

Acknowledgments

I GRATEFULLY ACKNOWLEDGE the financial assistance received from the Columbia Council of the Social Sciences, which covered the expenses connected with the preparation of the manuscript.

For their generous help, I am greatly indebted to–

Dr. Schulze-Wechsungen, of Berlin, for support in the organization of the prize contest.

Dr. Richard Sallet, formerly of the German Embassy in Washington, who was instrumental in securing the manuscripts of the autobiographies.

Miss Barbara Tolnai for invaluable assistance in the preparation of the study.

Professor R. M. MacIver of Columbia University, Professor Willard Waller of Barnard College, Dr. Sallet, and Miss Lucine Rousseau for their constructive comments on the manuscript.

Columbia University   T. A.

Contents

APPENDICES

Foreword, 1986

I N EARLY 1934, just over a year after Hitler's assumption of power in Germany, Theodore Abel, a sociologist from Columbia University, managed to convince the authorities of the new Nazi state that Americans—indeed, the world—knew far too little about the National Socialist movement, and especially about its followers. Who were the millions who between 1928 and 1933 had transformed the NSDAP (Nationalist Socialist German Workers' Party) from an obscure peripheral party into the largest and most popular political movement in Germany? What had motivated and influenced them? What had attracted them to National Socialism? These were important questions and they might be most informatively answered, Abel suggested, if the rank-and-file supporters of the party could explain matters in their own words. Abel, therefore, proposed an essay contest for "the best personal life history of an adherent of the Hitler movement." All participants in the contest had to have been members or adherents of the NSDAP *before* the Nazi seizure of power in January 1933, and cash prizes were promised for "the most detailed and trustworthy accounts." The contest rules also specified that respondents provide accurate and detailed descriptions of their "family life, education, economic conditions, membership in associations, participation in the Hitler movement, and important experiences, thoughts, and feelings about events and ideas in the post-war world." It was a project of considerable scholarly imagination and initiative, and miraculously the Nazi authorities gave their consent. Indeed, the Reich Ministry of Propaganda, the party press, and the local branches of the NSDAP all actively publicized the contest. Announced in June 1934, the project ultimately yielded approximately seven hundred autobiographical essays that ranged in length from a single handwritten sheet to eighty typed pages. Because political survey research did not exist during the Weimar era, and public opinion polling was out of the question in Nazi Germany, these essays—despite obvious biases—were of great potential value for any analysis of National Socialist support. It was on the basis of this extraordinary collection that Abel wrote *Why Hitler Came into Power.*

For a variety of reasons Abel's book did not appear until 1938, and the critical reception to it was decidedly mixed. Although virtually every reviewer praised the project's originality of approach and the author's objectivity in dealing with such highly controversial material, most questioned the reliability of the respondents—Nazis, after all—and lamented the book's methodological shortcomings, especially Abel's failure to make a more systematic content analysis of the essays and to link political attitudes with social-psychological characteristics.[1] Perhaps equally important, by 1938 the world

----

[1] See, for example, Harold D. Lasswell's highly critical review which praises the "ingenious idea" behind Abel's project but legitimately questions his failure to use cross tabulations or other statistical procedures to determine relationships between expressed attitudes and social characteristics among his respondents; in *American Journal of Sociology,* 44 (1939): 1003–1004. A. J. Zurcher acknowledges the book's originality but raises doubts about the nature of the sample; *American Political Science Review,* 33 (1939): 509–510.

was less concerned with understanding the appeal of National Socialism before 1933 than in coping with an ominously powerful and increasingly aggressive Third Reich. As a result, Abel's book virtually slipped from view. Rarely cited in contemporary studies, it was surprisingly ignored in the massive postwar literature devoted to the very questions of political sociology raised in his research.

Although methodological reservations about the nature of Abel's "sample" may have contributed to the book's meagre influence, his interpretation was also out of step with the prevailing wisdom. Abel's material simply did not fit neatly into the dominant interpretation of National Socialism as a "revolt of the lower middle class." According to that traditional view, the NSDAP was essentially a lower-middle-class movement supported by elements of the undereducated, economically marginal *Kleinbürgertum* (petty bourgeoisie) desperately afraid of proletarianization during a period of acute economic distress and social dislocation. The appeal of National Socialism was, to use Harold Lasswell's classic formulation, "the psychological reaction of this lower middle class" to the political traumas of the postwar era and the loss of its economic position and social status.[2]

The essays of the Abel collection certainly provide ample evidence of such petit-bourgeois discontent—indeed, the book contains some of the most powerful expressions of that mood to be found anywhere in the published literature. Yet in examining the essays, Abel was struck by the wide *variety* of motivational factors at work among the respondents, many of which could not be easily subsumed under the interpretive rubric of "lower-middle-class revolt." Although Abel classified the majority of the respondents as lower middle class,

---

[2] See Lasswell's article "The Psychology of Hitlerism," *Political Quarterly,* 4 (1933): 373–384 and Svend Ranulf, *Moral Indignation and Middle Class Psychology: A Sociological Study* (Copenhagen, 1938).

the presence of individuals from different social backgrounds in the collection—workers, civil servants, and even a smattering of professionals—also seemed to suggest that the NSDAP had found some resonance beyond the confines of the *Kleinbürgertum*. Keenly aware of the limitations of his data, Abel correctly refrained from generalizing about the social composition of the NSDAP on the basis of his sample alone. He had, however, seen enough to convince him that the almost exclusive emphasis on the lower middle class and its putative psychological makeup was simply *inadequate* to explain the social dynamics of National Socialist mobilization. Abel therefore explicitly attacked the prevailing "psychological interpretation" of the lower middle class and noted instead the diversity of the NSDAP's social appeal (see Chapter 8).

If that view left Abel's contemporaries and a subsequent generation of scholars unsatisfied, it has struck a very responsive chord in the research of the past decade on the social composition of the Nazi membership and electoral constituency. Indeed, in some ways Abel's book may be viewed as a forerunner of the current wave of revisionist scholarship that has recently mounted a serious challenge to the deeply entrenched lower-middle-class interpretation. Significantly, that revisionist assault began in 1975 with the publication of Peter H. Merkl's *Political Violence Under the Swastika,* a lengthy attempt to subject the Abel essays on file at the Library of the Hoover Institution at Stanford University to precisely the sort of rigorous statistical analysis originally demanded by Abel's contemporary critics. In his analysis Merkl quantified the Abel materials and greatly clarified, elaborated, and extended the implications of Abel's own rather tentative findings. In the process he raised new doubts about the adequacy of the lower-middle-class interpretation by concluding that the motive forces behind a commitment to National Socialism were hardly confined to *kleinbürgerlich* status anxiety but were "highly differentiated," and in fact seemed to possess "few common denominators."[3] Merkl's book was soon followed by a steady stream of dissertations, journal articles, and, in the early eighties, books that employed a variety of advanced statistical methods to determine the social composition of the Nazi electorate and membership. These studies have allowed us to identify the social bases of the Nazi following with far greater precision than was ever before possible. Although thematic emphasis and methods differ, these works are in fundamental agreement that support for the NSDAP extended far beyond the lower middle class to elements of the socially established *Grossbürgertum* (upper middle class) as well as to sizable segments of the blue-collar working class. At the height of its electoral popularity in 1932, the NSDAP had managed to transcend the basic cleavages of German political culture, mobilizing a mass following that was without precedent in its extraordinary social diversity. Despite some methodological and substantive differences, a new consensus has emerged in the literature of the past decade that sees the NSDAP less as a distinctly lower-middle-class phenomenon than as a remarkably successful catchall party of protest.[4]

---

[3] Peter H. Merkl, *Political Violence Under the Swastika: 581 Early Nazis* (Princeton, 1975).

[4] The socially diverse composition of the Nazi membership is treated exhaustively in the works of Michael H. Kater, especially "Sozialer Wandel in der NSDAP im Zuge der nationalsozialistischen Machtergreifung," in Wolfgang Schieder, ed., *Faschismus als soziale Bewegung* (Hamburg, 1976), pp. 25–67; and in Kater's *The Nazi Party: A Social Profile of Members and Leaders, 1919–1945* (Cambridge, Mass., 1983). The NSDAP's socially heterogeneous electoral constituency is examined in Thomas Childers, "The Social Bases of the National Socialist Vote," *Journal of Contemporary History*, 11 (1976): 17–42; and his *The Nazi Voter: The Social Foundations of Fascism in Germany, 1919–1933* (Chapel Hill, 1983). See also Richard F. Hamilton, *Who Voted For Hitler?* (Princeton, 1982), who insists, rather unconvincingly, that the lower-middle-class emphasis is not simply inadequate but utterly misplaced. See in addition Jürgen W. Falter, "Die Wähler der NSDAP 1928–1933," in Wolfgang Michalka, ed., *Die nationalsozialistische Machtergreifung* (Paderborn, 1984), pp. 47–59.

Yet if great strides have been made in isolating the social sources of Nazi support, none of this recent research has been able to break significant new ground in ascertaining the important motivational factors behind a vote for or membership in the party. We therefore know a great deal more about who supported the NSDAP than why. What attracted members of the upper middle class to the party? Why did many workers turn to the NSDAP? What had drawn them? What role did the NSDAP's ideological positions play in its popular appeal? How important were Nazi propaganda tactics and organization? These are obviously important questions for any study seeking to explain the sociopolitical dynamics of Nazi success, and it is precisely this set of central issues that Theodore Abel's work addresses.

Without survey data it is of course impossible to answer these questions with certainty, but the best material for approaching them remains the hundreds of autobiographical essays that constitute the heart of Abel's book. Though hardly representing a valid statistical sample and containing obvious biases that must be kept in mind, these essays offer the single most valuable source we have (or ever will have) for evaluating individual grassroots opinion within the National Socialist movement.[5] Moreover, the skepticism of Abel's original reviewers about the reliability of the respondents' essays is not, I think, really justified. Objections that the party may have censored the materials or that contest respondents may

---

[5] The NSDAP Hauptarchiv also contains several hundred "*Kampfberichte*," reports written by Nazi activists on their struggles during the period before 1933, which are also of considerable interest. These reports were collected by the *Gauleitung* (regional Nazi leadership) of Hessen-Nassau in 1936–37 and range from one to fifty pages in length. Although some provide important recollections about the NSDAP's activities at the grassroots before the Nazi *Machtergreifung* (seizure of power), they are far less informative about social backgrounds and attitudes than the Abel essays. See the Hoover Institution's Hauptarchiv microfilm collection, reel 27, folders 528–531.

have tailored their essays to impress an American audience or higher Nazi authorities certainly seem plausible. Yet the scholars—including myself—who have analyzed the Abel materials at the Hoover Library in recent years have all been struck by the unexpected frankness and unintentionally revealing content of the *vitae*. If the party censored the essays, it did a very poor job. Indeed, the portraits of the individual Nazis that emerge from them are by no means flattering, though that can hardly have been their original intent. In addition, it is quite easy to spot the ambitious essayist striving to impress his readers, and Abel has avoided the pitfalls of citing these in his book.[6]

The reader who looks beyond the admittedly limited statistical significance of the "sample" to the insights into individual motivations to be gained from the essays discovers the true value of Abel's highly original project. It is one of the book's great virtues that its author was sensitive to the surprisingly broad range of motivational factors involved in the appeal of National Socialism, and that he chose to illustrate that multiplicity of motive forces by allowing the respondents to speak for themselves. Thus throughout the book one hears at first hand the expressions of wounded national pride, fear of social decline, frustrated career ambitions, hatred of the Marxist left, fear of big business, belief in the *Volksgemein-schaft* (people's community), and faith in the Führer, among other factors, presented in the words of individual converts to National Socialism. I know of no more powerful or revealing grassroots testimony in the vast literature on the NSDAP. Equally important in light of recent research, one hears the views not only of the predictable petit-bourgeois bank clerks

---

[6] In addition to Merkl's use of the Abel files in his *Political Violence under the Swastika,* the essays have been analyzed by, among others, Claudia Koonz, "Nazi Women before 1933: Rebels against Emancipation," *Social Science Quarterly,* (1976): 553–563; and Childers, *The Nazi Voter.*

and shopkeepers but of workers, farmers, and professionals. Although other scholars have used Abel's materials profitably, none have surpassed the compelling presentation in his original book. When viewed in conjunction with the recent literature on the social bases of Nazism, his work constitutes a primary source of great significance. As such, Theodore Abel's *Why Hitler Came into Power* makes a major contribution to the ongoing effort to understand the complex sociopolitical dynamics of National Socialism's remarkable popular appeal. Almost fifty years after its original publication, the book deserves our attention. It is chilling but essential reading.

WHY HITLER CAME
INTO POWER

Chapter I

Introduction

WITH THE STAGE SET by recent events for German domination in central Europe, the consequences of Hitler's
ascent to power have ceased to be a matter of conjecture. After
1933 the question which agitated people most was, "What will
happen now that Hitler is in power?" Today, anyone who
has studied the record of the last five years can answer this
question with reasonable assurance.

However, the clearer the meaning of Hitler's control over
Germany becomes, the more one is inclined to turn back the
pages of history and ask why Hitler came into power in the
first place. The spectacular rise of the movement lead by
him remains a puzzle. Existing explanations are often mere
guesses, or are based upon preconceived theories.

Many of the shortcomings of current interpretations of the
Hitler movement may be attributed to the inaccessibility of
relevant material.[1] Published documents, newspaper files, and

[1] Among the more outstanding contributions in the English language
are: Heiden, K., *The History of National Socialism.* London: Methuen,
1934; Hoover, C. B., *Germany Enters the Third Reich.* New York:
MacMillan, 1933; Schumann, F. L., *The Nazi Dictatorship.* New York:
A. A. Knopf, 1935; Shuster, G. N., *Strong Man Rules.* New York: D.

impressions derived from interviews and personal observation rarely suffice as the fountainhead of valid conclusions. Consequently I have sought to improve upon the understanding of the Hitler movement by contributing new evidence for its analysis.

In studying the immigration problem, the effect of the depression on the family, the causes of crime, and so forth, sociologists—particularly the pioneer in the field, Florian Znaniecki—have obtained valuable material from life histories. In connection with the Nazi movement too, there are questions to which autobiographical data alone hold the proper answer. I have, therefore, assembled the autobiographies of six hundred followers of Adolf Hitler and have used them as the source material of my own interpretation.

Who were the people who joined the Hitler movement? What past experiences or factors in their backgrounds account for their membership? On what basis did they justify their participation? Just how was the movement promoted? What difficulties did it encounter? What were the activities of individual members? What popular reactions might serve as clues to the causes of the movement? On all these questions the life histories shed considerable light. Furthermore it is my hope that the direct testimony of eye witnesses and participants may make the Nazi movement more real and vivid to the reader.

During a visit to Germany in the summer of 1933, I was struck by the willingness of most people I encountered to discuss their political experiences. Determined to exploit this source of information, I announced a prize contest designed to induce Hitler's followers to submit their autobiographies. The announcement of the terms of the contest, launched early in June 1934, was as follows:

Appleton-Century, 1934; Roberts, S. H., *The House That Hitler Built.* New York: Harper's, 1938. See also Clark, R. T., *The Fall of the German Republic.* London: Allen & Unwin, 1935. Florinsky, M., *Fascism and National Socialism.* New York: MacMillan, 1936.

400 MARKS IN PRIZES

For the Best Personal Life History of an Adherent of the Hitler Movement

Any person, regardless of sex or age, who was a member of the National Socialist party before January 1, 1933, or who was in sympathy with the movement, may participate in this contest.

Contestants are to give accurate and detailed descriptions of their personal lives, particularly after the World War. Special attention should be given to accounts of family life, education, economic conditions, membership in associations, participation in the Hitler movement, and important experiences, thoughts, and feelings about events and ideas of the post-war period.

The prizes will be awarded to authors who have submitted the most detailed and trustworthy accounts. Style, spelling, or dramatic story value will not be considered. Completeness and frankness are the sole criteria, so that even the simplest and most undramatic story will receive full consideration.

The prizes will be awarded as follows:

First Prize .... 125 marks
Second Prize .... 50 marks
Third Prize .... 25 marks
Five Prizes .... 20 marks each
Ten Prizes .... 10 marks each

The prize money is deposited in the German Bank. The contest is organized under the tutelage of the sociology department of Columbia University, whose members will be the final judges. The purpose of the contest is the collection of material on the history of National Socialism, so that the American public may be informed about it on the basis of factual, personal documents.

The contestants whose contributions are published in part or in full will receive an additional honorarium of two marks per printed page. Manuscripts will not be returned, and must be submitted on or before September 1934.

This announcement was distributed in the form of a bulletin at all local headquarters of the National Socialist party and was also published in the party press.

Unable to obtain financial assistance, I was forced to provide from my own meager resources the funds to cover the expenses of the project. As a result, the number of essays submitted was smaller than it might have been under more favorable circumstances. Nevertheless, 683 manuscripts were contributed, a result as unexpected as it was gratifying. The wealth and variety of material contained in these life histories fully justified the undertaking.

The autobiographies were submitted in the fall of 1934. Owing to unforeseen circumstances beyond my control, the shipment of the manuscripts to the United States was delayed for over two years. Hence, also, the two-year delay in the publication of this study.

1. *Who Wrote the Life Histories?*

An analysis of the age, occupation, and class affiliation of our contributors, as well as the year they joined the National Socialist party, is summarized in the following tables.[2]

TABLE I. AGE DISTRIBUTION [3]

Age group	Age in 1934	Number	Per cent
1. Post war generation	20–26	75	12
2. War generation	27–33	165	28
3. War volunteers	34–40	138	23
4. War conscripts	41–59	197	33
5. Old generation	60 and over	25	4
		600	100

[2] Among the manuscripts submitted were forty-eight written by women. Because of their relatively small number, these biographies were not considered in the current study. An analysis of the women's contributions will be published in a separate article. Similarly excluded from consideration were a score of biographies one or two pages in length which contained very little information. Thus six hundred life histories remained as the basis of this study.

[3] The World War being the most important background factor of the Hitler movement, the war period was chosen as the basis for the differentiation of age groups.

TABLE II. OCCUPATION

Occupational group	Number	Per cent
Industry, mining	171	29
Government service	96	16
Clerical occupation	85	14
Agriculture	59	10
Trade	51	8
Professional	50	8
Personal service	46	8
Not reported	42	7
Total	600	100

TABLE III. CLASS AFFILIATION[4]

Class group	Number	Per cent
Workers, skilled and unskilled	209	35
Lower Middle Class	304	51
Upper Middle class and aristocracy	45	7
Peasants	42	7
Total	600	100

TABLE IV. DATE OF JOINING THE N. S. PARTY[5]

Year	Number	Per cent
Not reported	18	3
1920-24	42	7
1925-27	124	21
1928-29	127	21
1930-31	223	37
1932-33	66	11
Total	600	100

In addition to this data the autobiographies contain data on education, employment, membership in various associations, place of residence, marital status, wartime service, participation in military activities after the war, first contacts with the movement, the main reason for joining it, expressions of anti-Semitism, and so forth. (For details on these points, see Appendix II.)

[4] Income, occupation, status of the family, and occupation of the father were used as data for assigning an individual to a particular class.

[5] The full name is National Socialist German Workers' Party. Its abbreviation in German is N. S. D. A. P.

By taking the modal values of these data, we arrive at the following fictitious average type of follower of the Hitler movement: He is male, in his early thirties, a town resident of lower middle-class origin, without high school education; married and Protestant; participated in the World War, but not in the military activities during the revolution of 1918 or later outbreaks; had no political affiliations before joining the National Socialist party and belonged to no veteran or semi-military organizations. He joined the party between 1930 and 1931, and had his first contacts with the movement through reading about it and attending a meeting. He was strongly dissatisfied with the republican regime in Germany, but had no specific anti-Semitic bias. His economic status was secure, for not once did he have to change his occupation, job, or residence, nor was he ever unemployed.

Obviously, extracts from statistical tables cannot give a complete or a satisfactory picture of our contributors. I hope, however, that a reading of the quotations in the following pages and a perusal of the biographies reproduced in full in Part III, will remedy this defficiency.

2. *General Comments*

In view of the controversial subject matter of this study, several questions must be considered before we proceed with the results of our investigation. The first point at issue is the documentary value of the autobiographies. Is the information they contain reliable, and is there any serious omission of relevant data? Secondly, there is the question of objectivity. Does the study as such imply any judgment on the part of the author?

A widespread doubt of the trustworthiness of a people held in check by a dictatorship was, in fact, one reason why I was unable to obtain financial assistance on this project. A disbelief of the possibility of getting anything in writing from anybody, together with the assumption that the effort to do so might jeopardize my liberty, were among the objections advanced against it. The last two arguments are shown by the record to have been groundless; the first, however, may still be valid.

I am aware of the grounds upon which the reliability of this source material might be questioned. Chief among them is the argument that the contributors have written their stories with an eye on some party boss who might, by chance, read the document. In several autobiographies such a motive is clearly marked. They were written by individuals who were on the defensive because they joined the party only shortly before it came into power, and wanted to show that they had long been good National Socialists. In this study I have discounted all cases in which there were indications of deliberate deception on this or similar grounds.

A general presumption against the reliability of the source material, however, is more apparent than real. A large part of the material, such as the descriptions of childhood years, the job of making a living, the everyday incidents of life—not to mention such obvious items as age, occupation, and so forth —is politically as well as ideologically neutral. As regards political activities, on the other hand, we must bear in mind that the majority of the contestants were proud of what they did for the party or the movement. A main reason for distortion is therefore eliminated, since, unlike an outsider, the autobiographers are not likely to look upon any phase of their activities as "murder," "fanaticism," or "prejudice." Furthermore, most of the contestants were typical converts to a cause; and while any statement about motives must always be open to question, converts are more likely to confess the truth as they see it than deliberately to falsify their motives and feelings. Thirdly, a vast majority of the writers are ordinary, unsophisticated people, a circumstance which would predispose them to present a straight-forward story rather than fiction and deception. Finally, I attach considerable weight to the fact that contributors were under no compulsion to write their life histories. It is reasonable to suppose that the main inducement was the prize; consequently all participants would make an effort to conform to the rules of the contest. A perusal of the autobiographies reproduced in Part III of this study will give the reader an opportunity to judge for himself whether or not the histories show any evidence of intentional fabrication.

Granting the reliability of the information, however, the charge may still hold that the contestants have deliberately omitted certain facts. Everybody knows the all-too-human proneness to exaggerate one's own role, and to idealize the group to which one belongs. A strong presumption exists, therefore, that the authors of the life histories might have omitted certain information which would put them or their group in an unfavorable light. Undoubtedly many contributors did omit evidence of internal dissensions in the movement: acts of mismanagement, critical attitudes toward policies, and so forth. But even such omissions are not so numerous as one might expect. Many of the writers frankly state their disagreement with certain policies, as, for example, anti-Semitism. They speak freely of their doubts and fears, and of attitudes, feelings, and activities that are not always compatible with the devotion and loyalty expected of a follower. Many contributors, furthermore, report inadequacies of leadership and the presence of individuals of questionable character and intentions among the leaders. Data on intra-party activities and the several "palace revolutions" are scanty, since none of the contestants seems to have been directly involved in these conflicts. Lack of information rather than deliberate dissimulation may, therefore, account for this as well as other omissions. On the whole, I am less inclined to deplore the fact of deliberate omission than the incompleteness of some accounts, owing largely to the difficulty the contestants had in expressing themselves.

Misunderstandings of my position are bound to arise in connection with such a study as this. Consequently, I would like to defend myself against two errors in particular. A number of the statements and conclusions quoted from the autobiographies are wide open to argument. In presenting these facts and opinions without comment, I do not intend to convey the impression that I agree with them. I record them simply as data significant to the understanding of the movement, irrespective of whether they are "true" or "false."

A further misunderstanding might arise from a well-known phenomenon: that the more complete an explanation, the more likely it is to be taken as an implied approval or disapproval of a given fact. Mme. De Stael immortalized this curious psychological fact in the words, "To understand all, is to forgive all." I therefore declare myself willing to bear the accusation of impartiality, but plead "not guilty" to a charge of intended approval or disapproval of the movement.

The study is divided into three parts. Part I gives a brief history of the Nazi movement, with emphasis upon those aspects which are treated most extensively in the life histories. Part II attempts to ascertain the factors that have influenced the growth of the movement and to evaluate their relative significance. Part III contains six life histories. Their reproduction in full is intended to supplement the illustrative material used in the historical and analytical parts.

PART ONE

Historical

Chapter II

The Background of the Hitler Movement

ITLER'S FIRST APPEARANCE before the German public as the prophet of a new order occurred on February 24, 1920. On this date, which marks the beginning of the movement, Hitler proclaimed the program of a new political organization, the National Socialist German Workers' Party. In the speech which he delivered on this occasion he announced as the goal of this party a "fight to death" against the regime in Germany that had emerged from the aftermath of the World War. But in voicing this determination, Hitler was expressing a sentiment which had agitated thousands of his compatriots since the armistice. Hitler was not, therefore, building his movement upon a void. He was founding it upon a widely prevalent state of opposition and discontent in Germany, which many others before him had attempted to utilize for concerted action.

What was the source of the antagonistic attitude toward the new German government? In what way had it manifested itself before Hitler made his bid for leadership? The answer to these questions will reveal to us the background of the Hitler movement, which we need in order to understand its history. Taking our cue from the wealth of data mar-

shalled in the autobiographies, we shall consider in this chapter
the two major events and the reaction to them which, in my
estimation, determined the nationwide sentiment that Hitler
voiced in his opening address. These events were the revolution of 1918, and the signing of the Versailles treaty.

1. *The "Revolution" of 1918*

We realize today that the abdication of the Kaiser and the
proclamation of the Republic on November 9, 1918, were precipitated by two main factors: first, there were the reversals at
the front—the smashing of the main lines of defense of the
Germans, together with the sudden surrender of Bulgaria and
the crumbling resistance of the Austrian troops, which opened
a fatal gap on the left flank of the Germans; second, there was
the weakening of the home front, due to lack of food, supplies,
and fuel, the general exhaustion and a growing sense of futility
in regard to the war.

Conditions in Germany during the war are vividly described in these excerpts from the autobiographies:[1]

[4.3.4.] I was, of course, tired of the war, and eager to be at
home [writes a simple front-line fighter]. But even then I had
no premonition of the imminent horror. As I came home that
third Christmas, I saw hungry, dispirited faces, a people to whom
nothing mattered any longer. The most anybody could wish for
was a square meal and being left in peace.

This impression is further borne out by the reminiscences
of children of the war now grown to manhood.

[2.3.2] Sometimes I had to scurry around eight to ten hours—
occasionally at night—to procure a few potatoes or a bit of butter.
Carrots and beets, previously considered fit only for cattle, came
to be table luxuries.

[2.3.2] Hunger was upon us. Bread and potatoes were scarce,
while meat and fats were almost non-existent. We were hungry

---

[1] For an explanation of the key numbers in brackets, turn to the
insert at the end of the book.

all the time; we had forgotten how it felt to have our stomachs full.

All family life was at an end. None of us really knew what it meant—we were left to our own devices. For women had to take the place of their fighting men. They toiled in factories and in offices, as ostlers and as commercial travelers, in all fields of activity previously allotted to men—behind the plow as well as on the omnibus. Thus while we never saw our fathers, we had only occasional glimpses of our mothers in the evening. Even then they could not devote themselves to us because, tired as they were, they had to take care of their household, after their strenuous day at work. So we grew up, amid hunger and privation, with no semblance of decent family life.

Up to the end of July the majority of the German people were still hopeful of a victorious issue, or at least an honorable peace. The realization that the lines were crumbling was a profound shock, for which the nation was not prepared. The bad news led to a serious breakdown of morale and a growing resentment against the government that had misled the people with false hopes. A vain attempt was made to stem the tide of demoralization by belated and hastily conceived reforms. The stringent war regulations which gave the military absolute control were lifted; the Prussian three-class election law was made more democratic; a new government, under the liberal Prince Max of Baden, superseded the government of Herting, which was in reality controlled by Ludendorff. Based as it was upon a coalition of the major Reichstag parties, the new Government was hailed as the "first real Government of the people, proclaiming to the world the birth of a new Germany, free from the fetters of a world policy misdirected for decades, and independent of reactionary potentates and militaristic second-Kaisers."

But the democratic cloak under which the monarchy tried to hide its despair soon became threadbare. The death knell of the regime was sounded when the government was forced on October 6 to sue for an unconditional armistice. The result was the complete breakdown of authority that goes with a sudden fall from prestige. Because the state was unprepared for the emergency, it soon became paralyzed. The police power of the state virtually vanished, as public officials, bewildered and crushed by the sudden turn of events, ceased to exercise their duties or were ignored when they did. Soldiers on furlough refused to go back to the front; there was a mutiny in the navy. Food riots and mob excesses became daily occurrences. There were mass demonstrations and political meetings of all sorts at which violence, revolution, and dictatorship were preached. But there was no person or group ready to take over the control of the government that had dropped from the helpless hands of the old regime. Its opponents, the Socialists and radicals, were equally unprepared for the emergency. The Socialists had been waiting for the "natural course of evolution" to bring them into power; when this power was suddenly thrown into their laps, they did not know what to do with it. The more radical Socialists, under Ledebour and Liebknecht, claimed that they had started preparations for the revolution as far back as 1916.[2] Indeed their agitation was responsible for the strike of the munitions workers; they also had a hand in the propaganda at the front that was designed to undermine the morale of the soldiers. But, like everybody else, they were unprepared to assume the reins of government when the old regime collapsed. In addition to this, they made the fatal mistake of confusing the German situation with that in Russia in 1917 and of trying to proceed along the route followed by the Russian Bolsheviks. But, as subsequent events clearly demonstrated, there was no true spirit of revolution, no mass support for radicalism in Germany, despite the uprising against the established government. In spite of the bloody street fights in Berlin and other cities, the efforts of the Communists to establish a soviet government

---

[2] *Cf.* R. Mueller's statement before the Council of Workers and Soldiers in *Die Deutsche Revolution.* Leipzig: F. Meiner, 1919, p. 204.

in Germany collapsed for lack of support. The reason is obvious: what happened in 1918 was not the result of a general change of sentiment or allegiance to new ideas of law and order. The majority of the people were in a holy wrath against the regime for having brought about an intolerable situation. They favored banishing the regime as a punishment for its failure, and as an act of penance on their part for the mistaken sense of loyalty they had reposed in it. But they had no wish to change the structure of society. They longed to go back to work, to recapture the old state of stability and order. To change the rulers and leave practically everything else intact was the wish not only of the powerful middle class, which was the main source of resistance to a radical revolution, but also of the majority of the workers, who remained true to the doctrine of moderate state socialism under the aegis of a parliamentary government—that is, the program sponsored by the Social Democratic party.

The lack of revolutionary fervor was evident even at the time the revolution was supposed to be in full swing. The *Frankfurter Zeitung* wrote on December 11, 1918:

Never has there been a movement which originated from so many chance occurrences. Voltaire was able to predict the French Revolution. But nobody really wanted a revolution in Germany, and had anyone predicted it in 1914, he would have been considered ridiculous. The fact is that the German revolution, originating as a mutiny in the navy, later joined by soldiers and workers, is leaderless. Does this revolt dispose of the old faith in authority? For four hundred years we have known nothing but obedience to bureaucracy. Frederick the Great declared he was tired of ruling over slaves; Bismarck complained about the submissiveness of German character. Snobbish superiority has always characterized the ruling classes. Has the idea of a free people now become a reality?

In the light of subsequent events the prediction of the "Sage of Heidelberg," Max Weber, made at the height of revolutionary fervor, is an accurate answer to this question. "The prevalent liberal ideas are for most Germans only a drug to relieve the terrible tension created by the breakdown at the front," he wrote.[3] Liberal thought was doomed to vanish shortly, for, as Prince Max of Baden declared a short time previously (September 18, 1918), "The lack of liberty in Germany is due not so much to the institutions of the Reich as to the general passiveness of the people in the face of authority, and their unwillingness to assume personal responsibility for the fate of the Fatherland."

What were the outstanding features of the "Revolution of 1918"?

The ferment and disorganization imminent on the collapse of authority shortly after the opening of negotiations for an armistice first manifested themselves in a mutiny in the navy. The sailors refused to obey orders and to man their ships, suspecting that they would be sent out in a desperate effort to stave off the inevitable surrender by some "miracle of heroism." They assumed command of seaports and established sailors' councils.

As soon as news of the mutiny became known, soldiers on leave and workers in various cities got together and organized similar councils. These councils took over the local governments without resistance, and hoisted the red flag on public buildings. Mass demonstrations of workers and soldiers demanding the abdication of the Kaiser and the proclamation of the Republic were held in all cities. Events reached their climax in Bavaria on November 8, when a Republic was proclaimed and the Kaiser was forced to abdicate. The next day a general revolt of workers swept Berlin. The troops sent out against the rioters went over to them in a body. Around noon a bulletin announcing the abdication of the Kaiser was released by the Chancellor. Scheidemann, leader of the Social Democrats, proclaimed the Republic to the throngs assembled in front of the Reichstag, in the following words:

[3] An article in the *Frankfurter Zeitung* for November 22, 1918.

The monarchical system has collapsed. The greater part of the garrison has joined our ranks. The Hohenzollerns have abdicated. Long live the German Republic! Ebert is forming a new government in which all socialistic groups have joined hands. Let nothing disturb the triumph we have achieved. Maintain peace, order, and security.

The proclamation of the Republic was followed for a time by a reign of chaos in Germany. The new government lacked power and authority to enforce order. Executive power was wielded arbitrarily and extravagantly by local soldiers' and workmens' councils, and by the provisional governments of Bavaria, Saxony, and other regions. The central government pursued a confused and vacillating policy. The empire was threatened with disintegration when powerful groups acted for the separation of provinces from the Reich. Strikes and riots occurred all over the country. The most critical situation was precipitated by the growing split within the ranks of the radical parties that supported the new regime. Factionalism finally ripened into open strife between the Social Democrats, who favored a moderate republic, and the Communists, or Spartakists, as they called themselves, under the leadership of Liebknecht and Rosa Luxemburg, who, aided and abetted by Soviet Russia, demanded the establishment of a dictatorship of the proletariat.

Civil war broke out. In a series of bloody battles in Berlin, Halle, and other cities, the Spartakists were defeated by regular troops and volunteers who rallied in support of the Republican government.

The defeat of the Spartakists decided the burning issue of the day: namely, whether or not executive power should be vested in the soldiers' and workmen's councils to retain the "achievements of the revolution." Resolutions of civic organizations and front-line soldiers, demanding the convocation of a national assembly that would decide the future form of government, were pouring in. The Spartakists alone maintained that the revolution "stands or falls with the continuance of the councils," and that, in the words of Karl Liebknecht, "the calling of a National Assembly signifies the defeat of the working class, and the suppression of the revolution." The issue was finally decided by the councils themselves, at their Berlin congress, December 16-20, 1918. The delegates voted overwhelmingly in favor of the National Assembly after the resistance of the radicals had been broken by the suppression of their armed uprising.

The National Assembly, meeting at Weimar on January 19, 1919, adopted a new constitution and elected a president. The return to parliamentary government brought some order into the existing chaos. But the repercussions of the revolution continued to harass Germany well into 1924.

Throughout the months of ferment following the war there were two stabilizing factors. There was on the one hand the popular resistance to radicalism, the continued adherence to the old order of things, and the readiness of the people to content themselves with a superficial change in the form of government as long as they were allowed to resume the normal routine of life, with peace and bread. On the other hand there was the army, particularly the soldiers at the front. The most significant feature of the German "revolution" was the fact that the army at the front remained intact, maintained its discipline and order, and marched back in a fashion unparalleled in the history of defeated armies. There was no panic, no mutiny. A soldiers' council was formed, but it functioned in close coöperation with General Headquarters.

From the first, the soldiers in the front lines opposed a radical revolution. They favored a moderate socialist government, and led with the demand for a national assembly. The general reaction of the army is succinctly stated by one of our informants:

[3.3.3.] Then came the thing we soldiers of the front could never have believed: the very men we had for years defended, for whose sake innumerable comrades had given their lives, while they led a life of ease and profits, betrayed us. My division, together with our commanding officers, who through the years had fought side by side with us, spurned the revolution and the soldiers' councils. With a roll of drums we drew over the Rhine to Eilenburg, where we were discharged in January 1919.

This attitude of the front-line soldiers precluded a repetition of the Russian Revolution, which was made possible to a large extent by the disorganization of the army. The returning soldiers were enthusiastically welcomed by the population. Their continued discipline gave the people new hope.

The returning troops, as a rule, dissolved the soldiers' and workers' councils, with the consent of the community. The following notice, in the *Frankfurter Zeitung* for November 27, 1918, is typical of many newspaper reports of this time:

Regiments of the Sixth Army, marching through Lennep, removed the soldiers' and workmen's council. The red flag on the municipal building was hauled down and burned amid the rejoicings of the population. In its place the Prussian war flag was hoisted. Sailors and workers of Remscheid, who came armed with machine guns, were taken prisoners.

Events like this, more than anything else, reveal the mental state of a great section of the German people. The bearing of the soldiers from the front and the reaction of the population to the soldiers' rough treatment of the symbols of the revolution clearly demonstrate the weakness of the new revolutionary spirit.

2. *Reaction to the Revolution*

Since we are concerned here with the revolution only insofar as it concerns the Hitler movement, our main interest is in the negative, or unfavorable reactions to it, which were symptomatic of the general dissatisfaction it evoked. That there were positive or favorable reactions as well, particularly at the outset, goes without saying. This is clear from the result of the elections for the National Assembly in January 1919, in which the coalition parties, the Social Democrats, the Democrats, and the Catholic Center party polled the impressive total of twenty-three million out of thirty million votes. Many who later changed their affiliations supported the coalition in order to express their approval of the abolition of the monarchical regime. Others voted for it because they hoped that a democratic form of government would be an incentive to the Allies to grant a just peace—an illusion from which there was soon to be a rude awakening. With greater sincerity the workers gave their votes because of the social legislation establishing the eight-hour day, unemployment and old-age insurance, and improved working conditions, enacted by the new government soon after its inauguration. Finally the liberals, sincerely in favor of the new regime, voted for it because they believed, as one of their spokesmen put it, that "the achievements of the revolution pave the way toward the freedom, happiness, and well-being of the German people."

Opposed to the revolution as a matter of course were those individuals and groups who had vested interests in the defunct regime: the military caste, the conservative party, the Pan-Germans, and numerous government officials. These people lay low, for the time being. Just before the eventful days of November 1918, they endeavored to stave off disaster by trying to win support for the establishment of a dictatorship and the continuation of the war. They urged a defensive *levée en masse,* "that would cause a flow of new physical and moral power from the homeland to the wall in the West." Billboards everywhere displayed the Hindenburg appeal, "Heads up, you softies at home, the army will do it yet. The homeland must stand behind the army, strong, united, and ready for sacrifice. We can defy every storm if it does." They regarded the army as undefeated, and capable of indefinite resistance. So they propagated the idea of the "stab in the back," which was later forged into an effective propaganda slogan.

The *Deutsche Zeitung* of October 13, 1918, says:

The reply of the Government to Wilson's offer of armistice conditions is a testimonial of shame. Bring in your banners, you brave soldiers! You were not defeated by the enemy, but by the crumbling home front. The most tragic feature of the present situation is the realization that Germans have fought against Germans.

In numerous protest meetings held by nationalists all over the country, democracy was accused of "having betrayed the Fatherland out of weakness and innate timidity."

These appeals, exhortations, and protests were swept away by the tide of events. Groups opposed to the new regime were beaten because they were panicky and disorganized. But instead of withdrawing, they bided their time in the hope of a chance to come back. Their hopes were strengthened by the fact that the new government retained most of the officials of old Imperial Germany, that loyal troops under the leadership of commanders of the old regime were used to combat radicals, and that so-called "patriotic" organizations were encouraged and supported. In the absence of a platform capable of allaying popular suspicion, the nationalists could not muster sufficient support to dislodge the new regime. But they showed their hand in numerous disturbances, such as the attempted *coup d'état* of 1920 (usually known as the Kapp *Putsch*), assassination of leaders of the new regime, notably Erzberger and Rathenau, and they were responsible for the formation of the Black Reichswehr, as well as for other semi-military organizations.

The autobiographies give us a new clue to the negative reactions to the revolution. They show that this response was not limited to the reactionary group, and that the possible abrogation of vested interests was not its sole source. Many workers and members of the lower and middle class are found to have responded negatively to the revolution, and at least 10 per cent of these relate their negative reaction definitely to their subsequent joining of the Hitler movement.

Some of the negative reactions hark back to the fact that the conduct of the revolutionaries impinged upon the dignity of the individual. A soldier reports:

[2.3.2.] Troops were once again returning to the Fatherland, yet a disgusting sight met their eyes. Beardless boys, dissolute deserters and whores tore off the shoulder bands of our front-line fighters, and spat upon their field-gray uniforms. At the same time they muttered something about liberty, equality, and fraternity. Poor, deluded people! Was this liberty and fraternity? People who never saw a battle field, who had never heard the whine of a bullet, openly insulted men who through four and a half years had defied the world in arms, who had risked their lives in innumerable battles, with the sole desire to guard the country against this horror.

For the first time I began to feel a burning hatred for this human scum that trod everything pure and clean underfoot. Young as I was, I determined I should never have anything to do with these people.

Another soldier gives an account typical of many of the recollections cited in the autobiographies:

[4.3.4.] On November 15, 1918, I was on the way from the hospital at Bad Nauheim to my garrison at Brandenburg. As I was limping along with the aid of my cane at the Potsdam station in Berlin, a band of uniformed men, sporting red armbands, stopped me, and demanded that I surrender my shoulder bands and insignia. I raised my stick in reply; but my rebellion was soon overcome. I was thrown, and only the intervention of a railroad official saved me from my humiliating position. Hate flamed in me against the November criminals from that moment. As soon as my health improved somewhat, I joined forces with the groups devoted to the overthrow of the rebellion. I participated in the storming of the *Vorwaerts* Building and the *Marstall*, as well as in other Berlin skirmishes.

Non-combatants, too, underwent similar experiences, as is

shown by this extract from the autobiography of a youthful storm trooper:

[2.3.1.] On the ninth of November, 1918, I was going to choral practice. That day marks my awakening as a nationalist. I was wearing the cap of a choir student, adorned with a red-white-and-black cockade. I had just entered the Burgstrasse, when two men approached me, and though I was but a child, tore the cap from my head and boxed my ears. The cockade was deemed sufficient provocation. I went on in tears, not so much because I had lost my cockade, but because those fellows had been mean enough to attack a child. The bitter resentment of that moment made a lasting impression on me.

At choir practice they dismissed us immediately, with the remark that we would be notified when to come again. Instead of going home, however, I remained in the neighborhood of the Lustgarten, with one of my friends.

By eight o'clock the great Lustgarten was crowded with people. Red flags were waving everywhere. Presently there was a stir throughout the throng. The man who had had so much to do with the new turn of events, Karl Liebknecht, arrived. I stood right next to his car, and listened to his speech.

Suddenly a shot rang out somewhere. A terrible panic followed. Troops loyal to the Emperor rushed out of the *Marstall* building and fired in the air. The mob, hitherto so bold, dispersed in all directions, leaving an impression of utter cowardice. I myself was thrown and badly trampled. Finally, by nine o'clock, I reached home. My mother was waiting for me at the door. The excitement had spread to everyone.

I shall not dwell upon details, but the impression upon my youthful mind was a frightful one. I felt a profound hatred for these people, a hatred constantly strengthened by recurring incidents.

Many former soldiers assert that they looked upon the revolution as a negation of the very aims by which they had justified their participation in the war. Here are some typical expressions of the resentment thus aroused.

[4.1.2.] During the spring campaigns of 1918, our regiment fought in the vicinity of Nojon. After the retreat I returned to Munich with my regiment in December 1918. The sad picture of Red rule made a most painful impression on us front-line fighters. We could not and would not believe that this issue of the war was what we had fought and striven for through four and a half years. We would not be reconciled to the apparent fact that all our struggles and sacrifices had been in vain.

There was something heartening about the grateful, affecttionate reception the rank and file of the people accorded us everywhere, particularly in the territories that faced hostile occupation and foreign rule immediately after our departure. Back in my country, which had become so strangely unlike itself, I felt a passionate longing for a new order, built on our front-line experiences, which might resurrect our tortured Fatherland.

[4.2.5.] Despite the efforts of the leaders to ingratiate themselves with the workers, the revolution of 1918 was a crime not only against the workers but against the entire people. What became of peace, freedom, bread? So many catchwords, thrown to the furious masses, so that the so-called people's tribunals might have a better hold on them for their own sinister purposes. I need not emphasize that this criminal and forcibly induced development was a slap in the face of every decent German. Were these the fruits of my sixteen years of service in war and peace? Was it for this that the fresh youth of Germany was mowed down in hundreds of battles? It almost seemed as if that might be the answer—treason to Fatherland and people celebrated veritable orgies. All that still reflected the glory of the heroic deeds of our old army was derided and trampled in the gutter. My soul rebelled against this shame and baseness. My soldier's honor was blemished by the ignominy of this home-coming. Shallow pacifists inflated themselves and sputtered high-sounding phrases. Spineless men and the sickening off-shoots of exploiters triumphed over the decent part of the population.

"The soldiers of the German army fell on the field of dishonor," said a university professor, without fear of being torn to shreds. Deliberately, systematically, they were trying to stifle all the finest sentiments of honor and greatness a people or an individual can possess. Unfortunately these poisoners of the people succeeded only too well in infecting a large number of decent comrades through their words and writings.

Another important source of resentment in connection with the revolution had its origin in the fact that many Germans looked upon it as a negation of the moral precepts and the patriotic sentiments to which the educational system of the old regime had conditioned them. A young soldier writes:

[2.8.5.] No one who has not himself experienced it can imagine what went on in our young hearts when, on the night of November 9, 1918, we were roused from sleep with the words of treason and revolution,. Who had betrayed us? Our fathers, our brothers? No! A thousand times no! We looked at each other aghast, and, with no particular information at hand, we realized that if these things were true, there must be something decidedly rotten somewhere; the enemy must be behind the front as well as before us. We grew more and more wide-awake as news kept drifting in. We waited in vain for orders to strike out against the traitors; presently we were able to ascertain that our own officers had left us. A few days later soldiers wearing arm bands appeared among us. The ragged uniforms that they wore bore ample evidence of what had happened.

The so-called soldiers' council presented all manner of requests and orders, demanded that we remove the decorations from our uniforms, and so forth. In reality it was politely put up to us that we proceed to map out our own dismal existence. When, however, we were ordered to give up our flag in exchange for a red rag, our patience gave out. Shame reddened our cheeks and anger constricted our throats. Clearly there were people at work intent on turning things upside down. Heroism had become cowardice, truth a lie, loyalty was rewarded by dastardliness. We shouldered our weapons and put this extraordinary delegation behind lock and key. Tearfully our captain called on us, and told us all was lost. A few hours later we heard that a battalion of Spartakists was advancing. Thereupon we hurriedly mounted machine guns, to defend our barracks against any attack. Our officers, however, pleaded with us to abandon any idea of defense, in order to avoid unnecessary bloodshed. Some days later the Eighty-first Regiment of Frankfort entered Wetzlar, and took up quarters in the south wing of the barracks in which we were quartered.

It might appear that the soldiers themselves had brought on the revolution, and were therefore responsible for the frightful things that followed. Nothing could be further from the truth. This very first event of the revolution shows unmistakably that only a minority of the soldiers favored the revolution (this applies to the Eighty-first Regiment, too). Unfortunately they succeeded in checkmating the majority. More degrading cowardly sights than I have witnessed during those days cannot very well be imagined. We drafted many a plan to rid ourselves of the councils, but each time we lacked a leader. We were rescued at last when a recruiting officer of the Huelsen Volunteers managed to slip inside the barracks and describe to us the true state of things in our beloved Fatherland. We gave him our word that we would go along and help him fight the bandits who wanted to reduce Germany to a shambles. As the youngest member of the staff of the volunteers, I took charge of half a company.

During the occupation of some districts of Berlin, I became intensely aware of the horrors of a fratricidal war. Between skirmishes I drilled my troop with a view to avoiding unnecessary bloodshed. I gave the command to take aim with the precision of a drill sergeant; nor did the effect fail. For, the moment they suspected they were face to face with trained soldiers, the red horde sought the safety of cowards in the distance.

The knowledge that we were serving the people gave us the strength to fight. Only those who have known similar experiences can understand what we felt when, in self-defense, we had to turn our guns against them. Nothing can ever undo the harm wrought by fiendish aliens.

Yet we soldiers labored under another, deeper anxiety. We gladly fought to restore peace and order in the Fatherland; but we had no inkling of what went on behind the scenes in the government buildings. All we knew was that the government was in the hands of unknown, obscure men, who could not possibly win popular support, since all their measures so far only invited further disaster. Ebert, Bauer, Mueller, Noske, and the rest, whatever their names were, simply didn't register with us, and we silently hoped for a new leader. The general strike of March 1919 rendered the situation still more hopeless. Still we persevered. Recurring disorders left us no peace. Life was full of weariness and humiliation.

3. *The Versailles Treaty*

The significance of the negative reaction to the revolution is overshadowed by the far more general and more deep-seated reaction against the Versailles Treaty and the Republican regime that signed it. The conditions of the Treaty affected deep-rooted social values which carried a strong emotional connotation. From the point of view of a movement, impaired or threatened social values are far more significant than individual values. For social values, being shared by individuals as members of a group, are common factors in the life organization of many people. Consequently they serve as powerful rallying points of concerted effort to oppose any danger that threatens them. The significance of social values is furthermore enhanced by the fact that they permit an individual to disguise intentions emanating from purely personal feelings under the cloak of socially approved sentiments, and thus to justify extreme conduct.

Chief among social values is the group as a going concern. Associated with it are other values involved in the maintenance of the group and of the conditions that make the adequate functioning of the group possible. Such social values are the purpose of the group, its social position in relation to other groups, its traditions, ideals, symbols, and so forth.

When the group is a nation, the emotional connotation of social values is called "nationalism." This feeling is more positive than patriotism, or love for one's country for its "beautiful streams, valleys, and mountains." It is more than a mere desire to keep the nation intact. It is primarily a strong positive feeling for the accomplishments of the nation, its position of power, the men and institutions and the traditions which are associated with the glorified events of its history. It involves a certain amount of ethnocentricism, a feeling of superiority of one's nation over other nations, which might turn a nationalistic sentiment into chauvinism when the claim for superiority becomes associated with a claim for exclusiveness and consequent hostility to all other nations. The feeling of nationalism is strongest in a country where the educational system makes it a primary point of emphasis. This was true of the educational program in pre-war Germany. L. I. Snyder describes the nature and extent of nationalistic education in Germany as follows: [4]

Germany embodied her national aspirations in her school system perhaps more than other continental powers (p. 129).

The German educational system emphasized that the school existed, first of all for the State. . . . Obedience to authority, loyalty to the crown, even docility, were encouraged, because they favored the power of the State. Through the primary and secondary schools the prospective citizen underwent a vigorous training which always stressed the glory of German civilization, German ideals, German politics, German industry, German *Kultur*. . . . The spirit which tempered the national army was accepted without question in the educational system. There was but little need to force the system upon the population. It was accepted gracefully as a national requirement. . . . Cleavages in the German caste system were definite and rigid, but in the matter of duty to the Fatherland and loyalty to the crown every student, whether Junker's son or butcher's scion, was made aware of his Germanness (pp. 124-5).

The provisions of the Versailles Treaty cut to the quick the prevalent, highly developed sentiment of nationalism. Inasmuch as it curtailed the power of the nation, deprived it of its prestige, attacked its traditions, and impaired its integrity, it was regarded as a fatal thrust against social values held and shared by the vast majority of Germans. A negative reaction to the Treaty and to the regime that accepted it was almost universal. This feeling was practically unaffected by the antagonisms that divided the German people on other issues. Reactionaries and Communists joined hands in opposition to the Treaty. Newspapers, irrespective of party affiliations, attacked its terms and demanded its rejection.

---

[4] *From Bismarck to Hitler: The Background of Modern German Nationalism.* Williamsport, Pa.: The Bayard Press, 1935.

The democratic *Frankfurter Zeitung* blazed forth in big headlines on May 1, 1919: "U N A C C E P T A B L E !" The same issue carried the comment that the terms "are so nonsensical, that no government that signs the treaty will last a fortnight. Germany is crushed."

The *Berliner Tageblatt* predicted prophetically: "Should we accept the conditions, a military furor for revenge will sound in Germany within a few years, and a militant nationalism will engulf all."

The socialist *Vorwaerts* demanded rejection of the Treaty, and the communist *Freiheit* wrote that "no proletarian party can welcome such 'peace.'"

Stormy protest meetings were held all over the country and petitions were sent to the government imploring it to reject the Treaty. "We prefer to sacrifice everything and fight to the last man rather than accept as cowards a peace that is against our honor. Contemptible is the nation which does not offer its life gladly for the sake of its honor." This resolution, adopted by the students and faculty of the University of Breslau, was characteristic of the thousands that swamped the government. "Inhuman," "unbearable," "enslavement," "disastrous for the world," "cruel injustice," "shame," were the terms applied to the Treaty. The feelings of the people were deeply stirred. Mass demonstrations comprising all classes were held all over the country. Thousands of people milled in the streets of the big cities day and night. A period of mourning was declared. All places of amusement were closed. Patriotic songs suppressed during the revolutionary days suddenly became popular again, and were sung everywhere. People listened eagerly to nationalist agitators who denounced the government openly without interference by the police.

In retrospect it is clear that the affair of the Versailles Treaty was the primary factor in the debacle of democracy in Germany. It discredited the leaders who for months maintained that only a new, democratic Germany could count upon a just peace from the Western democracies. This became the main-spring of all subsequent attacks on the republican regime.

"We denounce the regime because it brought about the downfall of the Reich. It permitted the revolution to destroy the military and economic power of the nation, so that only paper protests remained possible. The people have already judged the destroyers of the Reich. Through political and military sabotage the revolution has made the German nation impotent to defend its honor. It has betrayed the people by beguiling them with the promise of a 'just peace.'" These words, spoken in 1919 by Count Posadovsky, a leader of the reactionaries, became a chorus that was repeated over and over again in years to come. It made no difference that President Ebert eloquently denounced the Treaty and sided with the patriots, that the socialist leader Scheidemann resigned from the cabinet because he refused to sign the "death warrant." Nor did it matter that adherence to the treaty was the only course left open to the government, in view of the threatened invasion of Allied troops, along with a continuation of the blockade, which was taking hundreds of lives daily. The tide was turned from then on against the democratic republican government. The first indication of future events was contained in the election *following* the acceptance of the Treaty of Versailles on June 6, 1920. The parties that voted for signing it—the Social Democrats and the Center party, lost a total of eleven million votes, three million of which went to the Communists, and another three million to the Nationalists, both of which were parties that had voted against the Treaty. Thus the main support was withdrawn from the government parties, which never regained a sufficient majority to rule effectively.

Negative reactions to the Treaty of Versailles are indicated in practically every one of the life histories. We need only quote a few to illustrate the general reaction. As in the case of the revolution, they also show that resentment in each instance was directed against the government.

[4.6.4.] The unhappy conclusion of the war, the spiritual, moral, and physical collapse of the front, together with the bankruptcy of the German government, led us straight into the arms of the Marxists. Weary as we were, we resigned ourselves to their leadership, and permitted them to seize the reins of government. We trusted the siren voices of the seducers, and looked to the life of "dignity and beauty" promised us.

Yet with the renewed strength of our minds and bodies our eyes too grew sharper, and we saw and felt the burden the Marxist traitors had placed upon us in the Treaty of Versailles.

We front-line fighters would not accept the things our country offered us. Our hands were clean! Under the right leadership—which unfortunately was no longer there—we might have swept the worm gnawing at the vitals of our people out of sight. Never, never could we conceive how people who called themselves our fellow Germans could deprive us of our last remaining national possession, our national honor.

[2.8.2.] To my way of thinking, the German people had a universal mission. I knew that Germany had brought forth great men in every walk of life, whose deeds had frequently influenced, even changed, the course of the world. I knew that my people were possessed of great inner strength which, together with keen determination and courage, had produced warlike heroes as well. I was likewise convinced of the honor and truthfulness of my people.

I therefore considered it a bitter injustice that this nation, exposed to an overwhelming number of foes, should thus be humiliated, in a manner that did little honor to the conquerors themselves. It seemed to me unbearable to think that there had been men who acquiesced in Germany's alleged responsibility for the war. Could a nation that had become great through decades of steady efforts for peace, suddenly precipitate such a conflagration? Could men who in their own country led lives of usefulness and devotion, and who, as I had ample opportunity to observe, reared their children in love and piety, suddenly turn barbarians in the land of the enemy?

[3.7.4.] When the revolution broke out on November 9, 1918, I lay seriously wounded in a hospital at Trier. I am grateful to fate for sparing me the shame and humiliation that brutal, subhuman mobs inflicted upon my wounded comrades in the streets. I'll never forget how a comrade, whose arm had been amputated, rushed into our ward, and threw himself weeping upon his bed. The red rabble that had never heard the whine of a bullet fell upon him, and deprived him of all his insignia and decorations. We all cried with anger. So this was the Germany for which we had given our blood and bodies; this was the Germany for which we had suffered the torments of hell and defied the world for years! No, that could never be!

I sought solace in the thought that things would change once our comrades returned from the front. Presently I became reconciled to the thought that Germany was now a republic, and that the people had taken their fate into their own hands. So long as the leaders of this Republic kept faith with the people, the front line fighters would be on their side. Though we had lost the war, Germany remained, and the front line fighters felt a particular call to help bind the nation's wounds, lest the sacrifices of our comrades, fallen beside us, shall have been in vain.

When the negotiations with our former foes, which proved so frightfully humiliating to Germany, began, it became clear to me that the new leaders trod in ways I could not follow. I felt a deep-seated opposition to their policy of compliance, their desire to conciliate the French through a show of our evident good will. A policy of that sort, in my opinion, must lead to bankruptcy of our people.

Having fought and bled for my people for two years at the front, I could not agree with this international trend. We front line fighters had no need of lessons in socialism. Had we not for years been the very embodiment of active socialism, in our comradery, our every deed? My bitterness increased as I was forced to recognize that the government deliberately sought to stifle all patriotic thought and activity. It was a joyous day indeed when I heard the *Stahlhelm* had been founded at Magdeburg by comrade Seldte (1919). I joined this comrade without further delay.

4. *War Prisoners and Occupation*

In addition to the revolution and the Treaty of Versailles, there were a number of other things about the aftermath of the war to which people responded negatively. Their influence, however, was not quite so extensive. Among these were the experiences of the prisoners of war and the people in the occupied territories. The usual sequence of negative reactions followed by active resentment against the government held true here, too.

The story of war prisoners is graphically told in the following biographic excerpt:

[2.2.3.] So passed the years up to the World War. Now we were face to face with something that affected not only individuals, personal interests and Germany, but all men and all nations.

On the second of May I became a soldier. I joined the army willingly. After ten weeks of training in the garrison at Duesseldorf, I was sent to Champagne on the western front, in the middle of July 1915, in active regiment number 39. I was not long at the front, for in the autumn of 1915 I was severely wounded and carried off to a French prison camp.

There were over a hundred wounded comrades in Montauban, in the south of France. After my wounds were healed, I was taken, along with a number of comrades, to work in a mine. We were much dissatisfied with the working conditions in the mines, the primitive methods in use, and above all, the ten hour day (which applied to French miners, too). We particularly resented the fact that in the French mines there was no way of washing all day, and we had to go home black and dirty—an unknown practice in Germany. We were rather amused by the careful watch the French guards kept over us, knowing as we did that no such thing was done in Germany. My fifty-four months of work as a prisoner were a great experience for me.

Then in 1918 came the end of the war, closed on the note of freedom and liberty for all people—even the Germans as set forth in Wilson's Fourteen Points. It meant also the end of our dull existence as prisoners of war. During our captivity we read French, Italian, and English newspapers, and learned that the enemy did not want to do away with the German people, but with the Prussian militarism, the Kaiser, and the monarchy. The French, too, gave us the same impression. We believed that freedom was ours. But a great surprise was in store for us. The French prisoners of war were promptly returned to their homes from Germany. There was no hatred between us, since their lot had been much the same as ours. Like us, they had been prisoners, robbed of their freedom, cut off from a normal existence.

In 1919, we hoped we might return to our homes and families. But this was not the case. We stayed on through the summer, long after the Reichstag had ratified the Treaty of Versailles. Once the Treaty was ratified, we believed we would be free to return home. Wilson's Fourteen Points, furthermore, led us to believe that America would not permit the enslaving of the German people. This was also an error.

There was a great deal of bitterness among the German people when the German government ratified the treaty of peace in the summer of 1919, and our fate still remained uncertain. Opposition to the German government and its methods was rampant. We felt as though no one troubled about us. After all we were no thieves and murderers, but soldiers who had fallen into the hands of the enemy in the course of duty. We no longer believed in the mythical tales of freedom, liberty, and voice of the people the whole world was speaking of. As we approached the end of 1919, we came to the conclusion that all this talk about freedom, liberty, and popular expression had nothing to do with Germany.

In the summer of 1919 we were working in the devastated areas. Christmas 1919 still found us on French soil. One can readily imagine the mental state of the prisoners of war, for Christmas is the greatest of holidays to Germans. Here, on the one hand, all the world was speaking of peace, freedom, and democracy, while 600,-000 to 800,000 prisoners of war were still being kept in duress a year after the armistice. A great bitterness consequently arose against the government and its liberal and Marxist protagonists.

Finally, at the end of January 1920, we were sent home. This ends the account of my experiences as a prisoner of war. I was confined for fifteen months after the signing of the armistice. During this time the foundation of many of my later political beliefs was laid. The same was true of thousands of men, who, like me, were held long after the establishment of peace. We had all heard of liberty, peace, and democracy, only to find that under Marxist rule reality differed from these slogans.

The following excerpts describe the situation in the territories occupied immediately after the war. The indications of popular reaction are typical of those in other autobiographies dealing with the subject. A young party member writes:

[2.7.3.] Once again the classroom benches were emptied, and hoary men and beardless boys took up weapons, for the Polish rebels were within forty miles of Bromberg. Yet every time their attacks were forcibly repelled. The year 1919 arrived, and with it the fate of the eastern provinces grew more and more uncertain. A miniature war was raging just outside the city. The schools were closed. Now came my chance. All public buildings had a private guard, consisting of their employees, each of whom received a Laufer rifle. Despite my eleven years, I could not rest until I, too, had obtained such an assignment. I was lucky, having been assigned to guard duty at the local government building. Thus for two months I was able to serve the Fatherland.

Classes opened again, despite frequent interruptions. The days that followed were unforgettable. It was fairly evident by that time that Posen would be ceded to Poland. At the beginning of June 1919, a delegation of foreign diplomats visited Bromberg to ascertain the general feelings of the populace. Despite the express prohibition of the principal of our *Gymnasium,* the entire school marched in a body, flags flying, through the streets of Bromberg. There were no parties in those days; all were Germans, who loved their country above all, and were ready to defend it to the last. Tens of thousands marched through the streets—soldiers, peasants, yeomen, boys and girls—to prove to the strangers that Bromberg was German, and wished to remain such. My father stood on the balcony of the Bromberg public library, opposite the foreign visitors, and addressed the huge gathering, telling them what was in store for us. Presently a cry, as if from one throat, arose: "We want to remain Germans!" accompanied by the defiant hymn *A Mighty Fortress Is Our God.*

Three days of the same scene: flags and masses, who would not be cheated of their Fatherland. Yet all was in vain. The government had yielded, and our fate was sealed.

At the beginning of September the first troops left the city. At the same time a considerable part of the population also packed up their household goods, to seek asylum elsewhere. On the eighteenth of January 1920, we assembled in the auditorium of our high school to bid farewell to the old Fatherland. Once again *Deutschland über Alles* was sung. The following day another few thousand citizens left the city, the soldiers who had not yet gone evacuated, and a committee of citizens took charge of the city. On the twen-

tieth of January the rear guard of the garrison withdrew, and at
ten o'clock the ringing of the bells announced the entry of the
Polish troops. We sat behind curtained windows, and paid no
attention to anything. We saw our mother weep, without quite
understanding what it meant to lose one's country, since all that
was something new in our lives.

The same tragic tenseness makes itself felt in yet another
excerpt:

[2.3.2.] And then the breakdown! A great deal collapsed for us
boys, soldiers in our hearts. I recall how one of my father's acquaintances, on sick leave, came to the house wearing an armband of
the soldiers' and workers' council during the early days of the
upheaval. My brother and I wept with anger, and refused him
admittance to our house.

Then came the news that Wiesbaden, our own lovely resort
city, would fall in the occupied zone. We received appropriate
rules of conduct at school; but we all knew that none of us would
ever salute a French officer. Better hide behind a strange doorway
than doff our caps to the enemy.

The advance guard of the French arrived. And if we had no
direct knowledge of misery in war time, we did then. Traffic was
at a standstill, food became scarce, and the conduct of the army of
occupation was in no wise conciliatory. There was more or less
open friction everywhere, with dire results to us Germans. Sepa-
ratism reared its head for the first time. My teacher, Klaus Kraemer, was appointed minister of education of the Rhenish Republic.
The entire school went on strike, and the teachers lost all control
over us. We refused to have anything more to do with our former
teacher. Shortly afterwards, when the same Kraemer appeared in
front of the school during a vacation period, he barely escaped a
thrashing. No one travelled on the state railway, run by the French
with the assistance of several Germans whom we considered traitors.
It would have been as good as taking one's life in one's hands,
since no one knew when a train would be derailed. In any case,
to patronize the railway would have been treason in our eyes;
rather suffer discomforts for hours enthroned on barrels high up on
freight trucks—but travel by train—never!

It was only by aid of the French that the Separatists were able
to hold their own as long as they did. But once popular resentment

reached its peak, the French themselves could do nothing against it. Armed with the fire hose, the sole weapon left them, the people drove the remaining Separatists from among them. It can easily be understood that these malefactors received no gentle treatment. As for the French, they proceeded to pacify the populace by mobilizing the Spahis, who ruthlessly rode down all who did not take a timely refuge in neighboring buildings.

A general atmosphere of discontent and unrest was thus created in Germany as a result of a series of actions bearing upon the personal and social values of individuals and groups. It indicates the presence of a vast store of energy, ready upon proper manipulation, to flow in the direction of counter-revolution.

5. Counter-Revolution

The autobiographies show that various types of individuals tried to make use of the opportunity offered by unsettled conditions. Apparently many people felt the urge to leadership, and a number of our informants engaged in initiating and managing sundry groups before they joined the Hitler movement. These counter-revolutionary groups, military and semi-military organizations, and political parties functioned independently of each other, each hoping to subordinate the rest and to become the center of a national movement.

a. *Military organizations*

The military organizations which sprang up in Germany after the war had their inception in the so-called *Freikorps,* organized by high army officers, and composed of loyal soldiers and volunteers, recruited through newspaper advertisements and street placards.

"What's the use of studies, and what's the good of business or a profession?" read a typical appeal, signed by former Admiral Lettow-Vorbeck. "Enemies within and beyond are burning down our house. Help us, in the spirit of German comradeship and loyalty, to restore our power of national defense!"

At the beginning the *Freikorps* were sanctioned by the republican government. The general demobilization ordered by the Allies left the government without an adequate military force to protect its borders, particularly in the East, and to subdue the Communist uprisings in industrial centers. At the same time the need for immediate action was too urgent to permit forming the Republican militia of "loyal socialists" suggested by the workers' and soldiers' councils.

The *Freikorps,* nominally under the command of the Minister of war, Noske, usually bore the names of their leaders (Merker, Eulenburg, Ehrhard, and so on). Actually these regiments often acted on their own initiative, in violation of government orders. Strongly nationalistic, their members often expressed a hatred of the revolution, and a determination to oppose the consequences of the Treaty of Versailles. One of the results of this opposition was the guerilla warfare in Upper Silesia, 1919-20.

The *Freikorps* leaders were men of the old regime who not only sought to prepetuate its military traditions, but in many cases openly conspired to restore the monarchical regime. In due time the government recognized the danger of these counter-revolutionary formations. But having blundered at the outset, it had to tolerate them as long as the threat of communism was effective. By the same token the *Freikorps* supported the government as long as both were confronted by the common enemy. But as soon as the Spartakists were defeated they turned against the government, and staged the Kapp *Putsch* in 1920. The government was saved at that time by a general strike, the inefficient management of the *coup d'état,* and by the fact that many members of the middle class were suspicious of the *Putsch,* closely identified with leaders of the old regime. The *Putsch* was suppressed. But it was only the rumbling of an inevitable eruption that was to follow sooner or later. The government heeded the warning and realized it was astride a volcano. Few people realized however, that the *Putsch* was the beginning of a fight for the very existence of the republican regime. Undismayed by this first setback, its opponents struck again and again, until they learned the lesson of their failures: namely, that to win mass support they had to advocate a new program rather than the restoration of the monarchy, and find leaders untainted by the stigma of the old regime. Hitler, more than any other, saw the handwriting on the wall that doomed the old regime, and profited from the lesson.

After the Kapp *Putsch* the *Freikorps* were ordered to disband. Many of the leaders, however, refused to retire to civilian life. They organized secret military groups, so-called *Wehrverbaende*, which formed a network over the length and breadth of the country. These secret organizations engaged in many counter-revolutionary activities. Most notorious among them were the Ehrhard Brigade, which wore the swastika as early as 1920, and the "Organization Consul," whose activities were revealed in the course of the Fehme trials of 1925-26. Certain of these groups, constituting the so-called Black Reichswehr, enjoyed a semi-official status, at least so far as the Reichswehr was concerned. These groups were regular military units formed in defiance of the Treaty of Versailles, which limited the standing army of Germany to one hundred thousand men.

Little is known of the activities of these secret troops. The following account written by a former leader of the Black Reichswehr affords some insight into their aims and functions:

[2.3.2.] I met a fellow cadet at Niederauslitz, and together we set out on our new task. We concentrated on patriotic societies, and proceeded to attract able-bodied men and former front soldiers of all groups. Thus the minor groups that only served to divide our strength were soon eliminated, while the *Stahlhelm*, the *Deutschnationale Jugendbund*, the *Bismarckjugend*, the *Junglandbund*, the *Jungdeutsche Orden*, the *Wehrwolf*, and so forth, held promise of future power. We knew the material at hand, good able-bodied Germans. Thus the network was spread over Ostmark. It was a difficult undertaking, but the results repaid our efforts. I went to Küstrin, where I organized the Black Reichswehr with second Lieutenant Schulz and six other comrades.

Nineteen-twenty was made memorable by the Kapp *Putsch* and the communist uprising in the Ruhr. It was a year of inner confusion and civil war. Germany consisted of two armed camps, lined up against each other. Nineteen twenty-three marked the occupation of the Ruhr and external complications.

The government was in a predicament throughout 1922-23. It was at this time of greatest need that the Black Reichswehr was organized. Had there been no Treaty of Versailles, had it not been for the fact that the imperialists, who gained the upper hand in France in 1923, stretched out their hands for the Ruhr and the Rhineland in order to destroy Germany, there would have been no Black Reichswehr.

To understand the events that threatened the very existence of Germany, we must go back to that period of history. The French had forcibly occupied the Ruhr. Inflation was assuming fantastic proportions. Obtaining food from day to day was a problem, as money would devaluate overnight. The Poles were a standing threat in the East. The Reich seemed to be on the point of breaking up. It was then that Poincaré spoke the dread words: "I can wait for chaos to do its work." Meanwhile in England the crown jurists had declared that the occupation of the Ruhr was illegal. Thus France herself had violated the Treaty of Versailles!

Nevertheless, successive German governments could arrive at no definite course of action. It was at this time that the work of Major Buchrucker and Second Lieutenant Schulz began. The undertaking was a difficult one: it called for skilled officers and men. Beginning with small units in Küstrin, it developed into what was later known as *Arbeitskommandos*. Eventually they were established in almost all communities of Brandenburg. The members were designated as civilian employees and workers; nevertheless they wore their Reichswehr uniforms, along with the proper designations of rank. In due time they undertook to round up all army supplies in the Province of Brandenburg, and store them in military supply houses. At the same time they had to take the utmost care lest these supplies fall into the hands of the Prussian police, who would have been only too glad to place them at the disposal of the Marxist hordes.

The *Arbeitskommandos* resorted to all means, legal and illegal, in their work. Committee members would wear uniform or mufti, as the occasion demanded. A great deal of material was assembled, which now had to be reconditioned. These supplies formed the nucleus of equipment for an army corps to protect the east of Germany against the danger of a Polish invasion. The organization grew and spread beyond the borders of Brandenburg under the name of *Schwarze Reichswehr*. Another task of the *Arbeitskommandos* was to assemble likely material not only for a possible mobilization, but also for training the troops. The manoeuvres took place under the auspices of the *Arbeitskommandos*.

Our chief difficulty was to keep everything secret; nevertheless we succeeded. Former members of the Black Reichswehr will no doubt recall numerous incidents of this time. The rampage in and around the centers of our activities attracted considerable attention, and numerous victims of the Marxist virus did their best to get at the bottom of this phenomenon. They even went so far as to set the Interallied Commission on our trail. Each time, however, the Interallied Commission had to withdraw without results, only to set on us the more furiously on the next occasion. Two distinct trends were noticeable among police officials, too. There were men constantly on the watch for anything they could report to the Marxist government, who would even deliver our store houses to its minions, while others went out of their way to avoid taking notice, and willingly helped us along. Our work was strenuous, but our men gloried in it. They realized that lasting results would have to come of our work, and acted accordingly. A great deal of money was required; this we obtained through our own efforts. Our contributors often viewed us askance, and demanded that we defend them against domestic disorders as well as external aggression. On every such occasion the officer in charge would point out that the Black Reichswehr was no garrison, and that every German had a patriotic duty to perform.

Ostmark was the territory most closely identified with the activities of the Black Reichswehr. It was our most important scene of action; it supplied the greatest part of our equipment, such as food, money, and supplies, and most important of all, it sent us the flower of its sons, who threw themselves heart and soul into the service of their people and their country. Thus a spirit of comradeship, discipline and loyalty held sway in the ranks of the Black Reichswehr. Every bit of this was necessary to the successful achievement of our task; in addition, it helped to keep away spies and traitors. While the spirit of the front line predominated, members of the then young N.S.D.A.P. carried the new idea to the hearts of these knights of the land. The Black Reichswehr constituted a community of its own, including all social strata. Thus it became the proving ground of National Socialism in the Ostmark, while today its rank and file actively fight and work for the Third Reich.

The secret military organizations were financed by heavy industry. They were strongly anti-Semitic, and formed the mainstay of the extreme rightist parties in the Reichstag. The government made numerous efforts to suppress them, especially after the assassination of Rathenau. The decree for the protection of the republic in particular was aimed at the secret military formations. All efforts at supression, however, proved ineffective, while the decree was invalidated by the military and nationalistic bias of the courts.

According to the autobiographies, 18 per cent of our informants participated in some form of post-war military activities, such as the fights against the Spartakists, the Kapp *Putsch,* the guerilla warfare in Upper Silesia, or the skirmishes during the Ruhr occupation in 1923. Sixty per cent of these were young men aged between seventeen and thirty in 1914, and two thirds belonged to the middle class.

A striking perspective of the mentality and emotions of the post-war generation is afforded by this story of a member of the youngest generation of front soldiers, subsequently a volunteer fighter in the Baltic provinces.

[1.7.5.] Completely disconcerted, a bourgeois generation faced the new world of 1918. It had managed during the war, adapting itself to all the unaccustomed limitations, suffering bitter need in the belief that some time, after peace was made, it would be able to continue down the broad, comfortable avenue it had traveled before. Now it found itself confused and frightened, in an arid meadow. In place of the imposing goal, they were confronted by unknown apparitions. An entire bourgeois generation stood and waited, in the hope that some time these spectres must disappear, and the broad open road must once again open before it.

There was a gaping abyss between fathers and sons. We soldiers of the front had never known the fabulous comfortable road; nor did we feel any longing for it. Fighting had become our life purpose and goal; any battle, any sacrifice for the might and glory of our country. The new state of affairs, to be sure, was a surprise to us. But we couldn't sit on the side lines, like people in a trance. Somehow we had to take a hand in affairs, one way or another.

There were those of the Marxist school among us. Like the rest of us, they had done their duty in the field. Now as red flags waved and processions marched, the mottoes and ideals of their fathers came back to them. They entered the soldiers' councils, spoke, organized, and tried to erect the free workman's state, dreamt of by Marx and Engels, LaSalle and Bebel. They fought with idealism and enthusiasm, until they finally fell back into the life of parasites, lolled comfortably in easily conquered arm chairs, and made good living their goal. Others turned away in disgust and roamed from leader to leader, from party to party, only to meet everywhere the spirit of Jewish materialism that their courageous soldiers' hearts could not accept.

And there were the rest of us—nationalists by education and tradition. We knew nothing of politics, yet we felt that therein lay the destiny of Germany. Slowly we came to recognize that we must learn to think in terms of politics if Germany was to live.

In the days of the revolution, discipline predominated. "Don't shoot," commanded the governor of the fortress of Kiel. Though convinced of the necessity of repelling Bolshevism, we didn't shoot. Then the sentries were withdrawn, weapons turned in; defenseless, bound by the command of our superiors, we young officers of the Imperial Marine stood face to face with the mob and its alien leaders. For more than four years death had been a matter of course for us; but we could not understand dishonorable surrender. Nor did we want to. What chance had we to resist?

On foot I made my way in the streaming rain to Neumünster. At least the infantry might undertake the battle against the reds. There too I was faced with disappointment. "Discipline! No bloodshed!" On to the office of the commanding general in

Altona I went. The same hateful word, "discipline," greeted me there too. In my native city I made a last attempt to contact an anti-Bolshevist troop. The old commander silently laid down a telegram before me: "No resistance!" Already men with red arm bands stood on guard; automobiles flew red flags. Deserters were hoisting red rags on the roofs. Offices and barracks were opened to them without resistance. "Discipline." It was the end.

One must bear these things in mind to understand the course of our lives, to comprehend how two generations became estranged in a few days. In those days our trust in the old leaders, in the old generation, was destroyed, struck dead. We had to take our fate in our own hands.

To feign indifference to the new conditions was impossible. The attempt failed miserably. Disgusted with the red cloths, drunken heroes of liberty, and uniformed bands of thieves, I turned my back on everything. Naturally only Kurland remained now.

Kurland meant to become a soldier again, to be allowed to fight again. It meant forming a decent troop which might one day clear up the mess, and finally it meant making primeval German land German again. So we marched, sang, and fought. But once victory was in our hands, Germany betrayed us. Germany? To us the Berlin of ministries was not Germany. Germany was ourselves, only we—no matter where, no matter under what flag.

Without further thought we surrendered our German citizenship, became Letts, and filled our pockets with the freshly printed rouble notes of the new Latvian Republic. Again we conquered, on the battlefield, only to lose once more at the parley tables. No matter. Under the Russian flag, we remained Germans. Only our uniforms were different; and soon we were fighting without pay. We suffered many privations, but we saw how our depleted group remained steadfast, until retreat was forced upon us by treason and unequal circumstances. We were back again, across the border, where Ebert and Noske ruled. They would see! Kapp was the name of our new leader, our next disappointment. Gritting our teeth we had to leave the conquered ground as our leaders disappeared. We were put to work in Pomerania, to protect the landed estates, to us the strongholds of nationalism. Soldiers were to become farmers. Confidently we set to work, only to realize before long what a world separated us from those "nationalists." At first we only sensed this. Still we did not want to resist these important landowners, whose ancient noble blood we felt we ought to respect. After all, they were *Deutschnational,* just as we were. Like us, they were fanatical opponents of Bolshevism. And yet our emotions were different. They spoke of Germany, but they meant money and privilege. They envisioned us not as free farmers, but as serfs. Unaccustomed as we were to expressing ourselves, we could find no words for our feelings.

Then—it was the summer of 1920—a summons came to us in Pomerania. Cheap paper . . . shabby print . . . slogans. . . . The contents didn't matter to us, but the signature aroused our enthusiasm. We had found what we had been seeking since the end of the war. *Deutsch-sociale Partei* was the name of the organization soliciting our support. It was German, of course . . . German, patriotic, nationalistic . . . that was what we were, and so too were the gentlemen with whom we could not agree. But there was another word that aroused our enthusiasm; the word connected with "German," instead of being coupled with democracy and liberalism as was usually the case. Socialism, enlightenment, the development of the communal spirit. . . . Once more we could respect every German as our brother. We sensed and we knew that if we succeeded in animating these printed words, if we could unite the concepts of nationalism and socialism, we would have a banner under which we could lead the German people to freedom.

The separatist movement, which sought to sever whole provinces from the Reich, was a standing thorn in the flesh of German nationalism. Particularly rampant in the occupied territories, it helped, along with the resentment felt over the occupation, to send thousands of young men and ex-soldiers into the nationalist camp. Practically all our contributors coming from the occupied territories responded, either by joining some military formation in Germany proper, or, where this was impossible, by resorting to local measures of retaliation. The following excerpt from the autobiography of a teacher illustrates one type of response:

[1.3.3.] Following the French invasion in 1923, the separatists once again gained hope of tearing the Rhineland from the Reich under the protection of French bayonets. At the time I was teaching at Altendiez an der Lahn, in the district of Wiesbaden. Day after day I had to suffer the sight of the French black troops marching from the one-time garrison city of Diez to their training place at Altendiez. These daily encounters with a foreign soldiery cut me to the quick. The provocative conduct of the French noncoms, whose fluent German bespoke their Alsatian origin, only made the hurt smart the more.

I taught the children under my care never so much as to look at these black fighters. If, by chance, they happened to pass by the school during recess, teachers and pupils would turn their backs, and remain standing like so many pillars of salt. The German-speaking officers and non-coms well understood this mute protest of German youth and its teachers, and not infrequently gave vent to their anger in the foulest language.

Our suffering was aggravated by the fact that in this hour of need there were people ready to take advantage of their German nationality to stab the Fatherland in the back and advance the French lust for power. There were a few of that ilk in Altendiez. Their leader, one Herr Knispel, was afterwards forced to flee, and ultimately made his home in America. The unpatriotic conduct of these people was the last straw for me. Everyone who identified himself with our suffering Fatherland proceeded to oppose these treasonable deeds. Here at last was a chance again to serve Germany to the best of our ability. And though we were at war with fellow Germans, we only fought the more bitterly; for the pestilential growth had to be cut off, lest the whole nation perish.

Along with two other loyal Germans, I organized a guard to watch the French railway at Diez, and to ascertain who of our people used the trains. The following day each of these would get a typewritten warning through the mails, to stop using this German railway fallen into French hands. There was an unmistakable indication, too, that force would be used if the recipient did not obey. Usually, however, the warning sufficed. Shortly afterwards there was not a soul at Altendiez willing to make use of the railway.

We paid special attention to the trucks of the separatists. If any such vehicle was reported coming from the direction of Bad Ems—usually they chose the hour of the nightfall—we would hastily throw a heavy chain across the highway, and lie in ambush nearby. I may say, too, we didn't treat these lads too gently.

In case of trouble, we hid all suspicious implements in the ice house of my father-in-law, who ran a butcher shop. The hollow walls, which insulated the ice house against outside temperature, held many a thing hidden to the eye of the uninitiated. As Herr Knispel's house was little by little demolished, however, the occupation finally resorted to the expedient of posting German citizens outside the house, who were to answer with their lives for the safety of the great separatist leader. Nevertheless the forces of destiny are not to be bridled forever.

On the twentieth of July, 1923, at nine o'clock in the morning, the French expelled me, thus putting a forcible end to my activities. I was given until 1:00 p.m. to cross the line of demarcation with my wife and five-months-old son. Before leaving, I had to give up the keys of my apartment to the French at Diez.

Exactly one year later, to the day, on the twentieth of July, 1924, the order of expulsion against me was rescinded.

While the indignation of Germans under foreign occupation was undoubtedly genuine, adverse economic conditions in many cases considerably affected their behavior. This second kind of response is particularly apparent in the following account of an unskilled worker:

[2.4.5.] Nineteen eighteen was the year of the breakdown. I lost my job. Relief was unheard of. The "conquerors" marched into the country. The Rhineland was occupied. Americans held sway at Linz. Spartakus raged in unoccupied Germany.

I arrived in Stettin in the spring of 1919 as a voluntary sanitation worker. On the way back I saw the following inscription on a billboard in Berlin:

WHO WANTS TO SAVE THE FATHERLAND?
THE LUETZOW FREIKORPS!
JOIN THE LUETZOW FREIKORPS!

Jobless and uprooted, I remained, to join the Luetzow Freikorps in Berlin. We received our training at Zossen and at the Wunstorf shooting galleries. The Commander, Major Hans von Luetzow, sent me to Linz to recruit volunteers. I returned with a troop of twenty-one Rhinelanders. The fratricidal war in central Germany, including the battles of Jena and Brunswick, followed.

"Why this war among brothers?" our comrades frequently asked. "Why should German workers fight against German workers?"

At the same time the Reichstag committee on war guilt was investigating General Field Marshal von Hindenburg, Ludendorff, and others. The day the Field Marshal was acquitted, the fifth squadron of the Luetzow Freikorps along with the Ehrhard Brigade passed in review before him. As a result we gained the undying hatred of Red Berlin, while Major von Luetzow was imprisoned for a fortnight.

Following our refusal to take the oath of loyalty to the Weimar Constitution before the Minister of War, Gustav Noske, we were transferred from the first national defense district of Berlin-Brandenburg to Westphalia, to avoid dissolution of the Freikorps. The Kapp *Putsch* found us at Schwelm, where we were stationed together with the Lichtschlag Freikorps. The first division of the Luetzow Freikorps was thereupon forcibly transported to Solingen (then under English occupation) and interned. What remained of the second division, which, like the Lichtschlag Freikorps, was almost entirely annihilated, was driven through Heiligenhaus-Duesseldorf back to Wesel. During this time I was at the hospital in Linz, having contracted an attack of the grippe shortly before.

What political wisdom had I gained at the time of my discharge in March 1920? Following the course of political and anti-Semitic lectures held under the auspices of the Luetzow Freikorps, I came to the conclusion that German workingmen were deliberately being deceived by so-called labor leaders (Jews), to forestall a union of all people of German blood, irrespective of class.

b. *Semi-military organizations*

To the semi-military groups belong the organization of veterans formed after the war. Of these the Stahlhelm was the largest and most disciplined. Organized by a manufacturer of soda water, at the height of the civil war in 1919, its first aim was the suppression of radicals in the mining and industrial centers of Germany, notably Halle and Magdeburg. The Stahlhelm never lost its counter-revolutionary character, and functioned as a bulwark of conservatism as its strength grew throughout the nation.

Second in importance to the veterans' organization were the numerous youth groups, such as the *Bismarckbund,* the *Koer-*

ner-Bund, Wiking-Bund, Jungdeutscher Orden, Wehrwolf, and so forth. Led by former officers, these groups were designed to inculcate the spirit of nationalism and racial superiority, and at the same time to promote military training among the young. Many organizations disguised as sport clubs served the same end.

Closest in spirit to national socialism was the so-called Artamane movement, whose activities are described in the following quotation. Approximately one third of our contributors belonged to this or other youth groups.

[2.2.3.] In 1921 I joined the then little-known youth movement of the Hawk and the Eagle, led by the German poet Wilhelm Kotzde. Its basic precepts related to national defense, race, and nationalism, and an absolute rejection of the poisons of civilization and the proprieties of a society infected by the virus of alien thought.

With youthful fervor we wandered over Germany and the border provinces. We met many prominent men, such as the well-known students of race problems Kreitschek and Günther, historians like Professors Hüsing, Schultz, Hahne, Halle, and others. Our conversion to National Socialism was a matter of course, as we found it to be the only right thing for us. It was not so much a matter of owning a membership card; rather we sought every occasion to defend the ideas of Adolf Hitler, particularly in the face of overwhelming opposition.

In 1924 Professor Willibald Hentschel issued a call to the German agricultural high school movement, the nationalist youth, and the entire membership of the national defense movement, to protect the German clod against aliens from the east, and to halt the flight from the land, by settling in the eastern provinces. We preached the basic truth enshrined in National Socialism: namely, that a people that deems it a disgrace to till its own soil must, in the natural course of events, be annihilated by the people to whom it leaves this task. Loyalty to the soil is tantamount to biological wisdom. He called this volunteer corps *"artam,"* so from the Aryan. A number of patriotic organizations helped in the realization of his ideas.

I, too, heeded the call. I persuaded my father to permit me to go to Germany, and join the Artamane movement. In the summer of 1925, I joined one of the groups in Saxony. In the summer we lived in Spartan simplicity and cultivated the soil. During the winter we were free to attend courses at the agricultural high school, or to continue our education at the Artamane leadership courses. A number of prominent men were connected with the movement, among them Himmler, leader of the Artamane, Günther, and Darré.

c. *Political groups*

Prior to the advent of national socialism, the parliamentary representation of the counter-revolutionary movement was negligible. Such opposition parties as the conservative *Deutsch-Nationale Volkspartei* accepted the new regime, and after 1924 actively participated in the government. It played the game of politics by the usual procedure of compromise and opportunism. The conservative party in the Weimar republic was the continuation under a new name of the party of the old regime. But there were several new parties, with radical, uncompromising policies that came into being after the war. Strongly anti-Semitic, these parties stood for a militant nationalism. They advocated far-reaching agrarian reforms (Damaschke's scheme), the nationalization of trusts, and the abolition of interest. Among them was the so-called German Socialist Party, led by Julius Streicher and Runge in Saxony and Bavaria, and by Kunze in Prussia. The predominantly anti-Semitic faction was represented by the *Deutsch-Voelkische Freiheitsbewegung,* under the leadership of Ludendorff, Graefe, Wulle, and others. The main support of this movement came from the *Schutz- und Trutzbund,* which comprised most of the rabid anti-Semites of Germany. Organized in 1919, it had for a time a following of several hundred thousand.

A brief survey of the counter-revolutionary groups shows how extensive and ramified were the activities through which certain parts of the population sought an outlet for their dissatisfaction with the new regime. If we consider that the supporters of these groups probably went into the millions, it becomes clear that a powerful tendency toward change existed long before the Hitler movement reached the first rung of success. But this tendency was highly diffused and uncoördinated. Many leaders were competing for power. There was no program to unite the different groups and enable them to win mass support. Anti-Semitism and militant nationalism, the two elements common to the movement, were still ideologically apart. Nationalism itself was a class issue, closely bound up with the desire of the followers of the old regime to stage a comeback under the pretense of promoting community interests. It remained for the Hitler movement to achieve the synthesis, and thus create a rallying point for the coördination of counter-revolutionary tendencies.

Chapter III

The First Period: 1919-1923

1. *Origin of the Movement*

How did the National Socialist party get its start?

According to all accounts, the party traces its origin to one of the many "political circles," or debating groups, that sprang up immediately before and after the war ended. These circles were in most cases casual gatherings of acquaintances who met to give vent to their dissatisfaction with existing conditions. The one that ultimately developed into the National Socialist party consisted of a handful of workers who met in a Munich beer hall. The leader of the group was the machinist Anton Drechsler; the rest were fellow members of his railroad union.

Drechsler had written a few articles in a Munich newspaper in 1918 urging the workers to stand behind the Imperial government and hold out for a victorious end. As a worker, he favored the reforms advocated by the socialists; as a patriot, however, he opposed the Social Democratic party on the grounds of its internationalism. It was largely because of Drechsler's articles that the circle was formed, for workers who shared his aversion to a "proletarian international." Devoid of any program or plan of action, the circle was no more than a *Stammtisch* of colleagues, who sought each other's company in order to air their views.

Under a republic dominated by social democrats, it was inevitable that union members, grouped around the discredited idea of nationalism, should attract some attention. Thus at an early stage a number of intellectuals, interested in the revival of nationalism in Germany, joined the group. Among them were Dietrick Eckart, poet, journalist, and rabid anti-Semite, and his friend Alfred Rosenberg, a disciple of Houston Stuart Chamberlain and an enthusiastic voucher for the Protocols of Zion. A refugee from the Russian Revolution, Rosenberg met Eckart in Munich and became associated with him in publishing propaganda pamphlets. Eckart also brought with him one Count von Bothmer, who addressed the circle on his conception of socialism as "the identification of the individual with his community, in devotion and service to an organic whole, the nation." Another intellectual who lectured before the groups was the engineer Gottfried Feder, who was obsessed by a plan of monetary reform and "social justice." He advocated the nationalization of credit, abolition of interest rates, and a government issue of non-interest paying bonds for public works and the development of industries. The idea was that "community interest comes before individual interest."

This mixed crew of nationalistic socialists, anti-Semites and economic reformers in turn attracted the attention of military authorities who readily supported nationalist activities. Hitler, at the time stationed with a Munich regiment, was assigned to establish contact with the circle.

In his autobiography Hitler gives a vivid account of his first contact with the Drechsler group, which called itself, somewhat pompously, "The German Workmen's Party."

As I entered the meeting room of the former Sterneckerbrau, I came face to face with a group of twenty to twenty-five men, mostly laborers and members of the lower middle class. Feder was giving a lecture, but having heard it before, I was able to devote my attention to the assembly itself. The impression I got was neither good nor bad. As far as I could see, there was nothing to distinguish this group from the many debating societies that made their appearance everywhere. It was a time when anyone dissatisfied with current developments felt the call to organize a new party.

These "parties" usually disappeared without much ado after a brief existence. In most cases the founders didn't know the first thing about transforming a debating circle into a movement. They hanged themselves with their ridiculous babbitry. I judged this group to be of the same type.[1]

Following Feder's lecture, Hitler participated in the discussion. His speech, directed against a member who advocated the separation of Bavaria from Prussia, made a good impression. As Hitler made ready to leave, Drechsler pressed a pamphlet in his hand, with an urgent request for his opinion. Hitler accepted it, on the chance that he might "learn something more about this boring society without having to attend any further meetings." Hitler read the pamphlet the following morning. He reports his reactions and subsequent experiences as follows:

At the time I was living in a tiny room at the barracks of the Second Infantry Regiment that still bore clear traces of the revolution. I spent most of the day with the Forty-first Sharpshooters; the rest of the time I attended meetings and lectures before other army divisions. As a rule, I went home only to sleep. Since I was regularly awake before five every morning, I made it a habit to leave some bread crumbs and hard rind on the floor for the mice that haunted my room. I would then watch the tiny creatures scurry after their tidbits. Having known so much want in my own life, I could readily appreciate both their hunger and their satisfaction.

The morning following the meeting, too, I lay awake by five, and watched the rush. Unable to go to sleep again, I recalled the previous evening, and in due time I thought of the pamphlet a workingman had given me. It was a slim little brochure in which

---

[1] *Mein Kampf*, 18th ed. F. Eher, Munich, 1933, pp. 237-238. Not included in the American edition.

the author, the aforesaid workingman, described how he had emerged from the welter of Marxist teachings and union catchwords, only to return to the principle of nationalism; hence the title, *My Political Awakening*. I read the pamphlet with interest. In substance it was much the same as my experience twelve years earlier. It seemed as if I saw my own development unfold before me once more.

I was about to dismiss the whole thing from my mind when, about a week later, I received a post card, notifying me that I had been accepted as a member in the German Workers' Party. I was to attend a meeting of the executive committee the following Wednesday, and let them know how I felt about the matter.

This method of recruiting members was, to be sure, new to me. I didn't know whether to be annoyed, or to laugh the whole thing off. For one thing, I had no intention of casting in my lot with any ready-made party; rather, I intended to organize one of my own. Consequently this demand meant nothing to me.

I was about to send the gentlemen a written summary of my feelings, when curiosity got the better of me. I decided to attend on the specified day, and personally recount my reactions.

The executive committee met in the dilapidated room of a cheap beer hall.

The minutes of the previous meeting were read and accepted. Next came the treasurer's report—the total assets of the organization amounted to seven marks and fifty pfennigs—hailed by a unanimous vote of confidence. The chairman then read his reply to a letter from Duesseldorf and one from Berlin. Following this he announced the receipt of further correspondence from Duesseldorf, Berlin, and Kiel. This met with universal approval, as this increased correspondence was taken to signify the growing importance of the German Workers' Party. Next a long time was spent discussing the proper replies.

It was all frightful. Here was the club game at its worst. So this was the organization I was to join!

Finally they came around to the question of new members—the subject of my being roped in, to be precise.

Now it was my turn to ask questions. Apart from a few slogans, however, I found they had no program, no publication, no printed matter, no membership cards, not even a beggarly rubber stamp. Their sole possessions were their evident faith and good will.

Yet this was no laughing matter. Rather it was a typical example of the helplessness and despair that characterized the prevalent attitude toward all existing parties, their platforms and activities. For the thing that prompted these young men in their seemingly ridiculous antics was only the outward manifestation of a recognition, instinctive rather than reasoned, of the complete inability of the current party system to improve the lot of the German people and cure its inner ills. The typewritten slogans, too, bespoke a seeking rather than a concrete attitude. There was much that was hazy; a good deal was missing; nevertheless there was nothing there that might not have heralded a stirring awakening.

I knew what these people felt: it was the longing for a new movement that would be something more than a party in the ordinary sense.[2]

Should he accept or decline the invitation to become a member? Hitler mulled over the question for two days. His own analysis, cited in his autobiography, reveals the real motive that animated Hitler in his career:

I began to weigh the matter. I had long ago made up my mind to take an active part in politics. It was clear to me too that the way to do this was through a new movement: up to that time, however, I had had no occasion to begin. I am not the kind who starts something one day, only to quit and start another the next. This very attitude made it difficult for me to launch a movement that would either have to be the be-all and end-all, or had better not exist at all. There could be no way out for me. I was in deadly earnest. Even then I had an instinctive dislike for people who meddle with everything without seeing anything through. To me their busybody tactics were worse than nothing. Yet fate itself seemed to point the way this time. I should never have joined any of the standing major parties; the reasons for this will be taken up in detail elsewhere. This ridiculous little makeshift, however, with its handful of members, seemed to offer one distinct advantage: it had not yet frozen into an organization. Thus there were unlimited opportunities for individual activity. The smaller the movement, the greater the possibility of directing it in the proper channels.

---

[2] *Ibid.*, pp. 239-242. Fragmentary in the American edition.

This movement could still be given the proper impetus, form and goal, a possibility not to be thought of in connection with the larger established parties.

The more I thought about it the more convinced I became that it was just such a tiny movement as this that might be made a harbinger of the future welfare of our people. The same end could never be achieved through the standing parliamentary parties that either placed too much weight on old concepts or deliberately profited through the new lords. For the thing that was needed was not a new campaign slogan, but a new world philosophy.

It was a difficult decision, indeed, to set about transferring these ideas into concrete realities.

Then, too, what qualifications had I for the task?

That I was poor and needy seemed the least of my handicaps. What was more difficult to bear was that *I was one of the nameless millions who live and die by the whim of chance,* without so much as attracting the attention of their very neighbors. Added to this was the handicap of my insufficient schooling.

For the so-called intelligentsia are ever ready to heap unbounded scorn on all who have not plodded through the prescribed courses, to have their heads pumped full of facts. Their concern is not with what a man can do, but with what he has learned. To these illuminati the worst numskull backed up by the requisite diplomas is dearer than a shining light who has not been able to afford these expensive trimmings. Indeed I only erred on the side of kindness, as I judged most people to be better than they really are in the cold light of sober reality. The exceptions, of course, only shine the brighter for all that. By this token I learned to know the difference between the true sages and the everlasting schoolboys.

After two days of painful indecision, I finally made up my mind to take the step. It was the weightiest decision in my life. There could and would be no road back.

Thus I reported for membership in the German Workers' party, and received the provisional membership card number seven.[8]

Hitler's entry into the German Workers' party was the turning point not only in his life, but also in the development of the party itself. For it was the coming of Hitler that transformed the insignificant debating circle into the promotion

---

[8] *Ibid.,* pp. 242-4. Fragmentary in the American edition (italics mine).

group of a movement. There can be little doubt that it was his energy, perseverance, and personality that saved the group from the fate of similar organizations.

In exchange for his membership in the Drechsler group, Hitler exacted the promise of a free hand in propaganda. Just then he was not interested in organization, and willingly left matters in the hands of the executive committee. He wanted action. That meant lifting the party from its obscurity, winning public recognition and acclaim. It meant assembling a sufficient following to bring about the defeat of the hated new order. Finally, it meant for Hitler the achievement of status, and a chance to become a leader. He faced these formidable tasks alone and virtually empty-handed. Devoid of funds, helpers, or an audience that would listen to him, he had nothing but his burning ambition to start with.

There was one circumstance, however, that carried the chance of success, provided he could turn it to account. Bavaria, and Munich in particular, had just passed through the bloodiest social upheaval in its history. Beginning with the establishment of a soviet government, it ended, after a period of terrorism, assassination, executions, and general disorder, in a civil war in which the soviet regime was defeated. As a result, the people turned against the republican government. Its weakness in combating radicals, along with its general lack of authority, led to a popular revival of nationalistic sentiment, and, since many of the Communist leaders had been Jews, to a widespread anti-Semitic movement. Many turned a willing ear to nationalist agitators and favored collective action to restore the old order of things. Pamphlets advocating a plethora of programs found eager readers. Thousands were rallying to nationalistic, anti-Semitic groups like the *Thule Gesellschaft* and the *Schutz- und Trutzbund.* The Bavarian Citizens' Corps *(Einwohnerwehr),* organized by Escherich soon after the overthrow of the Communist regime, had no difficulty in finding recruits. The newly appointed "popular government" smacked of reaction, and gave tacit support to anti-socialist and even anti-republican agitation. A fertile ground thus existed for an ambitious propagandist who could strike the public fancy.

By the spring of 1921 Hitler had recruited thousands of members for the German Workers' party, and attracted other thousands to his weekly meetings. He raised sufficient funds for a special party organ, the *Voelkische Beobachter,* and spread his propaganda through a band of stalwart and devoted followers. Thus the foundation of the "conquest of Munich" was securely laid.

How did Hitler achieve these results? The fact that he appealed to popular sentiment explains only part of his success. The decisive factor was his propaganda tactics. Hitler had learned a valuable lesson from the Allies, as he admits in his autobiography. From the beginning he used devices that gave him a clear advantage over competitors addicted to the traditional methods of political agitation. He announced his meetings by means of glaring placards; he used trucks to distribute propaganda material in the streets of Munich. He made the city aware of his party by means of distinctive uniforms and badges. He organized parades and street demonstrations. Acutely conscious of publicity values, he forced the opposition to take notice of him, and fight him in the press and at its meetings. This he accomplished by invading social democratic strongholds, staging his meetings in socialist-controlled districts, and disrupting the meetings of his foes either by monopolizing the discussion floor or, on occasion, by use of force.

The outstanding feature of his propaganda, however, was the aggressive tone adopted by National Socialists in their speeches, pamphlets, and newspapers. There was no mincing of words, no politeness, and little concern with facts and logic in these outpourings. Aimed at the emotions, they struck heavily but effectively. The rapier play of fine wit was as foreign to them as any attempt at fair play.

While these methods did not appeal to intellectuals and the sedate upper classes, they made a powerful impression on those less concerned with manners and logic. The blunt, unadorned words of the speakers seemed to favor their interests, and pointed the way to fearless, uncompromising action.

At first Hitler had considerable difficulty in rounding up even a handful of hearers for his political meetings. For days he walked the streets of Munich, distributing typewritten invitations to passersby. The response was disappointing. Seven persons attended the first meeting; months later he was unable to push the number beyond thirty. Things improved, however, when funds obtained from penny contributions made advertising in the press possible.

About one hundred people attended the first advertised meeting. Some months later the number rose to four hundred. On the twenty-first of February 1920, Hitler called a mass meeting, widely advertised by placards, for the official launching of the party. Four prominent Nationalist leaders were secured as speakers, and an audience of nearly two thousand attended the meeting. Among them were a number of opponents, who came to break up the meeting. No disturbance, however, marred the occasion. In a two-hour speech Hitler interpreted the twenty-five theses of party doctrine, to the vast enthusiasm of his hearers. In his autobiography he describes this meeting somewhat lyrically, but with surprising foresight: [4]

When the hall began to empty, and I saw the masses streaming like a flood through the exit, I knew that the tenets of a never-to-be-forgotten movement were going out among the German people. A spark had been ignited, and from its flame in time must come the sword that shall regain life and freedom for the German nation. And amid the vision of coming resurrection, I foresaw the inexorable vengeance to be visited upon the traitors of November 1918. The movement was started on its course.

---

[4] *Ibid.,* p. 406.

From that day the success of the party was assured. Attendance at its meetings increased rapidly, and soon the largest hall in Munich was inadequate to hold them. Sooner or later, most people dissatisfied with the current order came under National Socialist influence, and the party became the leading counter-revolutionary organization in Munich.

Hitler obtained funds for propaganda activities and the purchase of a daily newspaper through public collections, and through the contributions of a few wealthy friends who sympathized with him. The bulk of his funds, however, came from the Reichswehr. Military authorities, as we pointed out previously, were interested in the development of a strong nationalist party, and they were impressed with the success of the National Socialists. Ernst Roehm, captain in the Reichswehr and an early convert to National Socialism, was instrumental in securing and consolidating this support. Through Roehm Hitler also established contacts with the Bavarian government, and assured himself of the favorable attitude of the civilian authorities, particularly the police, toward his subversive activities.

Hitler's aggressive tactics attracted many young men who had little prospect of settling down under existing conditions. Bound by personal loyalty to Hitler, these men, imbued with a fanatical nationalism, constituted the Fuehrer's most reliable following. Hitler recruited them from among his own comrades in arms, university students, and unemployed young men of the working and middle classes. Early in 1921 these followers were organized in regular fighting units, and effectively designated as political soldiers. Politics were thus brought home to them in the familiar terms of discipline and fighting. These units formed the nucleus of what later became the famous storm troops and special guards, the *S.A.* and the *S.S.*, which served as the shock troops of the party.

After the establishment of a field of operation, large audiences and devoted followers rallied to the party. Two main developments characterize the growth of the movement from this time to 1924: first, Hitler's ascendancy to supreme leadership both in the party and in the nationalistic circles of Bavaria; secondly, the abortive *coup d'état,* the so-called Hitler *Putsch.*

2. Hitler Becomes the Leader

When Hitler joined the Drechsler group, he was primarily interested in creating a movement, with himself as its prophet. He sought to realize an idea that absorbed him completely, and he considered himself the chosen leader to present it to the German masses. The desire to put his idea into effect and the wish for leadership are inextricably woven together. To promote the idea he had to promote himself; to promote himself meant to him promotion of the idea.

Once Hitler had seized control of the party machine, he never again relinquished it, despite several attempts to challenge his authority. Notable among these was the Strasser affair of 1932, in the course of which Gregor Strasser broke away from Hitler, alleging disregard of party interests. From the first Hitler made the party subservient to the establishment of a movement under his leadership. Thus he ran the organization as a promotion group, instead of a political unit.

This was most evident between 1920 and 1924. Several times during this period various nationalistic groups sought to join hands with the National Socialists and create a united front. Invariably, however, these negotiations broke down, because of Hitler's insistence upon unconditional surrender, and unquestioned recognition of himself as leader. Furthermore, little was done at this time to expand the organization beyond the confines of Munich. About one hundred affiliated organizations are recorded outside the city at the time, but they were unsupervised, and uncoördinated with the parent organization. Left to their own devices, these groups were little more than gatherings of sympathizers who had heard about Hitler, but had only the vaguest conception of his program. The autobiographies show that a number of these groups existed in the Rhineland, and a few even in Prussia.

Hitler's neglect of party concerns, however, is most apparent in his speeches. They contain no elucidations of the party program, no arguments in its favor. Instead, Hitler used his speeches to make dire threats against the government, foment the idea of resistance, and make converts to his leadership. Basing his speech on some local or national news story, he would invariably wind up with the same refrain: the German government was run by criminals who mulcted the nation and called down the disrespect of other countries upon Germany. The revolution was one gigantic fraud; its leaders were doubtful characters, deserters, pacifists, and traitors; officialdom was corrupt, and procurers were being made chiefs of police. He held the republican government responsible for the fact that "hunger was rampant," "the currency destroyed." He accused it of leading Germany into "voluntary slavery," of "defiling traditions and destroying national honor." He maintained that "the November republic is a negation of German history, for it has led to the dissolution of the old army, has befouled the old flag, and made Germany the playground of foreign interests." Hitler would then follow up these audacious accusations, which held his audience spellbound, by an appeal to his hearers to become militant nationalists, and prepare for armed resistance. "We demand conscription for everybody. If you believe you must be free, then learn that the sword alone can give you freedom." His task, he would say, was to restore nationalism in Germany. "If sixty million Germans have the will to be fanatically national, then weapons will sprout from their fists."

His climax, too, was always the same. The things all true Germans desired were the "defeat of the Red Monster," abolition of the Treaty of Versailles, the resurrection of a powerful and defiant nation, and the establishment of a *Volkstaat,* a truly German community, in which honesty and morality should prevail. All this, he pointed out, could be accomplished through the victory of National Socialism. For National Socialism was of the very essence of the German spirit. It did not work for elections, but prepared the ground for the coming collapse, "so that a young spruce may grow where the old stem falls." What the German people needed was not parliamentary leaders, but a single leader who would rise from the masses and carry out what he considered right even against the opposition of majorities. National Socialism offered such leadership. It alone could destroy Marxism.[5]

Clearly such speechmaking was calculated to lead to the conclusion that Hitler himself was the much-needed leader. Soon a veritable Hitler cult developed among his followers, who bestowed upon him the title "der Fuehrer." This veneration was contagious, enhanced by the enthusiastic receptions his audiences accorded Hitler. He became a favorite orator, particularly during the disastrous time of the inflation, and the French occupation of the Ruhr. Thousands fixed their hope upon the hero whose firm hand would "liberate the nation."

Characteristic of the prevalent sentiment was the celebration of Hitler's birthday in April 1923. Thousands flocked to the Zirkus Krone to listen to the national airs played by military bands, to watch the parade of storm troopers, and to second the speeches of adulation that greeted Hitler. At the height of the celebration Captain Goering, head of the storm troops, tendered Hitler the gift of an honorary sword, with the words: "To the beloved leader of the German movement for freedom, in the conviction shared today by hundreds of thousands of the most loyal Germans, that Adolf Hitler is the only man who can save Germany."[6]

While Hitler was thus establishing himself as a "leader of men" at the expense of party politics, he was intentionally or

---

[5] The citations are culled from *Adolf Hitler's Reden*. Munich: Deutscher Volksverlag, 1933.

[6] Hasselbach, U. v., *Die Enstehung der National-Sozialistischen Arbeiterpartei*, 1919-23. Thesis, Leipzig, 1931.

unintentionally doing the right thing for the establishment of a movement. For the history of the great movements of the past, such as the Reformation, Methodism, and the French and Russian Revolutions, clearly show that belief in a "man of destiny" is vital to the furtherance of social movements. The leader who is thus invested by his followers with the attributes of a man of destiny may be designated as a *charismatic* leader, following the terminology of Max Weber.[7] Such a leader is one supposedly endowed with "special grace" (Charisma), for the fulfilment of a given mission. His followers look upon him, not as an efficient manager, but as a prophet, a symbol of their aspirations, a legendary figure for whom they experience unbounded reverence and to whom they feel bound in personal allegiance. This the Fuehrer cult, together with the wildly emotional tone of his propaganda, achieved for Hitler.

3. *The Hitler Putsch*

German banks were paying four billion marks for a dollar when Hitler staged his first stroke against the government in the fall of 1923. The French were in the Ruhr. People everywhere were aroused over the inactivity of the government in the face of foreign invasion, as well as what appeared to be the deliberate engineering of a ruinous inflation. Rebellion was rife, particularly in Bavaria, where nationalistic organizations had strongly entrenched themselves, by tacit consent of the provincial government.

Early in September 1923 the national organizations of Bavaria formed a united front, in preparation for a *coup d'état*. Hitler succumbed to the pressure of nationalistic circles, and, reversing his position of no compromise, for once joined a coalition. Accordingly he placed his organization and the storm troops at the disposal of a staff of officers in charge of military preparations. The "political soldiers" thus became

---

[7] Weber, Max, *Gemeinschaft und Gesellschaft.* Tübingen: J. C. B. Mohr, 1922. p. 140.

ordinary fighters. The National Socialist party temporarily ceased to be the promotion group of a movement and became a military party. Apparently this slogan, "The fate of Germany will soon be decided by Bavarian fists in Berlin," put all other considerations into the background. Hitler was appointed political leader of the united front, and hailed as the "German Mussolini." [8]

Throughout the fall of 1923 feverish preparations were afoot in Bavaria, particularly in Munich. But the great "nationalist uprising" never came off. Hitler precipitated the action contemplated by military authorities with the tacit support of the Bavarian government. On the eighth of November he arrested the members of the government, and on the following day marched his troops against Munich. There, however, a volley from troops loyal to the government put an end to the *Putsch*. Hitler fled, was subsequently arrested, tried, and sentenced to imprisonment.

Whether Hitler's impetuous action, upon which he staked his life and reputation, was caused by impatience over delays, or the suspicion that his fellow conspirators might be using him for the separation of Bavaria from the Reich, is not known for certain. Matters pertaining to this point were discussed behind closed doors at the trial, and the records of these sessions are not available.[9]

---

[8] It is doubtful whether Hitler himself had any aspirations to dictatorship at the time. In his speech at the trial following the *Putsch* he declared: "The only man I could consider for the top position (the military dictatorship then planned) is Ludendorff" *(Hitler's Reden,* p. 101) and, "I considered myself at the time the drummer of the cause against Marxism. I was not looking for the title of a minister." *(Ibid.,* p. 118.)

[9] In a speech before the survivors of the *Putsch* in 1934, Hitler indicated that he had been inspired by fear of a separatist move. "We had to act in 1923," he declared, "because we were confronted with a last attempt of the separatists in Germany to realize their aim. . . . If we had not acted, they would have done so, on November 12 (apparently the date set for the general uprising), on the principle that 'Northern Germany will go Bolshevik in any case. Let us, therefore, sepa-

While the direct consequences of the *Putsch* were a set-back for the movement, indirectly it benefited from the publicity attending both the *Putsch* and the subsequent trial. Throughout the period from 1920 to 1923 the German press had practically ignored the movement. After the *Putsch*, however, it was forced to give columns to the event, as well as to Hitler's speeches at the trial. Hitler became a national figure overnight. One observer records his reactions as follows: [10]

[3.1.4.] I felt electrified as the word went abroad in the newspapers in 1923 that down in Munich a man by the name of Adolf Hitler, aided by a little band of followers, had tried, in an excess of patriotic zeal, to shake off Red rule and restore its honor to the German people. Tensely expectant, I pursued all news of political developments in Germany thereafter. I felt with increasing certainty that a man had arisen to lead the Fatherland toward a brighter future. Instinctively I knew that this currently obscure movement merited every support.

A large number of our contributors report that they established contact with the movement through press reports following the *Putsch*. Many were particularly impressed by the bold stand Hitler made at his trial, and became his enthusiastic adherents. A war veteran writes:

[3.4.0.] There was no point of contact with the men in power. For they had banished the glorious old black-and-white-and-red banner and substituted a flag in its place that meant nothing to the front fighters. What became of the memory of the dead? Their blood called to high Heaven for vengeance!

Then came a light in the darkness. A movement for freedom was founded in Munich. In 1923 we heard the name of Adolf Hitler for the first time. Who was the man? He was a simple front soldier, an Austrian who had fought and bled under the German flag. What did he want? The thoughts raced through

---

rate. . . .' I made the decision to attack four days before my opponents intended to act." Quoted in Ganzer, R. H., *Vom Ringen Hitlers um das Reich*. Berlin: Zeitgeschichte Verlag, 1935, p. 14.

[10] For an explanation of the symbols in brackets, turn to the insert at the end of the book.

my brain. Truth, honor, faith, discipline! What marvelous words! Unity of all people of German blood! How was he going to accomplish that? Then there was the Buergerbrau Keller session in 1923. A new government was announced. The old men in Berlin were deposed! *Here was a man of action!*

Then treason did its work and the undertaking collapsed. Trials followed in the courts. How that man Hitler spoke! Those days of his trial became the first days of my faith in Hitler. From that time on I had no thought for anyone but Hitler. His behavior moved me to give him my whole faith, without reserve. There was not much to weigh or study. All a man had to do was to think about the courage and heroism of his beginnings. The ideas of the leader cannot be got from books, be they ever so learned. The philosophy of national Socialism must take roots in one's very heart!

Ever since those days I have fought and striven for my Fuehrer, Adolf Hitler. I shall readily give my all for him at any time he may demand it.

In a less tangible fashion the results of the *Putsch* had a considerable effect on shaping the future policies of National Socialism. Hitler became convinced that his aim could not be realized unless he had the majority of the nation behind him. Consequently he intensified his propaganda, and directed his organization in conformity with legal procedure. Hence the participation of the Party in the Reichstag elections, and his own candidacy for the presidency. The *Putsch* furthermore convinced Hitler that he could not count on the support of other groups. The policy of no compromise was adopted as a standing principle, and afterwards became the germ of the totalitarian state.

Chapter IV

The Second Period: 1924-1929

1. *After the Putsch*

WITH THE IMPRISONMENT of Hitler in Landsberg fortress and the prohibition of his party, the leaders of the Republican regime felt that a death blow had been dealt the movement. There was a general opinion that, deprived of an audience and removed from the scene of action, Hitler would soon be forgotten; his followers could never forgive him the defeat he had precipitated.

Hitler, however, was far from acknowledging defeat. Nor was he discouraged. He looked upon the *Putsch* as an incident in his fight for political control, rather than a set-back indicating that the movement was wrong or that his aims were unattainable. His failure he ascribed to betrayal by his allies and his mistaken compromise with other nationalist parties. Resolved to lead the fight alone from that time on, Hitler more than ever believed himself the "man of destiny," chosen to put an end to the—to him—inevitable defeat of the Republican regime.

Hitler used his enforced idleness to perform a much-needed task—one he was unable to fulfill while campaigning and fighting. This was drawing together the loose threads of ideas into an integrated ideology. Thus the very government, eager to silence Hitler, provided the opportunity and paid the expenses for the writing of the book that was to become the Holy Writ of the movement.

It is difficult to say what would have happened had *Mein Kampf* never been written. Its importance is amply demonstrated by its effect on Hitler himself. Reflection upon his past, organization of his thoughts, and a detailed consideration of strategy and tactics made Hitler a much more effective promoter than he had been before the *Putsch*. As a result, the movement became more rational and purposeful in its planning and more statesmanlike in its activities, providing a broader and more secure basis for its growth.

A more direct effect of the book may be seen in its influence as a means of propaganda, a manual for party leaders, and an inspirational text for the followers of the movement. An early convert writes:[1]

[2.8.4.] My greatest political experience occurred when I bought and read a copy of Hitler's book. I saw therein a confirmation of the very views I had cherished, but which I could not express properly. Now I had the necessary equipment to take up the quarrel with my political opponents. I had found the cause to which I could devote my life, and I availed myself of every opportunity at the club, the office, and at home, to spread the ideas of Hitler.

Another aspect of the part played by the book is reflected in this statement of a storm trooper:

[2.6.2.] Our group, consisting of students and workers, merchants and clerks, held frequent meetings to discuss the ideas of our movement. Barring the party platform, there was very little written material to instruct us. But in 1926 our Fuehrer's work was printed. It became the central factor in our undertakings, and we often read the book aloud at group meetings. Even though most

---

[1] For an explanation of the bracketed symbols, turn to the insert at the end of the book.

of the men had never seen Hitler, he was no longer a stranger to us, for his written word brought him vividly to our minds.

Hitler composed his book as he paced the floor of his cell, thinking aloud for hours, while the devoted Rudolf Hess, initiator and prime mover of the *Fuehrer* cult, took notes. Hess joined the party in 1921 on the occasion of his first meeting with Hitler. The young man, who had shortly before won a contest sponsored by a German-American on the "cause of the suffering of the German people," looked upon Hitler as the very incarnation of the "coming strong man."

In his prize winning essay, Hess pointed out the need of a dictator and predicted his advent:

The greatness of a people is national consciousness, the will to self-assertion in the world. Napoleon had the powerful nationalism of the French Revolution to build upon. The German dictator must first arouse and cultivate it.

He pictured the dictator as:

. . . passionate, and at the same time self-controlled, calculating and bold . . . without inhibitions in putting decisions quickly into action, without consideration for himself or others, hard without pity, yet at the same time soft in his love for the people, untiring in his work; not a despot, but a great renewer and educator of the people, to dare to begin what must be! This is the greatness, the mark of leadership.

Hess saw this mark in Hitler, and he succeeded in converting others to his faith, which ultimately became the principal tenet of the movement.

While Hitler was busily composing in his cell, various things were happening on the political scene. Following the abrogation of the National Socialist party, many of its former members dropped completely out of political activities, while others joined one or another of numerous minor nationalistic groups. Still others organized new groups, which under various names attempted to carry on the policies of the outlawed party. While part of the membership thus remained intact, each of the petty group leaders entertained personal ambitions, and competed with and intrigued against all the others. From his prison cell, Hitler could not exercise sufficient influence to prevent factional strife. An effort to create a nationalistic front was finally made through the establishment of the *Deutsch-Voelkische Freiheits Bewegung,* under the nominal leadership of General Erich Ludendorff. In the first election following its creation, held on May 4, 1924, the movement polled six and a half million votes. The lack of a unified central authority, however, obviated any chance of a vigorous, clearly defined policy. The minor leaders continued to work at cross-purposes, with a resultant confusion in the ranks of the voters. Consequently, by the next elections on December 7, 1924, the *Freiheits Bewegung* lost three and a half million votes.

There were other reasons too, which contributed to the temporary eclipse of radical nationalism in Germany. The year 1924 inaugurated a distinct change in international politics which, in turn, profoundly affected the internal situation in Germany.

In August 1923, the most critical period of German history since the World War, Gustav Stresemann became Chancellor of Germany. The Ruhr was at this time under French occupation; communist governments held sway in Saxony and other provinces; Bavaria was threatening to secede from the Reich; economic life in general was paralyzed by the inflation. In the face of this, Stresemann declared a state of emergency and ordered the Reichswehr to take drastic measures against the anti-republican left and right extremists. As a result, the Reichswehr suppressed the provincial communist governments and frustrated the "march on Berlin" planned by the Munich nationalists. The threat of internal disruption thus eliminated, Stresemann directed his efforts toward the stabilization of the currency. Then he used his newly won prestige as a wedge for tackling the biggest job he had set for himself, the revision of

Germany's foreign policy. By adopting a policy of conciliation, he opened a new path for negotiations with the Allies. This involved a surrender to the Treaty of Versailles, including the demand for reparations. Consequently a series of new agreements were made between Germany and the Allies, notably the Dawes Plan and the Locarno pact, which in due course eventuated in the entrance of Germany into the League of Nations on a status of equality.

Hailed as a triumph of German diplomacy, Stresemann's achievements were regarded at the time as harbingers of a new era of international coöperation. Economic recovery being the goal, prosperity, apparently well on the way, became the touchstone of the new dispensation.

As a result of the Dawes Plan, enormous sums of money, chiefly from the United States, were pouring into Germany in the form of loans to the government, municipalities, and private corporations. With the consequent revival of industry and the virtual elimination of unemployment, there was a striking change in attitude toward the Republican regime. The national conservative parties present the best illustration of this shift in public opinion. Impressed by the results of Stresemann's policy, and appeased by Hindenburg's election to the Presidency, they signified their approval of the regime by entering the government, *via* posts in the cabinet. A wave of optimism swept all over Germany; when Stresemann spoke his famous line about the "silver lining on the horizon," he was voicing a prevalent sentiment.

Not that opposition was altogether lacking. Conspicuous among the foes of the government was Hugenberg, at the time building up his vast propaganda machine by securing control of hundreds of newspapers and the radio and movie industries. The *Stahlhelm,* largest organization of veterans, joined him and publicly denounced the national parties as traitors. Lastly there was Hitler, who from his prison cell denounced the government for its surrender to the Allies, and for the imposition of an unbearable burden upon the German people in the Dawes settlement. The opposition, however, was unsuccessful in rallying support for its policies. People in general looked upon agitators as fanatical irreconcilables who would not recognize that the war was over, and who retarded recovery by fomenting strife and hampering the government.

Few people recognized the precarious foundation upon which rested the new order of things, its maintenance dependent wholly upon the ability of the government to consolidate its position and to insure the continuance of prosperity. The newly won tolerance had no roots, and was much too dependent upon economic and political exigencies to survive even a temporary adversity. Disappointment at this stage was bound to evoke a violent reaction, all the more so because the element of self-incrimination for giving in too easily would be present. Instead of a genuine peace, the people had made a speculative truce with the government. The flood that was to sweep it away was not far off.

Nevertheless, as Hitler, determined to resume his political agitation, emerged from prison in November 1924, he faced discouraging prospects. His followers were scattered among wrangling groups; the party which succeeded his had been badly defeated at the polls; a sentiment inimical to nationalistic agitation pervaded the country. Hitler was convinced, however, that this sentiment would not last. He had no faith in the ability of the government to maintain prosperity by means of an increasingly top-heavy economic and diplomatic structure. When this collapse occurred, it was reasonable to assume that the people would turn against the political parties, groups, and individuals involved in the debacle, and adopt the leadership of those who right along had combated them. With this in mind, Hitler resolved, despite the heavy odds against him, to resume where he had left off in 1923, by leading an opposition party. Prominent in its platform were repudiation of agreements with the Allies, refusal to pay reparations, and opposition to loans from abroad, under the slogan: "Only by its own force can Germany regain its rightful position in the world." No *coup d'état,* no march on Berlin was contemplated. The bid for power was to be made by entering the parliamentary race and fighting for supremacy by legitimate means.

By convincing the government of Bavaria of his change of heart in regard to *putschist* activities, Hitler succeeded in obtaining a revocation of the ban on the National Socialist party. Consequently, on January 27, 1925, he called a meeting at that scene of many past triumphs, the Brauhaus. Over four thousand people came to welcome him back. On the platform he effected the reconciliation of his former lieutenants, who since his imprisonment had been fighting among themselves for Hitler's crown, and accepted their pledge of allegiance to him. In a three-hour speech Hitler outlined his plan, proclaiming his principle that supreme leadership and unquestioned authority in policy and dogma, from that time on, was to be vested in him alone. The meeting showed clearly that the Hitler cult had not lost its appeal, despite the defeat of 1923. The audience gave Hitler a rousing reception, and the Party was launched in high spirits.

A ban on his public appearance, which was to be in force for several years, prevented Hitler from resuming his old role of chief spellbinder. Intended to deprive the Party of its most effective weapon, this restriction turned out to be the same double-edged weapon that Hitler's imprisonment had been. Barred from public speech making, Hitler turned his full energy to the highly important task of organization. Between 1925 and 1928 he set into' motion the vast propaganda machine and set up the network of National Socialist cells and storm troop units which finally, covering all of Germany, made it possible to take over the administrative affairs of the entire country without a hitch.

Under a policy of long-range planning, the movement newly resurrected by Hitler began a long uphill fight for political supremacy. It reached its goal eight years later when, on January 30, 1933, Hitler was made Chancellor of the Reich.

2. Organization

The eventful years from 1925 to 1933 were characterized by struggles on many frónts by the National Socialist party: the fight for party members and voters, the conflict against hostile parties both right and left, the resistance to efforts at government suppression, and factional strife within the Party (for example, the Stennes and Strasser affairs). Political manoeuvres and intrigues, pitched battles, and aggressive propaganda dominated the scene as never before.

a. *Significance of the local group*

Undoubtedly the leaders, particularly Hitler and Goebbels, played a decisive role in the promotion of the movement, especially in the inspirational influence they exerted upon their followers. But headquarters was not the only place where results were obtained. Thousands of unsung workers and "unknown *S.A.* men," as Goebbels aptly called them, served the movement in the remote villages, and small towns of Germany, with little or no guidance from the central organization. Thus it was the so-called *Ortsgruppe,* the local group operating within a community, that constituted the keystone of the movement. The daily battles for the preservation and growth of the movement were carried on in the intimate face-to-face relationships of individual members of communities. For this reason the real burden of promotion rested upon the local party worker; its progress depending to a considerable extent upon his tenacity and initiative and his ability to adopt his procedure to local demands.

In organizing local groups, frequently the leader of a neighboring town, or the district leader himself, would call a meeting in a given locality, either by invitation or on his own initiative.

The appeal for members regularly made at the close of the meeting usually yielded several applications. The applicants would then constitute themselves into an *Ortsgruppe,* which was left to its own devices in propagating the movement. One organizer writes:

[3.3.3.] In 1928 I became acquainted with a young fellow countryman, a worker, who had already been in the Ruhr. He had observed the movement there, and had met a number of the leaders.

In the fall of the same year, the newly appointed district leader of East Prussia held the first National Socialist meeting in Stallupönen. That day several fellow countrymen, as well as myself, became members of the Party. The number was too small for a local group; my young compatriot and I, however, continued to work for the idea. In the end he undertook the leadership of the new local. While my illness made me unequal to the actual job of leadership, I did all I could to help him.

Worry about his livelihood was a great hindrance to the young leader, who had a wife and two children to care for, in the face of unemployment. In due time I was able to get him a position as an assistant in the post office, so that he was at least fr~ed of the struggle for his daily bread.

While the group leader presided over outside activities, I did the outside work, and also took charge of the treasury. The financing of the group was an important and difficult task, for there were no wealthy patrons in our ranks, and we could count only on the sacrifices of those friendly to us. These, however, were all little people.

Finally our work was crowned by success. The number of members grew, and at the elections the votes cast for the new movement mounted unexpectedly. We had finally overtaken the *Deutschnational Volkspartei,* which up to that time had headed the list.

Quite frequently, too, locals were organized on the initiative of someone in the community, as the following case illustrates.

[2.3.2.] Having heard of Hitler and his ideas, I pondered how it might be possible to organize the movement in the Palatinate in spite of the authorities of occupation. Early in December 1924, I sat down with two friends in a cafe in Otterback, to discuss the organization. We decided to draw up a program of our own, which we could submit to the French.

Leaving out everything offensive to the French, I drew up a platform (in reality the program of the Leader alone counted with us!) and I presented it to the French delegate at Kaiserslautern, on the thirteenth of December 1924. I was fortunate, for on the following day there was to be a Reichstag election.

I told the delegate we must instruct our representatives, and he permitted a founders' meeting, though under the supervision of French officials. I wrote to all the friends of the movement whose names I had been able to discover, and asked them to let me know whether they were to help in the organization. I received no answers. Then shortly before Christmas 1924, a man, who introduced himself as the Mayor of Dannenfels, called at my apartment in Kaiserslautern. I had written him too. We passed the entire afternoon together, discussing the situation. The following day we rode to Pirmasens, where a local group of the *Völkische Block* was already in existence.

Things did not come off right. We determined to proceed independently, and I invited a few followers to a founders' meeting in Kaiserslautern on January 7, 1925. Nine came on my invitation; two of them, however, left again. That evening we created the *N.S.D.A.P.* of the Palatinate, as an independent association at first, since we were forbidden to belong to any association from the right bank of the Rhine. Provisional officers were elected, among them myself, as secretary and treasurer. We had membership cards printed with the superscription *N.S.D.A.P.d.P.* and began to recruit members. At first, however, we gained adherents only from the circles of high school students and youths of the merchant class. On the first of April 1925, the first *S.A.* storm unit assembled under my leadership. We practiced at night in the woods, or met secretly in my apartment, as we were still being watched. I founded local groups at Wolfstein, Landstuhl, Neustadt, and Waldmohr; subsequently I once again contacted the members of Pirmasens and Zweibrücken."

An analysis of statistical data available for the 124 members who joined the Party between 1925 and 1927 reveals the following characteristics:

Age. Seventy-one per cent were between seventeen and thirty-two years old.

Social status. Forty-four per cent were workers, skilled and unskilled. An equal percentage belonged to the lower middle class, being men in clerical occupations and government service. Nine per cent were engaged in professions, such as teaching and engineering; only 4 per cent were employed in agriculture.

Education. Fifty-four per cent had only a public school education. Twenty per cent had gone to high school, or to professional school. Ten per cent had university training. Twenty-eight per cent report that they came from homes in which a strong nationalistic sentiment prevailed, while 7 per cent stated that their parents had been Socialists or Communists.

Military background. Forty per cent were veterans of the World War. Twenty per cent participated in various military activities after the war (*Freikorps,* Kapp *Putsch,* etc.) Twenty-four per cent belonged to semi-military organizations before they joined the movement.

Employment. At the time of joining, only 9 per cent were unemployed or in economic difficulties. The rest had secure positions.

We gather from these data that the promoters of the movement in its early period of organization were men predominantly in their twenties, mainly employed laborers and white-collar workers. More than half of them had never gone to high school. Military background was not a major factor in bringing these men into the movement; in this connection it is interesting to note that 26 per cent never joined the storm troops, being presumably promoters rather than fighters.

b. *Propaganda*

The main aim of the *Ortsgruppen* was the winning of new members and votes for the Party in the numerous local and national elections. Consequently their chief activities consisted of propaganda. This was often of a very personal kind, through face-to-face contacts in the routine of daily living. One fighter for the cause active in the early days writes:

[4.6.2.] At the back of my house there lived a functionary of the Communist party who was rather ill disposed toward me. The man had a dog, and so did I. Consequently we often met in front of the house, since we were in the habit of taking our dogs out at the same hour. One day the dog, to which he seemed very much attached, was hit by an automobile. When I heard his cry I went outside, and offered to bandage the dog. This was the more welcome, as the Communist seemed quite lost, while I had the necessary first-aid material in the house.

From that time on we were friends. I continued to discuss political questions with him, and finally I got him to the point where he consented to attend a meeting of the *N.S.D.A.P.* and listen to the "quacking," as he put it. The meeting was at Hasenhaide, Comrade Dr. Goebbels speaking. As we parted after the meeting, my friend the Communist said very little. I noticed that he seemed different from his usual self, and that he seemed to have heard something new at the meeting. Still it took some time before he came to the conclusion that the views he had previously held were not right.

One day he came to me, and told me he was sick of the crookedness of the Communist party and that he had become a member of the *N.S.D.A.P.* From that time on the Communist party persecuted him relentlessly, and threatened him every day. He could not remain in his old quarters, and shortly afterwards he moved. I never saw him again, but I am convinced he became a good fighter.

Personal propaganda offered the widest scope for individual initiative and enterprise, and it was here that the personality of the propaganda worker counted for most. A striking example of National Socialist field work will be found in the following quotation:

[4.7.4.] We, the early simple champions of the Third Reich, fought largely of our own accord. Ready to do all in our power, we frequently did things without being told to do so; in fact, there were a great many things no command could have forseen. Action, after all, is the outstanding preoccupation of the true fighter; but his action must be such as to serve the great cause to which he has pledged his support.

During my numerous trips, which frequently involved extended periods in the country, I found ample opportunity to spread the National Socialist doctrine. At first it was necessary to proceed with consummate caution, since the people, but lately betrayed, were wary of everything new. It was best if one could say with a good conscience that though one was acquainted with National Socialist teachings, and though one was sympathetic to the idea, one was not actually a member of the party.

By this stratagem I succeeded in the course of conversations with simple farmers to inoculate them with the National Socialist "serum." Later on, when one or another was more or less won over, there would be meetings in the tiny parlor of a little peasant cottage, to which all and sundry would come, without any suspicion of attending a political meeting. Conversations were always planned with a view to spreading National Socialist doctrines.

This method was particularly valuable, since many fellow Germans thus reached would never have gone to a large political meeting. Though it was never officially recommended or even recognized, it was highly effective, since it entailed work in the midst of opponents, or people not heretofore reached, with the result that all questions had to be cleared up immediately. Frequently questions were deliberately asked, in order to make possible the proper reply; and though we were at times hard pressed, our superior skill always gave us the advantage. For not only were we firmly convinced, but also, the idea was a very obsession with us. Consequently the fight always gave us renewed strength.

An important feature of propaganda activities was the distribution of literature and the placing of placards, which occupied a great deal of the party members' time. The following recollections of a propaganda worker afford some insight into these activities:

[2.3.4.] Propaganda in the north of Berlin! Only those who participated in it can fully appreciate what that meant! At half past three in the morning we had to report in the Viennese garden of an *S.A.* local at the Goerlitzer station. The very way from the Katbachstrasse, where I lived at the time, was fraught with danger. Still we proceeded to the appointed place.

Upon our arrival we were lined up in groups of six men each. Two of the groups were charged with propaganda material, two stood guard in the courtyard, and two were stationed at the front door. Then we received our commands and set out to work with renewed zeal. Rows of gray houses rose before us, with dark landings, five to eight mail boxes on each floor, every house five to six stories high. Systematically we distributed our propaganda material in every house. One day I found myself on the fourth floor of a house along with another comrade, when a female voice broke suddenly into abuse. "Nazi swine!" "Murderers!" "Blood-hounds" are only a few of the milder epithets she applied to us; other designations heaped upon us are unfit to print. After this introduction, we were showered with all available movable objects. Indeed a nice set of kitchen equipment could have been picked up then and there. Had not the situation been so serious, one might well have thought a wedding feast was on in the house. Neverthe-less we continued to do our work for the Fuehrer.

The dogged perseverance this kind of propaganda required will be seen from the account of a worker operating in a fashionable suburb of Berlin. This account has an added in-terest in that it reveals a type of mentality which, judging by its prevalence among our informants, must have been very common among the National Socialist party workers.

[4.6.2.] We were about to inaugurate the street cell system. To this end prospective cell foremen were invited to the home of the section leader, to be charged with their duties as officials of the Party. I, too, was of this number, and I was assigned the district of Eichkamp as the field of my activities. Besides me, there were three other party members in this district: my wife, Comrade Treff, and Comrade Walter.

A long and stubborn siege began. Eichkamp, stronghold of the Grzesinskis, the Aufhaeusers, Arnold Zweig, and Dr. Rosenfeld, had a Red settlement, including more than a hundred *Reichsbanner* members and numerous Jews. The majority of the inhabitants con-sisted of complacent burghers who had acquired wealth and honors through the inflation and the revolution, and were eager to preserve the *status quo* as long as possible. The rest were largely German Nationalists who, however, lacked the courage to come out in open opposition to the system. What would their neighbor Jew Levy or Jew Cohen say if they went so far as to acknowledge their adherence to that proscribed bugaboo of respectable bourgeoisie, the National Socialist party!

A great deal of education was needed here. First of all National Socialism had to be made popular. But how were we to go about it, poor as we were? The fact was, we didn't even have the necessary funds to procure propaganda material for Wilmersdorf. We had no money, and we could produce no printed matter. Very well, another way would have to be found!

Comrade Kuebler of Wilmersdorf, whom I knew well, took over the sale of the *Voelkische* and the *Illustrierte Beobachter* in the district of greater Berlin. I made arrangements with him to get 500 to 1000 copies for free distribution in Eichkamp. Soon my apartment looked like headquarters. The propaganda material, carefully stored away, was counted and sorted unto the small hours, for distribution the following evening.

In the dark of night two shadowy figures, armed with placards and a pot of glue, could be seen stealing through the streets of Eichkamp. No one would have recognized the one as the respectable official, a very exemplar of republican virtues throughout the day, while in the evening he was known far and wide as the Eichkamp Nazi chieftain. The two dark shapes, Comrade Walter and I, had thought of a neat joke. Cautiously we approached a slumbering villa, and in no time an announcement of Hitler's speech at the Sportpalast was pasted, with very good home-made glue, opposite the door of His Excellency, the Prussian Minister of the Interior. Ever after, Herr Grzesinski regularly had a double guard on duty at his gate.

Sooner than he could have wished, however, the bad, bad Nazis, slipped up behind them. On the twenty-first of November 1929, nine articles of my authorship appeared in the *Angriff*, somewhat as follows:

NEWS OF HERR GRZESINSKI

Berlin, November 19. Herr Grzesinski, chief policeman of Prussia, no longer feels safe in his week-end villa, at G. Street 6, Number 9, Eichkamp. Ever since the time last year that the damned Hitlerites pasted an announcement of a Nazi meeting to his front door, which only yielded to the wet terrorism of a thorough scrubbing, this charming nest, scene of so many hours with the beauteous Daisy Torrens, the lovable mate of the famous official journey to

Vienna, no longer seems what it used to be. Two policemen with nightsticks were regularly stationed at the house
thereafter. As the first of May approached, however, Herr
Grzesinski did not seem to feel safe, despite the twofold
guardianship of the law. Consequently he has had a detachment of Schuppo men installed for his personal safety
in a nearby warehouse.

Meanwhile National Socialism has been making rapid
headway in Eichkamp, by means of zealous newspaper
propaganda and placards proclaiming the ideas of the
Hitlerites. Herr Grzesinski himself seems at last to have
become aware of the goings on. Is he perchance expecting
some time to find a bomb in his garden, which might spoil
his taste for the charming Daisy? In any case, the two
Schuppo men no longer seem adequate to him.

Accordingly he has bethought himself of the old gendar-
merie barracks at number 143-144 Koenigsweg, where a
number of petty officials and their families now make their
homes. All of them have now been served notice, effective
April, 1930, so that Herr Grzesinski may, for his own as
well as his girl friend's safety, maintain a detachment of
police there. Thus while the Prussian Minister of the Interior and his lady friend may get atmospheric pressure, the
children of poor officials will have to pack up and return
from the clear fresh air of Eichkamp to the backyards of
Berlin. The friendly gardens will have to go to make way
for garages for armored cars. Now if such a thing had
happened under the ignominious old regime!

This number, distributed free of charge for propaganda purposes,
was left in the letter boxes of the policemen's families, as well as in
Herr Grzesinski's box.

Despite the Schuppo men in front of Grzesinski's house, four
or five of us, including my wife, worked steadily through dark
and fog, through rain and storm, in frost and thaw, and made
gradual progress. Elections came and passed. Every division had
to finance its own propaganda. Wilmersdorf had its own troubles.
What were we going to do? We went to the Nationalists we had
come to know in the course of years, and asked them for contributions. Thus we collected 50 marks. This was not sufficient, however, even to cover the cost of propaganda material. The amount

had to be deposited with the district propaganda division. What were we to do?

I got my last remaining funds together. Even so, the amount was not sufficient. On one pretext or another, I touched my col-leagues at the office. I had that much credit with them anyway. Thus the 100 marks was fully deposited. Now it was a question of calling for the propaganda! Some amusing incidents occurred in connection with this. It was the custom to demolish the placards of our political opponents, and paste our own in their place. Our greatest political opponent was the Jew Mendelsohn. Some nights my fence, door, and windows too, were pasted all over at his behest.

One night the government henchmen preceded us in putting leaflets into the garden mail boxes in the Heerstrasse. That made us angry. Carefully we hauled out all their propaganda, filling two large brief cases, and replaced it with our own material. We then tore up the leaflets of our opponents, and despite careful watch threw one half of them into Grzesinski's front garden, disposing of the rest amid Mendelsohn's flower beds. The fury of the Socialists passed all imagination.

The main efforts of the promoters centered upon the organi-zation of meetings. Hitler himself set the example. Directly the ban against him was lifted, he began touring the country indefatigably, addressing thousands of listeners throughout Ger-many. His appearances were an important factor in the spread of the movement, as they usually led to substantial increases in party membership and bolstered up the morale of party work-ers. But in the sum total of activities, this personal campaign was incidental to the spade work of the *Ortsgruppen,* who did much to keep their communities in a state of constant agitation through their continuous program of meetings. It was, in fact, this very intensity of National Socialist propaganda that enabled them to outdistance other parties. The *Ortsgruppen* leaders acted as if a crucial election were being held every day of the year. Party members devoted most of their leisure time to propaganda.

"My wife jokingly called me a 'guest' at her house, as throughout those fighting years I went home only occasionally to eat and to sleep," writes one informant. "As soon as I finished my work at the office, I would go to headquarters, there to begin a round of activities, such as attendance at meetings, posting of placards, propaganda marches, *S.A.* patrol, and so forth, which often kept me busy until the small hours."

Unemployed party members usually devoted their entire time to party work. The burden of supporting the family, in such cases, usually rested upon the shoulders of the wife. A typical instance of this follows:

[3.1.3.] My wife underwent untold hardships throughout these years. To enable me to pay my party dues, and spend an occasional penny, she worked hard at sewing, constantly harassed to provide a meager living for me and the family. Frequently, if I returned late at night from a meeting or a propaganda trip, I still found her bent over her work, happy to see me come home unharmed. This went on for weeks, months, and years. But she willingly endured it, for she too could not be robbed of her faith in the ultimate victory of National Socialism.

The meetings of the *Ortsgruppen* seldom were smooth affairs. Very often they eventuated in skirmishes with hecklers. Indifference of the community had to be combated. Then too, there were technical difficulties, lack of qualified speakers, inability to secure a meeting place, and so forth. The following description, not without humorous implications, presents an authentic picture of the tribulations of the small town or village *Ortsgruppe* leader:

[4.5.3.] I made my debut in Andernach, a small town in southern Germany, and presently I began to busy myself in the environs.

In the evening we marched from village to village. Meeting after meeting was called. Our greatest difficulty consisted of the lack of qualified speakers in the neighborhood of Mayen. Sometimes I was sent men I personally had to stop from making an address. Then we would be refused a meeting place. Often we had to run around a week before we could obtain the use of a hall. Once we had the meeting place, we had to start looking for a speaker.

At first the meetings were fairly well attended. Soon, however, people began to stay away, as the clergy attacked those who placed halls at our disposal. There was one place in the neighborhood of Mayen where 250 people came to the first meeting, while there were only half as many at the second, and not more than four people at the third.

I repeatedly told them, "The time will come when you'll run to meetings and beg to be enrolled." Their reply was invariably "Never!"

In Andernach too it was difficult to make any headway because of the Catholic party. My shop was boycotted. Children passing the store with their mothers would warn them not to go in there. "The Reverend Father says you mustn't," they would say.

Yet the more they persecuted us, the more stubborn we became. We arranged an impromptu meeting with Count R. in Koblenz. Once in Kruft three of us went boldly through the village streets, calling out announcements of our meeting. Three to four hundred people assembled within an hour. As we opened the meeting, the village chaplain called out: "Citizens of Kruft, beat up the Nazis! Run them out of your village!"

From Kruft we went to Niedermendig. There we had our first encounter with Communists. We had to flee from the village; the same thing happened at Obermendig. From Obermendig we went to Bell. In Bell we had an audience of twenty, and we left amid threatening roars. The Communists of Niedermendig and Obermendig followed us with speakers; we had to go back by way of Brohltal.

The day before an election we went with seven men of the Andernach local on a sound truck through the southern district of Mayen, and distributed printed matter. In the village of Plaidt we were pursued by Social Democrats, who destroyed our leaflets.

Four days before the election, Dr. Heller of Koblenz spoke at Andernach. The meeting was poorly attended. Dr. Heller said I could be well satisfied if I obtained 200 votes in Andernach; there was no room for a new party there. Election night, however, crowned our endeavors with success. Andernach had not abandoned us. We polled 771 votes.

Some time later we called a meeting at Mayen with district leader Florian from Duesseldorf and Heiliger. The meeting was managed and financed by the Andernach local. Three fourths of the seats in the room were taken, nevertheless the Andernach group managed to make a fiasco of the meeting. Heiliger had had just a few too many before the meeting, and found himself stuck in the middle of his speech. Florian from Duesseldorf, however, more than made up for Heiliger. From that time on, we never let Heiliger have more than one glass of liquor and one beer before a speech.

c. *Finances*

A standing difficulty many *Ortsgruppen* had to face was the lack of funds. Contrary to prevalent opinion, the work of the *Ortsgruppen* was not financed by large-scale capitalists and landowners. Hitler had, indeed, contacted several leaders of industry and finance as early as 1927, and gained the support of some of them. Still, whatever sums he may have obtained, the autobiographies show without exception that no money from this source reached the *Ortsgruppen*. Apparently these sums were used entirely for the support of headquarters, the maintenance of certain storm troop units, and the costly Reichstag election campaigns. The *Ortsgruppen,* on the other hand, were financed in the main by dues and contributions of party members and collections at meetings. Sometimes the leader of an *Ortsgruppe* had to pay expenses out of his own pocket:

[4.3.2.] I took care of finances myself. I paid debts out of my meager resources, and gave free room and board to every speaker who came to town. This was quite a burden, for they sometimes made my house their headquarters for weeks, from which they visited the surrounding towns.

The necessity of financing their own work entailed genuine sacrifices for many party members. A former engineer writes:

[3.6.2.] Having decided to devote myself to the cause, I had to give up my profession, as I had no more time for it. The Party was unable to pay me anything. I consumed my savings, and soon I was forced to borrow, and sell anything of value I possessed. To have enough money for the movement, I withdrew from all other organizations, and gave up all forms of recreation.

The same evangelistic fervor is evident in the following quotation:

[2.3.2.] Both as an *S.A.* man and as a cell leader, I was constantly on the go. We all had several jobs to take care of. And everything cost money—books, newspapers, uniforms, propaganda trips, and propaganda material. So it happened that many of us frequently went hungry. But nothing mattered, so it served the cause! Every one of us would have been glad to die for it, let alone go hungry.

Collections at meetings were the main source of income of the *Ortsgruppen*. That the technique of revivals was not foreign to these affairs is shown by the following account of a young man attending his first meeting:

[4.8.5.] At the end of his speech the leader made an appeal for contributions, since this movement, unlike the rest, did not have the support of Jewish money lenders. To this end two tables were placed near the exit, where all who wished could leave their contributions. As I stepped up to the table to give my modest bit, I saw to my amazement that there were only bills on the plate. Somewhat taken aback, I lit a cigarette and stood aside, as I had no more than three marks in my possession. Thereupon a white haired lady came up to me, saying, "Young man, if you smoked one cigarette less each day and gave five pfenning to the cause, you would be doing a good deed."

I never knew the exact amount of my contribution. I only know that I left the place with a sense of humility, and the knowledge that that woman was a true National Socialist.

Gradually the intensive propaganda, sustained by fanatical party members, penetrated to the inmost recesses of Germany; the message, pounding relentlessly at all ears, was slowly achieving results. From a total enlistment of 27,117 in 1925 the number of members increased to 108,717 by 1928. With the rise of unemployment and increasing evidence of the inability of the government to cope with the crisis, more and more voters turned a willing ear to National Socialist propaganda. In the Reichstag elections of 1928, the National Socialists polled in all

810,000 votes, or 2.6 per cent of the total vote. By 1929, however, there were indications in communal and provincial elections that the tide was turning. Thus in the *Landtag* elections in Thuringia in December 1929, the National Socialists gained 11.31 per cent of the electoral votes and were able to force the appointment of one of their deputies, Dr. Frick, to a ministerial post.

By 1930 the National Socialists' rise to power was an accomplished fact. Unnoticed to most observers, a distinct change in public opinion toward the regime was making rapid headway. To the surprise of everybody, including the party leaders, the National Socialist party that year obtained the support of over 6,400,000 voters, or 18.3 per cent of the electoral vote, and marched into the Reichstag as the second strongest political party. With this turn of events, which placed National Socialism on the map of international politics as well as of Germany, the movement entered its most difficult phase: that of violent, open struggle with its foes for ultimate supremacy.

Chapter V

The Third Period: 1930-1933

B EFORE 1930," WRITES one of our informants, "most people
looked upon us as immature hot heads, sacrificing their
time and money for a chimerical cause."

This attitude was as true of government officials and politicians as it was of the German public. Few of them paid any
attention to the Hitler movement; the vast majority never considered it a possible threat to their power.

1. *Opposition*

The unforeseen victory of the National Socialist party in
the elections of 1930 made short shrift of the feeling of amused
scorn and indifference toward National Socialism. The sudden realization that an ominous reaction against republican
democracy was afoot spurred government supporters into vigorous action.

In the years 1930-32, the government issued a series of decrees designed to curtail propaganda activities and hamper the
development of the National Socialist party. The text of the
first order, in part, was as follows:

Following the developments in the Communist party and the National Socialist party, both parties are to be regarded as organizations whose aim is the forcible overthrow of the existing order. Any official who belongs to such an organization or is active on its behalf, thereby violates his obligations toward the State, and is guilty of a breach of discipline. Membership in these organizations, participation in their activities, or extending any support whatsoever to them, is therefore forbidden.

The Ministry of State hereby calls the attention of all officials to this order, with the warning that in the future disciplinary action will be undertaken against all officials who fail to comply with its specifications.

The Ministry of State at the same time orders all authorities to report every case of contravention of this order to the proper minister.

After the elections, government ordinances became more stringent. In March 1931, Chancellor Bruening promulgated the first of several "emergency ordinances," which prohibited mass meetings and the public display of uniforms, at the same time making all pamphlets and placards subject to police censorship. Four months later this ordinance was supplemented by a decree which virtually abolished the freedom of the press.

From this time on, government ordinances became progressively more stringent. An order of October 1931 empowered the police to close all meeting places on the mere suspicion that they were being used for subversive purposes. This order was generally applied against storm troop homes and restaurants frequented by party members. As a climax to all previous orders came the dissolution of the storm troops (the *S.A.* and the *S.S.*) in April 1932.

The government decrees put the authority of the party leaders to a severe test. Intent on avoiding charges of illegality, Hitler ordered strict conformity with all regulations, threatening violators with expulsion from the Party. The general reaction was succinctly expressed by Goebbels: "Legal to the last rung of the gallows, then, we shall proceed with the hanging."

On the whole, discipline was maintained, but many ways of circumventing the decrees were found. Thus party members expressed their resentment of the uniform ban as follows: [1]

[2.3.2.] Then our garb of honor, the brown shirt, was forbidden. Nothing daunted, we marched in white shirts. For our conviction lay not in our shirts, but in our hearts. The government speedily recognized this, but not until it had forbidden us to wear white shirts too.

I still recall the time a police officer warned me prior to a meeting that white shirts were not to be worn. The policeman asked me to see to it that this order of the *Reichspraesident* was honored. I announced the import of the order, and five minutes later the *S.A.* appeared at the foot of the speakers' platform, clad in nothing but their trousers. Thus we escaped further chicanery. Shaking their heads, the police saw that we were not to be downed.

Even in regard to its employees, the government could only enforce its orders to a limited extent. Many heads of departments were secretly in sympathy with the movement and shut their eyes to the activities of their subordinates. Furthermore, many government officials chose the following way of extricating themselves from the dilemma:

[3.7.4.] When the government forbade membership in the National Socialist party to its employees, every teacher and official had to sign a declaration and affirm in word and writing that he was not a member of the Party and did not participate in its activities. I too signed such a declaration, but neither my colleagues nor I withdrew from the Party. We simply notified headquarters, so that in case of a check up our names would not appear on the list of party members. For the rest we continued to pay our dues and carry on our propaganda work, though we had to be doubly careful now.

The police, particularly in Socialist governed Prussia, frequently resorted to drastic steps against the National Socialists. There are numerous accounts of dramatic raids, culminating in

---

[1] For an explanation of the bracketed symbols, turn to the insert at the back of the book.

wholesale arrests, in the biographies. Hundreds of National Socialists were sent to prison between 1930 and 1932. Several of our informants report prison sentences ranging as high as ten years.[2]

The presence of National Socialist sympathizers among the police and the judiciary was one of the main obstacles to the effectiveness of court measures against the Party. Indeed locals were frequently informed in advance of police moves, and judges as often as not suspended sentences. A police officer, secretly a National Socialist party member, writes:

[3.7.2.] I had learned from friendly police officials that a bloody encounter was being planned, not by the Communists only, but also by the Marxist police, irrespective of whether or not the *S.A.* men should give cause for it. I immediately went to the local group leader and reported the danger threatening the forthcoming *S.A.* parade. All sections of the *S.A.* were thereupon promptly notified, and the planned provocation did not materialize.

The leniency of the courts is described as follows by another of our informants:

[2.3.3.] Several judges were friendly to us, and we insisted on having our cases tried before them. The following day we were free to resume our activities.

When decrees failed to stem the rising tide of National Socialism, the government ordered the dissolution of the storm troops. This order, however, came too late to produce any tangible results; as usual, it was circumvented by the storm troopers.

[3.3.3.] When the order was issued, we did not disband. We simply formed clubs and sport associations under innocent sounding names and continued our activities in civilian garb.

---

[2] Since the sentences, on the whole, were for political offenses, many of the prisoners were freed by the amnesty decree of the von Papen goverment in 1932. The rest were cancelled by Hitler when he came to power.

The main reason for the ineffectiveness of all preventive measures, however, was the fact that by the time they were enacted the movement was within reach of the final victory, and the field of action had been transferred from the street to ministerial salons; it was there that interminable secret debates finally ended in the appointment of Hitler to the Chancellorship.

Simultaneously with the repressive tactics of the government, various social institutions with which party members were affiliated also tried to use pressure methods against them. Notable among these were the Catholic Church, trade unions, and relief organizations.

[4.5.5.] The church made life difficult for us. The consolations of religion as well as burial in consecrated ground were both denied murdered National Socialists. For years the Center (Catholic) party had been log rolling and making compromises with the anti-religious Marxist parties. Our repeated avowals of the proximity of National Socialism to Christianity were branded false.

The bitterness of this strife may further be gathered from the following excerpt:

[3.3.4.] At a local mission we were barred from the sacraments, because we refused to leave the Party. A letter to the bishop was without avail. But the more the Center clergy persecuted us, the more fanatically did we fight for the freedom of the Fatherland.

In workshops and factories party members frequently came in for abuse at the hands of their fellow workers. One party member reminisces:

[2.3.2.] I found work again as an electrician. I tried to talk to my fellow workers about Hitler. At first they listened in silence. I was more eloquent now, and I could answer the *whys* and the *wherefores*. Suddenly they began to curse me, and one day I found I was ostracized. I greeted them as I entered the shop, but they all became silent and turned to their work. This was the most unpleasant experience in my life. Finally I found a follower in a young apprentice.

One day he told me that all the men had gone to the chief and demanded that he dismiss me. They threatened to call a strike unless he complied. But the master wouldn't be bullied. He felt it was up to him to choose his employees; anybody who didn't like that could go—there were plenty of people to take his place.

As a result they hated me more than ever. Then, one day, I left of my own accord—I couldn't stand it any longer. Shortly afterwards, however, the master sent for me; there was a great deal of work to do, and he trusted me. On this occasion I met a man I hadn't seen before.

"Say," he said, "I understand there's a Nazi among us. If I ever get hold of that fellow, I'll crush his skull with my hammer!"

Trade unions refused to apprentice workers known to be adherents of Hitler, and frequently obstructed their employment.

[2.3.3.] I was unemployed, but I managed to get through somehow. I found some kind German brothers who helped me from time to time, even though, not being masters in their own workshops, they couldn't give me a job. Vacancies in each case were filled by trade unions.

Some of our informants report difficulties in obtaining relief when their political ties became known. Others describe attempts to prevent them from collecting the dole.

[3.1.3.] The trips to relief headquarters to have our cards stamped were an ordeal indeed. We were beaten, kicked, and spit upon, while we waited outside the office, under the very eyes of the police. Despite all humiliations I gritted my teeth and refused to be robbed of my faith in a better future.

By 1930 the general public was openly taking sides for or against the movement. The rising volume of *"Heil Hitler"*s that greeted National Socialist parades mingled ominously with the rumble of disapproval.

[2.2.3.] People cursed and even spit upon us as we marched through Munich. The women were the worst of all. They grabbed us by our brown shirts, and tried to tear them from our backs.

[4.4.2.] "Blood hounds," "Hitler bandits," "blood suckers," "Kill the dogs!" were among the endearments with which they greeted us. This will indicate the type of reception that awaited us at many meetings. At times we could obtain no hall for our meetings, as every innkeeper knew he would lose his customers once he took in the "damned Nazis."

[4.5.3.] We were mocked and abused by our opponents. Indeed it was difficult to bear up under all this. If we went into a pub, all the guests would turn their backs, with the remark, "We won't have anything to do with the Nazi pest." Most of them were afraid they would become suspect if they had anything to do with us. This derision assumed such proportions that I avoided all pubs.

Stores and shops owned by National Socialists were boycotted, and members of the Party were frequently dismissed by their employers. Thus 12 per cent of our informants report that they lost their jobs or had their business ruined after they joined the *N.S.D.A.P.*

2. Conflict

Violence was common throughout the turbulent period from 1930 to 1932. Particularly virulent were the clashes between the National Socialists on the one hand and the Iron Front, composed of the pro-republican *Reichsbanner,* trade unions, workmen's associations, and the communist Red Front on the other hand. The technique of the battle front was combined with the methods of American gangsters in pitched battles, assaults, and attacks of all sorts between well-trained and, frequently, armed units. The fighters belonged largely to the younger generation, who, having the largest stake in the promise of a better future, chafed under the existing economic and political conditions. Loyalty to a cause or a leader had a strong appeal to young men, and adventure, too, was alluring. They readily risked their lives for the sake of the slogan, *"Schluss damit!"* ("Let's end it!")

Judging by the autobiographies and reliable contemporary newspaper reports, responsibility for the use of violence, which plunged Germany into a virtual state of civil war, rests equally with both sides. In their effort to "conquer the streets," the National Socialists sought to spread their propaganda in predominantly radical neighborhoods. The supporters of the government and other anti-Nazis, on the other hand, were equally intent on obstructing their propaganda activities. The clash between the two parties, each determined to annihilate the other, was thus inevitable.

The storm troopers felt it necessary to justify the fact that their aggressive tactics kept the country in a state of constant turmoil.

[1.5.3.] That we took recourse to drastic action and that many of our opponents came to feel the hard fist of the *S.A.* goes without saying. For we made it our maxim that "terror must be broken by terror"; furthermore, we felt that all opposition had to be stamped into the ground. We could show no consideration for the individual when the destiny of sixty million people was at stake.

[2.7.3.] We marched on and on, for Hitler, for freedom, and for bread. There could be no turning back for us. Our only thought was to show ourselves worthy of our comrades of the Great War, as well as of those of our ranks who slept beneath the turf.

The autobiographies contain many vivid details of the struggle. Frequently the opponents played more or less innocent pranks upon each other, for purposes of provocation, or in order to disrupt a meeting. Thus the following incident illustrates a less ominous phase of the struggle:

[2.3.4.] One night, about eleven, we were sitting in the throes of boredom, when Storm Leader Oehmig and I hit upon something to do. The idea was to hoist a standard onto some belfry or chimney. Chief Leader Devanter, who was present, was also enthusiastic. We went to his workshop, picked up a standard, and, fastening it to an old gas pipe, set out on the sly, about one in the morning.

We selected the old chimney of the Leopoldshall for the night's work. Three men stood on guard while Storm Leader Oehmig and I climbed on the roof and fastened the standard after some hard work.

With pleasurable anticipations of the long faces we were sure to see the following morning, we headed home along the Bernburgerstrasse, singing softly. Suddenly, at the corner of Gustnerstrasse, we came upon columns of Marxists. We separated, but met again at the corner of the next street, only to find that one comrade was missing. We hastened home for the car, to look for our comrade. On the way we were shot at several times, but the bullets went wild.

After finding our comrade, we were halted by the police; but we were released shortly afterwards. Around seven o'clock we learned that the flag we had so laboriously attached to the chimney was about to be hauled down. We repaired to the scene, and saw a man exerting himself to get the banner down. To avoid accidents, he dropped the standard down the chimney directly he had got it loose. The minute it hit bottom, however, one of our friends salvaged it, and threw it to us over the wall. We made away with it in a hurry, pleased over our little stunt and the annoyance we had caused the "comrades."

All this, however, didn't satisfy us, and we tried to think of something better to do. And so we hit upon the idea of hoisting a flag above the high tension wires, where no one could get it. Accordingly we donned gym shoes and slipped out softly with a flag. With the aid of a cord, we hoisted it high above the wires and I fastened it in place. There it remained for a fortnight, falling only when the cloth was ruined by wind and rain. But it had served its purpose.

Less innocent is the act of provocation described in the following excerpt:

[1.3.3.] The Socialist party called a mass meeting, with Captain Lieutenant Mücke as speaker. Three men, myself among them, were directed to break up the meeting with tear gas. We went to the meeting, each of us armed with a tear gas bomb and the certainty that if all went well—that is, if we didn't land in the hospital —we might expect to board at least three-quarters of a year at the expense of the State.

There were some 2,000 people at the meeting. Three hundred *Reichsbanner* men held the fort, aided by our beloved police. Each one of us felt strangely tremulous inside. Nevertheless, as Mücke entered the hall amid the crescendo of the local band and the joyous greetings of the Iron Front, I lit the fuse of my bomb. I myself was frightened as a flame of 15-20 centimeters shot out. An instant later, however, I hurled my bomb far away under the tables, and before the people around me could recover from their surprise, I made a dash for the door. The shouts and yells that broke out a moment later were my starting signal. I really did run that time.

I spent a quiet night, to be roused in the morning by the police. They took me to the guardroom, where I learned that my comrades had been apprehended before they could carry out their part of the plan.

After staunch denials, I finally admitted that I had thrown the bomb; but I maintained that there had been no understanding between my comrades and me. At the same time I refused to give the police any further information. I was allowed to go home that evening, as no one suspected me of wanting to get away. Rather than submit to six months' imprisonment, however, I took to the road, and left Hildesheim.

Practically all our informants have tales of attacks by bands or mobs to which they had been exposed at one time or another.

[3.3.5.] I was going along the Ludwig Wucherstrasse on my way from Rieleck, when I saw a procession of Communists coming from the opposite direction, carrying red flags and shouting 'Down with them!" We met at the head of the Kronprinzenstrasse. To avoid the parade, I turned up the street; but they must have seen my emblem, because groups of them suddenly appeared, and before I quite realized what was happening, I was surrounded.

The crowd roared "Kill him! Kill the fascist swine!" They trampled on me; someone took my walking stick from behind. I turned fast as lightning, determined not to let my attacker think that now he had my walking stick he could beat me with it. At the same time I ducked a blow at my skull, and parried with my left arm. I was in an extraordinarily precarious situation. I had to keep a cool head, and think in a flash. I gave up all thought of fighting off my assailant with a kick below the belt, as this would have meant certain death for me. They tried without success to snatch my emblem. The Communists swarmed thick and fast around me. My only chance of escape was in the direction of Saint Paul's. As a sportsman and runner, I had to make the attempt to burst from the clutches of the maddened mob. Beating out suddenly with both arms, I opened a path, and ran in the direction of the church. As I turned my head, I saw people stare after me, complete surprise written all over their faces. I thought they'd let things go at that, when the hue and cry rose from hundreds of throats "Kill the Fascist swine! Stop him! Kill him!" As I ran along the Kronprinzenstrasse, I saw people at the other end, ready to shut off my escape. I tried to concentrate all my strength, to reach the Kleiststrasse before they did. I ran as I never ran in the field, all my prizes notwithstanding.

With something of a headstart, I reached the Bismarckstrasse, turned to the right, and rushed into the first house there. I had scarcely reached the foot of the stairs, when I heard the Communists shouting outside, "Where is the dog? Get him!" I rushed up two flights of stairs, and rang a doorbell. A woman opened the door, and I dashed into the apartment, without so much as greeting her. She must have thought I was crazy. Unaware of what was going on, she said calmly, "You must have made a mistake, sir."

"No," I said, "please close the door quickly. I'll explain everything."

I walked into the study, and pointed out the howling mob beneath the windows. She brought me a drink of cognac.

"Take this," she said; "you're all out of breath."

Failing to find me, the Communists turned back, and, as the son of my hostess afterwards told us, rejoined the parade, still on the march.

An instance of group hostilities is vividly told in the following account:

[3.1.4.] After the parade at Hohengarten we went into the city, without knowing very much about the place. At the nearest crossing we asked a policeman the best way to the Hagenmarkt, as we had parked our conveyances there. The policeman directed us to the most dangerous section, a neighborhood of deserted streets. We came to a curb, where another street joined the main thoroughfare. Still not a soul was to be seen. But we had scarcely advanced some eighty paces when a mob armed with daggers, blackjacks, and pistols burst from the street behind us. We tried to run away, only to see another mob at the other end of the street. We were surrounded, and the only thing that remained was for us to sell our lives as dearly as possible. We drew our pistols, unstrapped our holsters, and took up our respective posts. "Murderers, swine, bums!" the mob was shouting.

At the command "Kill them!" our foes began to run toward us. At that point we, too, began to run. The pack was face to face with us. At that point, however, we discovered a weak spot, held by women and boys. We broke through at the cost of a blow or two and ran for all we were worth. As our pursuers came near, we beat about us with our equipment.

We scarcely dared trust our eyes when we saw a group of *S.A.* men coming to our aid down the main avenue. Two minutes later the Marxist scum disappeared. At the same time we received a sound scolding from our comrades for going to the Mauerstrasse and the Ackerstrasse, the very heart of the Communist section, in our *S.A.* uniforms.

To this day we thank God that we succeeded in getting away with life and limb. During another propaganda march at Dessau, we were showered with flower pots, beer bottles, and chamber pots. But together with the Köthen students, we managed to get even for this.

Still another case history of violence illustrates the aggressive tactics of the National Socialists and the extent to which the *S.A.* specialized in guerilla warfare:

[2.3.2.] After a spell of active work on behalf of the Party, I was transferred to Kuersdorf early in 1928. Yet there, too, I soon had to give up my job because of my political affiliations.

From there I went to Zechin, near Frankfurt, where I worked as a farmhand. While there, two *S.A.* comrades and I released our storm leader from prison. We had to flee by night when the authorities discovered this. A fellow party member, the innkeeper Haase, helped us in our flight.

The following morning we went to Cottbus. The local group there sent us on to Galau, where we all found jobs. On the eighteenth of October 1930, four *S.A.* men were wounded as a result of a clash with socialists. While at work the following day,

I was attacked by four *Reichsbanner* men. I received several knife wounds, so that I immediately had to place myself under a doctor's care. I also participated in minor skirmishes in the course of demonstrations at Cottbus, Vetschau, Senftenberg, Finsterwalde, and Luckau, where I once again rescued my Galau storm leader from the clutches of Communists.

The same day we got wind of an attack planned against one of my comrades and myself. I had been in the habit of driving through the village each noon and morning. That morning, however, I had to avoid the village, as the three Schreiber brothers of Galau had threatened that if I came by, it would be my last drive. Still, as no one could be found to warn my comrade, I made up my mind, in spite of all danger, to take the hazardous trip. Having been denied police protection, I obtained a shotgun, to defend myself in case of a serious attack.

I left Galau at 1:00 P.M., and met my friend at a quarter of two, to tell him an attack against him was scheduled for that evening. Having discharged my duty, I went on. As I drove past the Schreibers' garden, two of the brothers attacked me. One of them mounted the wagon, armed with a heavy object. After a brief struggle I had recourse to the shotgun and fired at W. Schreiber, mortally wounding him. I went on, and an hour later I was arrested at Cottbus. After four weeks of preliminary investigation, I was set free. On the eighth of July 1932, the jury at Cottbus sentenced me to six months' imprisonment for unlawful possession of arms, the plea of self-defense having been accepted by the court. This sentence was subsequently cancelled through the amnesty of Christmas 1932. Following this, I was transferred to Berlin, where I have been active ever since.

The killing of opponents was practiced equally by both sides. Between 1930 and 1932, several hundred National Socialists were stoned, shot, or knifed to death by Communists and members of the Iron Front. An account of one such killing follows:

[3.1.3.] July 10, 1932, was a black day for us, for it was on that day we lost our *S.A.* comrade, Decker. The scene of the tragedy was the small town of Beverungen on the Weser. Our comrades of that town had asked us to assist them at a propaganda demonstration. Naturally we consented, knowing as we did the reputation our Beverungen *S.A.* enjoyed among the Communists and members of the Catholic party. Communists and Catholics inevitably united in opposing us.

We gathered at the neighboring town of Launförde, separated from Beverungen by the Weser bridge. There were about three hundred of us there. In the heat of the midday, we received news that the Communists were planning certain moves. We promptly put ourselves in readiness and crossed the bridge in closed formation over to Beverungen. Along with another storm leader, I headed the procession. We knew that those across the river were armed, while we had no weapons with which to defend ourselves. But we had courage and the will to carry on through any adversity.

The nearer we came to the city, the more violence we saw. Crowds flanked the streets, their faces full of hatred.

"Leave the streets!" our commander shouted.

Anyone slow to move was promptly given a helping hand.

District Leader K. made a propaganda speech at the market place, and we returned to Lauenförde. In the meantime, some of our *S.A.* comrades, who had a long way ahead of them, were excused from further service, to permit them to go home on their bicycles. As they rode through Beverungen, they were attacked and thrown from their machines. The alarm spread to Launeförde, and we ran back to Beverungen, headed by comrade Decker. He was killed by a dagger thrown by a Communist. An *S.A.* comrade hurrying to his side was shot down by another group of Communists. We didn't know which way to turn. Finally the police stopped the rioting. Short prison terms were the only punishment imposed upon the murderers.

Collective acts of aggression ranged from chance encounters to pitched battles in streets and meeting halls.

[3.1.3.] Then came the elections! In the darkness of night small groups stole about to attach their placards in different places. Usually there were encounters with bands of Marxists and Communists, out on similar errands. Equipped with passwords and signals, four men, occasionally under escort, went about carrying glue pots and the like. They penetrated the enemy's camp, tore down notices, and replaced them with our own. Unexpected meetings gave both sides an opportunity to show their comradeship. There were smothered cries, shrieks, dull blows, and the whole thing vanished in the gray of dawn.

Street fights, particularly around 1932, were common occurrences.

[4.6.3.] Every *S.A.* man has a tale to tell. I was ordered to guard duty at a meeting. The storm leader happened to be delayed, and I had to take his place. About fifteen minutes before the meeting I met a number of *S.A.* comrades and we proceeded, nine men strong, along the Richard Wagner Strasse.

Even at a distance we could see a huge crowd gathered there. An acquaintance coming our way warned us to change our direction, as the Communists were assembled in full force; the order to attack us had already been given.

In close formation we marched through the crowds. Not a sound issued either from us or the Communists. Evidently they were impressed by the courage of a handful of men cutting through that mob.

I kept wondering when they'd seize one of us and make short shrift of him; incredibly, they let us pass. Perhaps they judged nine of us were too many for 250 of them to deal with.

Soon we came to know better. I turned my head to see if we were all still there. We were some fifteen paces removed from the crowd, when I noticed two men in *S.A.* uniforms running toward us down the street. I directed the others to wait, until they caught up with us. The men came nearer and nearer, right through the mob of Communists. But scarcely had they reached us, when a hail of stones rained down upon us. It was only then I noticed crowds of women, their aprons loaded with stones, which they handed to their men to throw at us. I was hit on the back and the elbows: all over, in fact; I carried bruises for weeks. The other comrades also were hit, but fortunately no one was disabled.

Since I was responsible for these men, and since there was no possibility of our being ambushed at the other end of the street, the most sensible course, it seemed to me, was to withdraw. The soldiers of Adolf Hitler were too few and precious to be unnecessarily sacrificed.

One of our elder comrades, decorated with the Iron Cross, First Class, particularly deplored the fact that we were doomed to flight. But we resolved to pay our opponents in full the next time.

When we arrived at the meeting, I had to give a brief report to the standard bearer, only to learn that a group of *S.A.* comrades, coming from the other direction, had scattered the Red mob. A few hours later the Halle *S.A.* arrived. Thus we were 400 men strong, and jointly we resolved to have a look at the Communist quarter around midnight.

We had scarcely entered the first streets when the street lights were extinguished by stones, and walking ahead with several other comrades, I was once again showered with stones. Yet as we rushed into the dark streets, there was not a person in sight. We groped around in search of an invisible foe, pelting us with stones from windows and rooftops.

Suddenly a command was given to attack us. But even after we had fired our guns to scare them, we couldn't tell where the Communists were. Unfortunately the police commanded us to turn back. I should have welcomed a bit of revenge for our forced retreat of a few hours before. Nevertheless, we were the better for the experience. We had learned that Communists attack only isolated political foes, when their own strength is overwhelming. Knives and daggers are their favorite weapons, occasionally supplemented by stones and revolvers of all calibers. They prefer to attack under the pall of night, when they are safe from recognition, and, provided they are in the majority, even murder their foes. These, briefly, are the methods of the alleged liberators.

When I looked in the *Klassenkampf,* official paper of the Communists, the following day, I found that the eleven of us had grown to one hundred and twenty, and that we had provoked poor working people, unfortunately too few in number to send us on our way as we deserved.

A typical description of the fights waged in meeting halls is presented in the following report:

[4.5.2.] The Trier *S.A.* received orders to go to Idar the following Sunday on guard duty. Early Sunday morning we rented a truck, and thirty of us went through Hermeskeil to Idar. There we were welcomed by the district leader, and entertained at the local National Socialist pub. Meanwhile other *S.A.* troops, from Saarbruecken, Coblenz, and the Palatinate, also arrived on the scene.

The parade began at three in the afternoon. We marched through Idar to Oberstein. In Idar the population greeted us with hands raised in salute. As soon as we entered Oberstein, however, the Red pack let out a howl. To be sure, we expected something to happen. But, since there were 500 of us there, we were in no way frightened.

There were three thousand people at the meeting, 90 per cent of them Communists. As a precautionary measure, the S.A. lined up in front of the speakers' platform, near the wall. Everything proceeded in a quiet, orderly fashion.

After four different speakers had had their say, the editor of the *Nahetalboten* asked for the floor, to open the discussion. That was the signal to attack the S.A. Instantly beer glasses flew at us from all directions. At the same time an S.A. trumpeter leaped on a table, and blew the signal to attack. A terrific battle ensued. We fell upon the mob with the legs of tables and chairs, and in ten minutes we cleared the hall. The Oberstein police went so far as to side with the Communists, and let loose at us with blank bullets. But even this did not avail against our resolution. The S.A. reassembled in a much damaged hall, and we found that several comrades had been so badly wounded as to require hospital care.

This ruinous partisan warfare was not halted until January 30, 1933, the day that Hitler assumed power. Sporadic skirmishes, to be sure, still occurred after this date. But the National Socialists now had command of the police power of the State, and they could legally pursue the extermination of their bitterest opponents.

[2.3.2.] The burning beacon of the Reichstag building, on January 27, 1933, lighted our way. We were prepared. I had gathered about me a group of the bravest of our storm troopers. Night after night we lay in wait.

Soon the time arrived. Firebrands flared in Berlin. At the same time came the command to fall to *(Packt zu!)*. Fall to we did, with a vengeance. This time it was a matter of them or us, and we were determined once and for all to rid Germany of the bloody terror of Bolshevist hordes.

We succeeded. A few months later our standard flew in all its glory side by side with the battle flags of our army, announcing to all the world the dawn of a new German day.

Even before the partisan warfare had been terminated, the odds were overwhelmingly in favor of the National Socialists. A final decision, however, could not have been reached without a prolonged struggle, more bloody and ferocious than anything that had happened up to that time. Not the least of the considerations that prompted President Hindenburg and his advisers to appoint Hitler chancellor was, probably, the conclusion that the National Socialists would not give in short of achieving their goal; civil war seemed inevitable unless power was given to them. Because of the strength and determination of the National Socialists, and because of the doubtful stand of the army, the outcome of such warfare would in all probability have been favorable to National Socialist ambitions.

3. *Victory*

During the period from 1930 to 1932, the movement grew rapidly, in spite of various obstructions placed in its path. Thus between January 1930 and December 1931, the number of members rose from about 400,000 to well over 800,000. The increased volume of public support was evident in the results of many elections of that period. In the provinces National Socialists were rapidly taking over control of local governments and municipalities. In the presidential elections of 1932, when Hitler was a candidate against Hindenburg, the former secured thirteen million votes, or 36.8 per cent of the total electoral vote, as against 18.3 per cent in 1930.

The accusation that the National Socialists were fomenting civil war made little impression upon a large part of the German people. On the contrary, aggressive tactics were bound to arouse the admiration of a citizenry nurtured in a worship of militarism. The fighting spirit of the National Socialists, moreover, had a special appeal at the time, in view of the spectre of Bolshevism currently haunting the middle and upper classes in

Germany: anybody who would boldly take the offensive against the menace of Bolshevism was welcome.

As we have previously pointed out, the crucial decision which, by raising Hitler to the Chancellorship, staved off an inevitable *coup d' état* on the part of the Nazis, was reached in protracted conferences behind closed doors. The task of revealing the details of these meetings must be left to future historians. Undoubtedly the situation was complicated, and there was room for intrigues and machinations of all sorts. The immediate issue, however, was essentially simple. At the end of 1932 the National Socialists held three trump cards: their determination to fight to the finish for political power; their widespread support among the German masses; and the fact that they were the strongest party in the Reichstag, even after losing 34 seats in the November 1932 elections. There was no gainsaying these facts. Nevertheless the opposition was determined to save as much as it could for itself in the bargain. Since the Chancellorship could not be denied to Hitler, the object was to keep as close control as possible over his actions. With this object in view a cabinet was appointed by the President in which all but two ministers did not belong to the National Socialist party. This scheme for keeping a check on Hitler's actions failed, as subsequent events show, for it ignored the fact that Hitler was not merely the head of a political party, but was the leader of a movement. A party might well be expected to conform to established procedure but a movement seldom adheres to regulations and precedents. Being revolutionary in character it is bound to sweep aside all considerations, once it gets into power, until it has completely asserted itself.

Hitler's followers knew this. They greeted his appointment as Chancellor as the crowning victory of their cause. They did not conceal their emotions at the advent of the long-awaited "day."

[2.3.2.] Promptly at ten o'clock the telephone rang.

"Hitler has just been made Chancellor," a comrade reported.

The joyous news was almost too much to encompass; yet it was reality. That night the National Socialist formations and societies gathered for a torch parade before the hoary old Field Marshal and the young Chancellor down the Siegesallee. The torches were lit, and the throngs set out on the march into German history.

An indescribable burst of joy awaited us as we marched through the Brandenburg Gate. Thousands of bareheaded spectators sang *Deutschland über Alles* and the Horst Wessel song. Renewed outbursts greeted us all along the Wilhelmstrasse. We passed in review before the hoary President, defender of the German Reich. Standing at the window of the Chancellery was Hitler, between Goering and the leader of the *S. S.,* Himmler. We marched on to the Kaiserhof, where we passed in review before the ranking *S.A.* and *S.S.* leaders.

Late that night we returned to our storm local, where we fittingly celebrated the event that had recompensed us for all our struggles and sacrifices.

The following day militant National Socialism turned to the grim and arduous task of establishing a totalitarian state.

PART TWO

Analytical

Chapter VI

Discontent As a Factor

M ANY different things hold the key to the success of the Hitler movement and what first attracted people to it. For it was not a single force, but the combination of many factors that gave rise to the movement. What were these factors, and what was their relative significance? The analysis presented in the chapters that follow purports to answer these two questions.

No startling revelations or hitherto unknown facts are disclosed in the biographical material used in the analysis. The wealth of relevant data, however, leads me to hope that my interpretation may be more complete and systematic than any made by previous investigators.

1. The Drawing Power of National Socialist Meetings

The autobiographies show that people's first contacts with the National Socialist party were made in many ways. Some of its later adherents learned about it through newspapers or the numerous pamphlets which the Party distributed in great profusion. Others became acquainted with it through friends, colleagues, or members of their families. The following quotations illustrate a few such types of contact:[1]

---

[1] For an explanation of the bracketed symbols, turn to the insert at the end of the book.

[4.8.4.] One day early in 1927 I bought a copy of a weekly, *Der Angriff* ("the Attack"). The name of the magazine attracted me. After a study of the first copy I could not wait to see the next, and I fervently read its attacks on the Republican regime. From then on I became a regular reader of *Der Angriff*, which brought me in close contact with the party fighting for a new Germany.

As the next quotation shows, *Der Angriff* was not always so effective in its appeal. But a trusted friend was instrumental in introducing the author of the following passage to the party.

[2.6.3.] In 1927 I obtained a copy of *Der Angriff*. Its language was harsh and uncouth, yet something about the contents attracted my sympathy. This feeling, however, was outweighed by my low opinion of National Socialists. I was under the influence of other newspapers that described them as scoundrels and called them a murderous plague. These accusations were so common that I thought there must be some truth in them.

Following this, in 1928 I became acquainted with a colleague of my own age, with whom I had frequent conversations. He was a calm, quiet person whom I esteemed very highly. When I found that he was one of the local leaders of the National Socialist party, my opinion of it as a group of criminals changed completely. My new attitude was further confirmed through my contacts with other National Socialists, after I had attended a meeting at the instigation of my friend. I came to value many of them as good comrades and honest, sincere fellows.

The influence exercised by individual members of families in drawing others into the movement is illustrated by the following excerpt:

[4.3.4.] One day I discovered that my seventeen-year-old son was a Nazi. Being myself a member of the conservative *Deutschnationale Volkspartei,* I promptly forbade my son to associate with these revolutionaries. The boy, however, paid no attention to this prohibition, and even had the nerve—or the courage—to come home in his brown uniform. Thereupon I gave him such a beating that my wife thought I would kill him. The boy, however, reassured his mother with the words, "Even if father kills me, I shall remain true to Hitler." That was a crucial hour for me. For a long time

I pondered how it was possible that my only son would be willing to let himself be killed for an idea. It struck me that there must be something about that idea, other than what I had heard about it. In all secrecy I bought myself a copy of *Mein Kampf.* Then I went to some National Socialist meetings, and I began to see the light.

Irrespective of the nature of the first contact, however, our contributors are unanimous in the contention that it was their attendance at the meetings that induced them to join the movement.

What was there about these meetings that impressed people so deeply? A provincial shopkeeper writes:

[3.7.4.] I happened to drift into a National Socialist party meeting during the election campaign. There I heard a Bayreuth teacher expound the ideals of National Socialism. His conviction and forcefulness made a profound impression on me. From that time on I attended all National Socialist meetings in my town. What I saw and felt at these meetings was that here were people with only one thing foremost in their minds, for which they would readily risk their lives: Germany. The shame and disgrace of our country, the ignominy and lies spread about everywhere, weighed upon them even as they did upon me. I became a passionate defender of Hitler's ideal.

The following words of a young worker contain a similar sentiment:

[2.3.3.] I found that the greatness of our people was preached at the meetings I attended. I learned to love the movement and its leader. I left the Socialist party, for now I saw clearly what I dimly sensed before: namely, that the Marxist leaders were mostly men who did not belong to our people. The significance of the Jewish question as a social issue dawned upon me.

A rural tradesman writes:

[4.2.4.] At the close of the war I resumed my trade, and began to work my small farm. Together, the two occupations assured me a decent livelihood. Politically speaking, I was practically neutral, since the long war and the death of my wife had left me with nothing more than the desire for peace. Furthermore, none of the existing political parties appealed to me. Consequently I paid no attention to what was going on in my country. Often, however, I did wish for a party that might unite the peasant and the workingman. In the absence of this, I felt, Germany was headed for ruin.

Having to some extent recovered from the war and the death of my wife, I began to see that, unless timely rescue came from some quarter, the policies of the German government were bound to lead to catastrophe.

No one knew anything about Adolf Hitler in our section of the country. Though the newspapers touched briefly on the Hitler *Putsch* of 1923, that too went by without affecting me. But I was profoundly shocked by the shooting of that fighter for liberty, Albert Leo Schlageter, in the Golzheim meadow, on the twenty-sixth of May, 1923. The following year, in the summer of 1924, I attended a celebration in honor of Schlageter at Laubach. There I heard an address by a female National Socialist from Munich. She spoke with profound sincerity, and for a long time afterwards I pondered over the things I had heard.

A year passed, and in 1925 another National Socialist addressed a meeting at Bettenhausen, near my home. I went home with the same enthusiasm as that with which I had left Laubach. *Now I had an aim and a purpose.* Then and there I began to study National Socialist publications.

The point of view of a physician is reflected in the following account:

[3.7.3.] I first heard of the National Socialist party in 1928. I became interested, and attended a meeting. There one Dr. Ley gave a remarkable analysis of governmental responsibility for the plight of Germany, at the same time outlining the aims and purposes of National Socialism. The speaker's ideas were so thoroughly after my own heart, that he seemed, in fact, to be expressing my own thoughts and desires. I was swept off my feet, and I made up my mind to join the party without delay.

Undoubtedly the eloquence of the speakers and the dramatic staging of the meetings were calculated to arouse the emotions. A number of our informants confess that they succumbed to the magnetic spell of famous orators such as Goebbels; others admit that they were roused to a fever pitch by martial music, stirring songs, display of banners, and other customary paraphernalia of mass meetings. The foregoing excerpts, however, taken from among hundreds of similar testimonials, clearly show that the instrumental factor in bringing most of our contributors into the ranks of the Party was the content of the speeches.

The following comment on oratory is revealing:

[5.0.3.] Honor to our great National Socialist orators, masters all, after their fashion! One and all, they have advanced the great cause. Our opponents frequently claimed the reason we grew so rapidly was that we had the best speakers. To this I say that we had the best speakers indeed, since our leaders, convinced of the greatness of their mission, spoke for a just and holy patriotic cause. That was the secret of the enthusiasm designed to open the eyes of indifferent masses. For I can say out of my own experience that the evening get-togethers of other parties were, on the whole, apt to be dull affairs, and the speakers seemed to orate only with a view to party coffers; thus, their high motives not withstanding— despite their stubbornness, I should say—they unconsciously aided the Marxist regime, to the greater confusion of the German people. Accordingly our opponents were in no position to appeal to any true German who in his soul longed for a German Savior, and sought to raise his eyes in trust and confidence to a truly great leader.

There is considerable justification for this implied claim. Rhetoric at best is only a vehicle for striking ideas; to make a lasting impression, any piece of oratory must touch off a responsive chord in the listeners. Experience with revival meetings and other instances of crowd behavior [2] readily substantiates this contention. Thousands of people "hit the trail" under the spell of some evangelist, only to turn their backs on it the following day. No matter how skilfully an orator plays upon the emotions of his audience, he cannot long maintain his hold unless

[2] *Cf.* Martin, D. E., *The Behavior of Crowds.* New York: Harper's, 1924.

he evokes convictions and deep-felt needs which the listeners, consciously or unconsciously, harbored long before coming face to face with the spellbinder.

The following quotation well illustrates this process:

[3.8.4.] The National Socialist party came to my notice sometime in 1930. Never before had I occupied myself with politics. At first I paid no further attention to the National Socialists, thinking they were one of the numerous political parties of which we read so much in the newspapers, but whose general ineffectiveness in the reconstruction of Germany was no incitement to enthusiasm. Nevertheless, I attended one small meeting, addressed by a National Socialist speaker.

The first impression of the gathering was not exactly edifying; we met in a small, dismal room, that had been unoccupied for some time. The speech itself, however, was stirring. *Much was touched upon that had long been in my subconscious mind, and was now called forth into consciousness. I went home deeply moved, thinking that if the aims and purposes outlined by the speaker were capable of achievement, then life would once more be worth living.*

The drawing power of National Socialist meetings provides an important clue to the factors which most effectively contributed to the growth of the movement. Thus in examining the testimony of our contributors, we find that the most influencial items of campaign oratory were as follows:

1. Expressions of dissatisfaction with the German government, together with attacks on republican institutions and office holders; in short, a campaign *against* the existing order.

2. A program based upon National Socialist ideology, providing a panacea for all ills and a way to restore Germany to a position of power in international affairs; in other words, a campaign *for* a new order.

To understand how the National Socialists were able to create a popular movement on this basis, we must bear in mind the widespread existence of an attitude favorable to their appeal long before the advent of National Socialist propaganda.

2. *The Basis of Discontent*

The general dissatisfaction with the Republican regime, following the aftermath of the revolution of 1918 and the signing of the Treaty of Versailles, has already been considered. After 1929 this opposition was reinforced by the belief that the growing number and severity of the problems confronting the German nation were largely due to the inefficiency of the government.

The war had ruined Germany's world trade. The inflation wiped out a considerable part of her capital resources. Reconstruction and the payment of reparations, together with a wide problem of social legislation exacted high taxes from the people. Employment was insecure and business hazardous, except for the few. The full force of economic disaster became particularly evident after the collapse of the brief period of prosperity from 1924 to 1928, made possible by lavish loans from the United States. The crisis that followed this spurious recovery soon took on catastrophic proportions. The number of unemployed began to mount rapidly and soon reached the staggering total of five million.

Since 1930 in particular workmen were driven onto the dole by the thousands; hundreds of peasants lost their land because of inability to pay interest on their mortgages; the middle class standard of living was rapidly declining; discontent and bitterness mounted to menacing proportions. The government vainly attempted to stem the tide by hastily decreed emergency measures—it had lost what little prestige it ever possessed, even among its supporters. The ranks of the radicals, both of the right and the left, were daily swollen with thousands of new members, desperately looking for new leaders and new institutions.

The threat to economic values in the daily lives of individuals is the theme most frequently recurring in the autobiographies. In 20 per cent of the autobiographies the inflation and its effects are registered as a major crisis in the life of the individual. The extent of economic insecurity may be surmised from the fact that 13 per cent of our contributors report changes of jobs two or more times. Twenty per cent became perpetual wanderers in search of better opportunities to make a living.

The younger generation was hardest hit by the prevalent insecurity. One half of our contributors between twenty and forty years old were forced to look for new jobs at one time or another. Twenty-one per cent of our contributors were unemployed more than a year, while a number of them had no jobs for practically the entire period from 1928 to 1933.

The following excerpts will give a general indication of the economic hardships recorded in the biographies:

[4.3.4.] My most urgent task in 1919 was to make my business a going concern once more. This was the more difficult, since throughout the long years of the war no one had had the time to concern himself with it.

After much effort, I finally succeeded in getting some orders. All my hopes, however, were dashed. The inflation put an end to my endeavors. I had no money to pay my help—my reserves were gone. Hunger and privation once more held sway in my home. I cursed the government that sanctioned such misery. For I was convinced at the time that inflation was not necessary on the scale on which it had been carried out. But it had served its purpose: the middle class, which still had had some funds, and which had steadily opposed Marxism without actually combating it, was completely wiped out.

Some of my friends with whom I discussed the situation suggested that I join one of the reactionary movements. Yet I declined with thanks, since there, too, I should have been an outsider. The only way out of our misery was to find a man who might succeed in uniting all Germans who still had some regard for honor.

A building contractor records his impressions as follows:

[4.3.5.] Activities in the building industry were steadily declining. At the same time there was the inflation, the deflation, and the constant exploitation of tradesmen and taxpayers. On the evidence of my undoctored bookkeeping records, I was a million-aire in paper marks, and accordingly I was saddled with all manner of forced loans, as well as the Rhine and Ruhr sacrifices. The latter swallowed my last possessions. I protested to the customs depart-ment that my sole remaining resources were involved, that I would have to dispose of all my stock and supplies to produce the necessary amount; but I was told that the sacrifice would have to be made. And so I sacrificed, thinking it was for my father-land. But conditions grew worse and worse. I should never have believed that any government could let a key industry like the building trades go so utterly to ruin; I kept hoping for help, which in my opinion could come only throuh radical reform, of the sort outlined in Gottfried Feder's *Soziale Bau- und Wirtschaftsbank.*

The reverses many of our contributors experienced as a re-sult of the economic situation are illustrated by the following excerpts, indicating at once the popular resentment against the government and the economic basis of participation in the Hit-ler movement.

The author of the following report was variously employed after his return from the front. Finally he became a clerk in the government sales division of naval supplies. There he found that:

[4.5.5.] Corruption and profiteering of the first water prevailed; Jews and profiteers grew rich, and lived in ease and luxury as in the Promised Land. The newspapers denounced every effort at a national awakening. Germany seemed doomed. All any front line fighter could do was to resign himself to existing conditions and try to shield his family from hunger and privation. The German wife and mother fought side by side with her husband in this struggle against an overwhelming fate. Strikes and revolts flared up everywhere. The fate of Germany seemed to be sealed. Momentarily there was the false boom of the inflation, the greatest swindle ever perpetrated on a decent, thrifty people. The world turned upside down. Diligence was penalized, while profiteers waxed rich. Public houses stocked with strumpets sprang up everywhere. All sluices of indecency were thrown wide open. The front line fighter and the decent part of the population waged a hopeless battle against this defilement. Parliamentarianism celebrated veritable orgies. Some thirty-five parties arose to confute the people, a very Witches' Sabbath! Devoid of political training, sick of body and soul, the German people reeled giddily after the different will o' the wisps.

(The entire stock of navy goods was sold to a Jewish purchaser, and our contributor lost his job. He became a salesman and struggled along as best he could.)

In 1926 I moved from Bremen to Muelheim on the Ruhr, where my inlaws were living. My father-in-law had died in the meantime. I had to accustom myself to my new life and in the very heart of the heavy industrial area. Apart from a solid middle class, the majority of the population consisted of workingmen and their families. Unemployment, already widespread, was on the increase. The suffering and despair of the people, subjected to foreign occupation and a number of communistic uprisings, was terrible. Scarcely a week passed, but huge processions of starving, excitable men would march through the streets. There was a constant tension in the air. One government followed the other. The Marxists held huge mass meetings. The population was split up into tiny parties. The atmosphere was teeming with all sorts of plans. There was no unity of purpose anywhere. It was almost impossible to find one's way in the Hell's Kitchen of Contradictory opinions. Divided by political views, interest, class and caste, the people were so many toys in the hands of the nation's enemies.

As often as not, opposition to the regime was directly connected with economic adversity. An elderly bank clerk writes:

[4.9.4.] Despite my lifelong conscientious service at the Reichs-bank and the repeated assurances of government representatives that the positions of officials would not be affected, I found myself temporarily retired on March 1, 1925, as a result of the famous order of retrenchment. More accurately, I was out on the street. If I lacked confidence in the government before this, I now felt an honest hatred for the system.

A young party member records his impressions as follows:

[1.8.2.] As a result of the military occupation, we boys naturally conceived a violent enthusiasm for anything that smacked of nationalism. We wore black-white-and-red ribbons in our lapels, until one day an order of the Minister of Education stopped us. Our Red classroom teacher sneeringly carried out the order; he was furious to see that we continued to wear our colors on the street.

Late in 1925 my father, who had been an inspector for the Koeln-Duesseldorf Steamship Company, lost his job, but soon found another with a charitable society in Duesseldorf. He had to deposit a guaranty of two thousand *Reichsmark* with the society; it soon became evident, however, that he had fallen into the hands of impostors, and that he would have to give up all hope of ever recovering his money.

A time of utter misery now set in for the family. I had to leave school. Once again we came to know hunger, for it was next to impossible to provide for a family of five on our meagre dole, while my father continued to live in Duesseldorf. An abysmal hatred flared up in me against the regime that could not provide employment for a family man who had done his duty in the war.

Further light is thrown on the situation by the reminiscences of a white-collar worker.

[2.3.4.] For a while I was unemployed. Then I worked by turns in the government service and in different banks. Nevertheless, I felt out of place in post-war Germany, and I fully resolved to leave the country. Indeed I should have done so, but for the bid of a Dutch firm that offered me a position just then.

We soldiers of the war, who had done our duty to the last, were the laughing stock of every deserter. If we happened to be Nationalists at that, we were exposed to persecution as well. People foreign to our land and race made up the government; the middle class was ruined through the scarcity of food and the depreciation of money; scoundrels and parasites cheated and robbed us, and in an incredibly brief time ruined undertakings it had taken a whole people centuries to build. People lacked the very essentials of living, and suicides were daily occurrences in the large cities. Yet at the same time, everybody was dancing around what appeared to be a Golden Calf. I was dismissed from my position with the State porcelain works, for not attending Rathenau's funeral. For some time afterward, I held an honorary post with the *Deutschnationale Volkspartei.* Yet my general inclination was

more and more to the right. My favorite newspaper was the Leipzig *Hammer* (anti-Semitic). Little by little the teachings of National Socialism were taking root in the people. But experience
had made me skeptical, and I would not immediately be convinced.

I joined the Party only in 1930. I made the acquaintance of a
number of comrades; and while many of them were of inferior
education, their selfless exertions on behalf of the movement made
them my friends. Having felt the results of the economic collapse
on my own pulse, I was only too happy to take my place in the
van of the movement.

Bitterness is rife in these words of a petty tradesman:

[2.3.3.] Business was falling off; I couldn't keep my shop going much longer. I took a job as a handyman. My place of work
was about an hour's walk distant. Whatever time was left to me
I spent in my bakery, so as not to have to shut the place completely. Nevertheless in 1926 I had to give up the shop, and see
my stock and goods sold for a pittance, because of my creditors'
Jewish partners. I moved to Schoenebeck, where unemployment
forced me on the dole. On these beggarly alms my wife and I
managed to subsist until 1927. From that time on till 1929 I made
a living as a peddler.

When we consider that on the one hand the policies of the Red
government, particularly the inflation and taxes, deprived me of
all means of livelihood, while on the other hand we soldiers of
the front were being ruled by a gang of exploiters ready to stoop
to any means to seize the starvation wages of our suffering, duped
comrades, it will become clear why a number of us welcomed the
activities of patriotic groups, particularly those of the Hitler movement. The combination of patriotic aims along with social reform
led many an old soldier and idealist under the banner of the National Socialist German Workers' Party.

Finally we quote the words of an unskilled laborer:

[3.3.3.] The terrible burden of the breakdown threatened to
bring all economic life to a standstill. Thousands of factories
closed their doors. Hunger was the daily companion of the German workingman. Added to this was the artificial whip of
scarcity, wielded by the Jews, which sent workingmen scurrying

from their homes to beg for food from the farmers. For no German family received more than twenty to thirty pfennigs dole per head in the terrible year of unemployment. Housewives will readily appreciate what it means to rear a family on that. The government carried its measures against the public so far that many an honest workingman had to resort to theft to obtain food. A case in point is the extensive pilfering of potatoes all through harvest time. Burglaries, too, became daily occurrences, and the police had their hands full protecting the citizens' property. All fellow citizens, with the exception of the Communists, yearned for better times. As for me, like many another, I had lost all I possessed through adverse economic conditions. And so, early in 1930, I joined the National Socialist party.

Like the economic factor, the effect of which persisted throughout the period from 1918 to 1923, the operation of the government was a standing source of dissatisfaction throughout the republican regime. Two things in particular invited criticism: the superabundance of political parties, with the consequent practice of *"Kuhhandel"* (political horse trading), and the numerous scandals such as the Barmat and Sklarek affairs, in which government officials were involved. The latter gave rise to general allegations of government corruption and mismanagement. Popular resentment of the many political parties was further aggravated by the fact that the public was not used to a democratic government, and distrusted the "ordinary man" in a high position. Accustomed as it was to one man assuming responsibility for government policies, people resented the frequent coming and going of ministers and the apparent immunity they enjoyed.

Thus from its advent in 1918 until its final dissolution in 1933, the German government was the object of persistent criticism on the part of a large section of the population. Excerpts from the autobiographies show furthermore that this critical attitude existed independently of National Socialist propaganda. Undoubtedly the latter helped materially in the focussing process by which everything unsavory was linked with the government.   But the ultimate reason why the campaign of vilification at National Socialist meetings appealed to the listeners was that they were in any case predisposed to blame the government for all ills.

3. *Opposition to Other Parties*

Discontent therefore was the foundation upon which Hitler and his followers built their edifice. Important as this foundation was, however, it is not sufficient cause to account for the popularity of the Nazi movement. There were, after all, other powerful contemporary groups and leaders who also appealed for public support by combating the government. Most important of these organizations on the right was the *Deutschnationale Volkspartei (D.N.V.P.)*, comprising big land-owners bitterly opposed to the agricultural policy of the government, industrialists who feared socialization, and conservatives generally, who longed for the re-establishment of the monarchy. The party had an efficient organization and large funds; it waged an embittered campaign against the government both on the floor of the Reichstag and in public meetings. Yet while many of our contributors were members of the *D.N.V.P.* before they joined the Hitler movement, the party had no permanent hold on them.

[4.7.4.] I was unwilling to join any of the old parties. Naturally I voted right at the elections, but I was never convinced of the merits of those elected. We in Germany had been deceived too often to warrant trust in any party. I had some regard for the parties of the right on the grounds of their "nationalism"; *but I missed the right attitude toward the people—the willingness to help.* Before elections we were always welcome; once the elections were over, however, the voter was something of a nuisance.

Similarly, another contributor writes:

[3.4.3.] After some good work at the outset, the spirit of caste and class came more and more to the fore in the German National party. I did not find there the thing I had sought. The gentlemen were ready enough to be Germans and nationalists, but they lacked the courage for socialism. The history of the German people had taught them nothing. Consequently I withdrew in the spring of 1923, and made every effort to contact some group that gave recognition to my own ideas.

A former nationalist speaker contributes these comments:

[4.7.5.] I saw more and more clearly that the German Nationalist party held to the unalterable conviction that the "common man" in service or industry had no right whatsoever to freedom, recreation, entertainment or the higher pleasures. I felt that this anti-social spirit would prove fatal to the *D.N.V.P.* I lost all pleasure in my work, and finally in 1932 I joined the Nazi party though I knew that, in accordance with their propaganda methods, my public appearances would, for the time being, come to an end.

The direct cause of my withdrawal from the old party was a point of policy expressed at the political education course for speakers which I attended. This was that the misery of the millions of unemployed should not be relieved by direct measures, but that all means should be used for the general improvement of economic conditions, which would ultimately lead to the elimination of unemployment. That meant in practice that unless the army of unemployed, out of work through no fault of theirs, could be absorbed by industry, they would have to starve. It meant furthermore years of bayonet rule, to deal with the desperation bound to follow. How different from this was the daring proposition that sprang from Hitler's warm, sympathetic heart! His idea was not to use the resources of the state to help industrialists and land owners, but to take advantage of them immediately to relieve the misery of millions of unemployed Germans!

A final criticism from another dissatisfied German nationalist further clarifies the stand of the *D.N.V.P.* and the reason it failed to win popular support.

[2.5.3.] To salve my German conscience to some extent, I attended the meetings of so-called nationalist organizations. But I went home dissatisfied, with no resurgence of inner faith. Later on, when this same party held some seventy to eighty seats in Parliament, its political aberrations and complete lack of integrity amply demonstrated to me that I had properly appraised this type of politics. All the national enthusiasm of this school could be adequately summed up in the words: "They well might, but would not!"

Clearly the main objection to the leading party of the right was its lack of sympathy with the needs and interests of the common man, the worker, the farmer, and lower middle-class shopkeeper and clerk. To the leaders of this party, "national" meant not the nation but a class and its rights and privileges. As time went on, more and more people came to the conclusion that in voting for the *Deutschnationale Volkspartei* they were only subscribing to an attempt to restore the order of caste and privilege characteristic of the Wilhelminian era. A clear indication of this is to be found in the drop of *D.N.V.P.* voting power from over six million in 1924 to less than two and a half million in 1930.

In addition to the *D.N.V.P.,* there were numerous other militant rightist groups, such as the nationalistic youth organizations and associations of veterans, notably the *Stahlhelm,* to which we have already referred in a previous chapter. Many of the objections levelled against the *D.N.V.P.* also applied to these groups.

[1.7.4.] In 1924 I was at last of an age to become associated with one of the groups fighting for Germany. At the suggestion of several of my classmates, I entered the *Wehrwolf* (a youth organization). For three years I worked for the rebirth of my country in the ranks of this organization; but in the end I could only conclude that no genuine spirit of fellowship—a prerequisite of success in any fight for the cause of a great people—was to be found in the *Wehrwolf.* All social classes of my home town were represented in the organization; nevertheless the power of class prejudice was inescapably evident. I still recall my uncle scolding me for associating with workers. "Keep to your own kind," he tersely summed up his words of wisdom.

Reactionary circles were well aware that we were fighting for a nationalistic Germany; still they continually excluded working-men from the national community. Yet even then I sensed instinctively that our country and our people could be resurrected only through the union of all Germans. At the elections, furthermore, it became evident that the *Wehrwolf* lacked all political foresight. The organization lacked an intrinsic unity of purpose, since the members had no idea which of the many "national" parties to vote for. It was quite evident that no purely military organization, such as the *Wehrwolf* sought to be, could achieve its aim without some degree of political wisdom; and so, I withdrew from the organization.

Equally open to criticism were other youth groups. The basis of this most frequently was lack of a well-defined policy and inadequate leadership. The following excerpt illustrates the gradual disillusionment of a once enthusiastic member of the *Wikingbund:*

[2.8.3.] A newspaper notice called my attention to the Wikingbund, under the leadership of Erhardt. Its patriotism and military spirit, together with the fact that Jews were excluded, induced me to join up. That was early in 1926. In the course of time I became more and more deeply rooted in the Wiking fellowship and looked upon my activities in the organization as far more important than the exercise of my profession.

I joyously accepted any task assigned me, and constantly strove, both through the newspapers and personal propaganda, to enlist new members. So I came to know my comrades, and so I came in intimate contact with the Socialist and Communist terror so often visited upon nationalists. Still, nothing could dissuade me from my course.

On Ascension Day, 1927, the Wikingbund was banned in Prussia; later on it was outlawed all over Germany. Yet though they abrogated our organization, the loyal comrades of individual groups continued together. *Unfortunately, as often happens under such circumstances, disagreements arose, so that we could not long keep our ranks intact.* In my *Wikingbund* days, I often attended meetings of the inter-patriotic society council, and noted that the various delegates seldom agreed on any point. *Nearly all the group leaders were former military officers, and each and every one of them felt a call to the general leadership.* Consequently neither this organization nor the *Frontbann* could ever accomplish anything. Indeed I may say that the quarrels among the patriotic societies, all of which subscribed to the ultimate aim of liberating Germany, had a bitter-

ness that might much more profitably have been used in combating
the enemy.

In the course of this inner strife the struggle against the regime
was neglected. The *Wikingbund* broke up. But a number of old
comrades continued to meet in Berlin, and together they formed a
new organization, the "Black-White-and-Red." Loath to desert my
old comrades, I too was a member at first. But in measure that the
monarchical question gained more and more prominence in the organization, I felt proportionately less interest in it.

Early in 1928 I attended the great turnout of National Socialists
in the Kriervereinhaus in Berlin. Dr. Goebbels' speech filled his
hearers with enthusiasm for the coming Third Reich. Then and
there I made up my mind to enroll in the Hitler movement; for I
realized that it alone could set Germany free and right existing
wrongs.

On the left, the Communists were bitter enemies of the
existing order. Frequently they used the very same arguments
against the government as the National Socialists, and often
joined hands with them in obstructive tactics on the floor of
Parliament. Supported by the Third International in Moscow,
they indulged in extensive propaganda.[3] Their program of a
new order and the promise of social betterment was calculated
to have a wide appeal, particularly among the unemployed
masses.

Yet while the Communists and the National Socialists were
the only parties with a persistently mounting enrollment
throughout the post-war years, the increases of the Communists
were never so spectacular as those of the National Socialists.
The Communist voting strength in 1924 amounted to 3,600,000,
while in November 1932, at the height of its power, the party
polled in all 5,900,000 votes. The National Socialists, on the
other hand, with a voting strength of only 900,000 in 1924,
came to the staggering total of 12,000,000 votes in November
1932.

---

[3] *Cf.* Rosenberg, Arthur, *Geschichte der deutschen Republik.* Karls-
bad: Graphia Verlag, 1935, p. 226.

What were the factors obstructing the growth of Communism? The reports of our informants shed little light on this question. None of those who were Communists before they joined the Hitler movement evinces a whole-hearted adherence to Communist doctrine at any time. For example, one converted Communist writes:

[2.3.2.] There were none but Communists, all of them members of the notorious "Red One Hundred," at my new place of work. Having worked hard all my life, I never paid any attention to politics. Presently, however, I, too, surrendered to the wooings of the comrades, and joined their ranks without ever grasping the meaning and aims of Communism.

In due time I enrolled in a trade school in a nearby city, where I came in contact with comrades of a different sort. There I experienced my first street fight, as I marched off with the Red Hundreds to break up the German Day observances. But the tide turned against us; we were beaten and put to flight.

That day, too, I saw for the first time the storm troops, with their bright red swastika banner. At the head of the procession they carried a picture of Hitler crowned with oak leaves. Their brave carriage and manly bearing immediately attracted me.

For some time afterwards I concentrated on National Socialist literature, particularly Theodor Fritsch's handbook of the Jewish question. Then I joined the ranks of the Nationalists.

A one-time parlor radical describes his conversion as follows:

[3.7.2.] The faith of my childhood collapsed when I was nineteen, as a result of my wartime experiences; I was a soldier on the Western front at the age of eighteen. Having known all phases of materialist thought, I was predestined to draw definite political conclusions.

I recall one characteristic incident at the Kaiserin Augusta Gymnasium, where I was preparing for graduation after my return from the war. Our history teacher had asked whether we considered Wilson's idea of a League of Nations capable of realization. Unequivocally, I replied with a loud "Yes." Having been a firm believer in the League of Nations, I regarded our teacher's evident skepticism as a direct attack upon my ideals.

In time I became more and more radical. Active Bolshevism

looked most attractive to me at a distance. I regarded it as the legendary Black Knight, who at the proper moment would play a considerable part in freeing Germany. In my revolutionary enthusiasm I transformed a classroom theme based on the text, "To you, O Gods, belongs the merchant, who goes forth in search of worldly goods, while goodness rides upon his mast," into a pean of praise for the coming world revolution. The composition described a wide arc as it flew from my teacher's desk, and landed at the footrest of my seat. All that, however, failed to impress me. Knowing my mental state, my German teacher kindly invited me to his house, and went on long walks with me. Even my religious instructor unexpectedly made his appearance one day, to advise and direct me. Yet out of the depths of my conviction I had to tell him I could never again believe in God.

Still, though I had fallen under the spell of communistic-democratic ideas, some inner instinct, as well as certain practical considerations, prevented me from engaging in active work on behalf of Bolshevism. I looked upon democracy as an historically necessary transition to the pure democracy of Communism. Consequently I could not envisage its arbitrary extinction before it had run its course. Moreover, the personal representatives of democracy could not inspire in me the respect I should have liked to have felt. I speedily discovered gaping loop-holes between their teachings and their conduct. And once one discovers the essence of a blunder and sees it soberly in its naked reality, even the mantle of loyalty and tolerance which one painstakingly draws over it loses its power of concealment.

The empty dryness of the Marxist press had begun to bore and disgust me. At this time of incipient doubt I happened to see a remarkable book in the show window of a bookshop. Remarkable the title seemed to me, and even more so the opening sentence, "O my brethren, what I love about man is that he is at once transition and destruction."

These words irresistibly captured my imagination. Strange words, yet there was something behind them. They fell upon my spiritual ear like a message from distant space; they found a kindred echo in my soul.

Each time I passed the bookshop after that, I always stopped a few moments to recall the motto that so powerfully moved my thoughts and feelings. Finally I saved up enough money to buy the book. Nietzsche, hitherto unknown to me, became my guide in philosophy and the motivator of my youthful spirit. In Nietzsche I rediscovered a bit of my primal self. His *Zarathustra* and *The Will to Power* induced a temporary spiritual intoxication in me.

Materialism and the shadowy world of Marxist democracy collapsed in me. The very inopportuneness of these concepts turned upon them and broke loose like a hammer upon their rotten foundations. It was only later I discovered that Mussolini, too, had been a youthful follower of Nietzsche, and in the most important sense continued to be one to this day.

(Our contributor subsequently identified the superman idea with Hitler, and joined the National Socialist party.)

Another of our contributors doubts that there ever was any genuine Communism among the German masses. This writer was active in various leftist organizations in the several factories where he served his apprenticeship, until he discovered that some of the labor unions secretly worked hand in hand with the employers' associations.

[1.0.5.] The idea of the class war and international solidarity was not deeply rooted in the rank and file of the Communist party. As far as I could see, these notions were limited to the party officials and the gang that waxed fat at the expense of the Communist working masses. The decent workingman who for any reason had been a member of the Communist or Socialist parties did not have to execute nearly so sharp an about face in January 1933 as some of the gentlemen of the right, particularly those of the *D.N.V.P.* and company. One day in 1931 I asked a Communist group leader whether he enjoyed taking orders from Moscow. The man replied he had never thought of his work that way. "Germany for Germans," he said. Could that man ever have sung the *Internationale* wholeheartedly?

Obviously, this statement must be discounted. But it contains one important suggestion: namely, that patriotism, loyalty to past traditions, and national pride, common to all classes of the German population, were the main reasons for the inability of the Communists to enlist many German workers on their side. Strong evidence in support of this hint is also contained in the life histories.

All things being equal, public support should have been more or less evenly distributed among the groups that fought the government. Consequently, the overwhelming success of the Hitler movement must be attributed to the special feature of the movement itself rather than to the milieu in which it operated.

Chapter VII

Ideology As a Factor

1. *The Idea of Gemeinschaft*

The leitmotif of the Hitler movement is contained in the slogan, *"Gemeinnutz vor Eigennutz"* (common good before personal advancement).

At the core of the concept is the idea of *Gemeinschaft,* an untranslatable term which combines the meaning of "unity," "devotion to the community," mutual aid, brotherly love, and kindred social values. The primary form of *Gemeinschaft* is the family, in which these social values are most easily realized because of the ties of kinship and mutual interest. But the National Socialists were not concerned with the family; they talked about the nation as a *Gemeinschaft.* They were thus expressing a desire for a social order, in which the organization of national life would follow the family pattern.

This ideal has been the wish of mankind since the time it emerged from the primitive stage of tribal civilization, when new communities—townships, nations, empires, not held together by bonds of kinship—began to be formed. Factional strife, abuse and exploitation, selfishness, and kindred evils of community life were attributed to the absence of such bonds of kinship.

But while many before had preached the desirability of restoring the family semblance in community life, the National Socialists alone succeeded in making it the rallying point, the gospel of a popular social movement. Usually in the autobiographies the idea of *Gemeinschaft* is linked with sentiments or intentions rooted in the personal experiences of individuals. Most of our contributors report that in early youth they were inculcated with strong feelings of patriotism through the influence of their families, their schools, or the youth organizations to which they belonged. This early conditioning made them peculiarly sensitive to the tragic outcome of the World War. Their dearest wish was to see Germany restored to its former power and splendor. Throughout German history, too, the lack of unity among the people, the division of the country into petty principalities, the religious schisms, and the split between the classes has been a thorn in the flesh of patriots. It was precisely to this feeling that National Socialists appealed with their proclamation of *Gemeinschaft*. The following quotation expresses a point of view common to many of our contributors:[1]

[2.7.3.] Seldom was our people united and great. But whenever it was strongly unified, it was unconquerable. This then is the secret of our idea, and in it lies the power of National Socialism: Unity is the goal of our leader, who wants to make the people strong, so it may become powerful again.

The unity the patriots aspired to was to be a unity of the German people, not of groups of nations or of the workers of the world. Consequently, the presentation of the *Gemeinschaft* ideal together with violent opposition to any form of internationalism, especially that of the Marxist variety, appealed particularly to patriots.

---

[1] The bracketed numerical symbols are explained in the insert at the end of the book.

[2.7.2.] I felt a deep-seated aversion to the idea of an "International." I was brought up as a nationalist, and I could never develop any enthusiasm for the utopian idea of a "unity of nations."

A carrier in a coal mine expresses his doubts as follows:

[2.3.4.] Young as I was, I was puzzled by the denial of race and nation implicit in Marxism. Though I was interested in the betterment of the workingman's plight, I rejected it unconditionally. Instead, I often asked myself why socialism had to be tied up with internationalism—why it couldn't work as well or better in conjunction with nationalism.

Another member of the working class, an old railroad employee, professes similar views.

[4.3.3.] As a railroad worker, I had ample opportunity to observe the prevalent confusion, particularly among workers. While I was in the army, I found that the best soldiers came from the working class; now I had to witness these workers being alienated from the Fatherland. Why then should Germany rend itself? I shuddered at the thought of Germany in the grip of Bolshevism. The slogan "Workers of the world unite!" made no sense to me. At the same time, however, National Socialism, with its promise of a community of blood, barring all class struggle, attracted me profoundly.

The appeal of the *Gemeinschaft* concept was not limited to opponents of internationalism only. Rather it was the social implications of the *Gemeinschaft* ideal, including the abolition of privilege, that attracted wide sectors of the population.

Many of our contributors expressed genuine dissatisfaction with the class system in Germany.

[4.6.4.] In the army rigid limits were set for the common mortal. He could not under any circumstances become an officer. This class difference seemed to me another obstacle to the realization of the true *Gemeinschaft*. For many an old sergeant and non-commissioned officer had proved that he was better able to take charge of a battery or lead a company in the field than many a young or even old officer. Thus, even in pre-war days standards were set which marked a man as a human being or less. In private life the prerequisite of humanity was an academic education; in the army it was the officer's stripes. All this, it seemed to me, was eminently unjust. Yet the system persisted through the post war days, until our Leader, Adolf Hitler, proposed to put an end to it.

The abuses of the class system are a frequent theme in the autobiographies. The following excerpt is typical of many of our contributors in a critical mood:

[4.3.4.] Contact with these people, who passed their lives at the grind from dawn to sunset, made my father wish that their lot, too, might be bettered. Why did the neighboring landowner have to have four horses to draw his carriage when two would have done as well? Why were hired men, working for a shocking wage, subjected to daily indignities?

All these youthful observations were more than confirmed when my father, as a young teacher of twenty-two, was employed at the house of a great landowner. As frequently as not, the lord of the manor used his whip on his working men—a most horrible example of the "divine right" of the Junkers! The class spirit of our "betters" once again appeared at its crassest, when these Junkers banded together in the pre-war conservative party, voted against a ship canal designed to open the way to the east, lest too much "enlightenment" be spread among the working masses.

Though my father dated back to the monarchy of old Fritz, he was, nevertheless, opposed to the mighty of his day, since he recognized that any contact with the people had long since ceased. The princely houses of his day no longer ruled for the good of the people, but sought only to perpetuate their power and bask in the flattery of the sycophants around them. A typical expression of the spirit of the time was the so-called "three-class" election law, which enabled people who paid a large tax out of their bounty to cast two votes, or even a third, according to the amount of their wealth or the degree of their "learning."

Character is determined neither by wealth nor by position; devotion to duty alone is the mark of true nobility. Consequently, the man who, by the sweat of his brow supports his family of four or five, is far more worthy of admiration than the man who, because of his business cunning, at regular intervals cuts coupons, nobly bearing up under the strain of making this terrestrial existence as pleasant as possible for his "lady" and his spoiled only child.

The philosophy of life with which my father sent me on my way never left me. Later on when, after attendance at a secondary school, I became a mason's apprentice, I was able to supplement this philosophy on my own initiative. I had been engaged to work on the workers' quarters of a heavy industrial plant. These quarters consisted of row upon row of damp dark houses with scarcely any room for yards where people, crammed close together, were forced to lead their joyless lives.

Tenants began to move in before we were through plastering the houses. The impression they made has never left me. Whole families came, with three, four, or more children, their sole luggage being one much battered travelling bag or a single cardboard box! The first few nights of their stay they would buy some packs of straw from the cattle dealer, and strew it over the floor for themselves. How, one asks, were these people lured from the peace of their villages? That is perhaps one of the saddest chapters on the conscience of big business.

It was an everlasting shame. These people had been bundled together *en masse* and transported like cattle in freight cars. Yet the social order of that day passed lightly over such things, since the bulk of the population on the whole was well off. Still, whoever went among the people in those days and exchanged political views with working people was bound to find again and again that they repudiated with disgust the conduct of that wild horde. The unbiased observer, moreover, could not but recognize that much of the unrest was due to the attitude of big business, which looked upon the working class as a plastic mass, to be shaped and kneaded without regard for the individual. Seldom if ever had professional classes been lined up against each other in such bitter strife, full of meanness and hatred.

The almost inhuman struggle by which the mighty of that day often ruthlessly drove the individual from his work and sent him scurrying from place to place under assumed names, depriving him of his home and family, and often sending him to prison under the heaviest bodily and spiritual duress, had to be overcome by an inner strength striving toward a goal that warranted all this suffering. Neither privation nor death of individuals mattered in this strife. All this constituted only an added cause for the survivors to fight, that their friends might not have died in vain, and that the great ideal of the people's community might all the more speedily be attained.

The general resentment against the class spirit often originated at the front or was reinforced by experiences there.

[4.7.4.] Nevertheless, the war had taught us one lesson, the great
community of the front. All class differences, staunchly entrenched
before the war, disappeared under its spell. Out there it was what
a person *was*, not what he seemed to be, that counted. There was
only a people, no individuals. Common suffering and a common
peril had welded us together and hardened us; that was why we
were able to defy a world for four years. My experiences at the
front, along with what I learned as a prisoner of war in France,
have determined my political outlook. Out there we actually lived
the inscription on the tomb of the great Swiss, Pestalozzi, "Everything for others, nothing for oneself," and its truth was graven on
our hearts. How often all of us had been helped out by some manifestation of friendship!

To many, the movement itself signifies a resumption of the
fellowship of the trenches.

[3.6.4.] When I joined the Party, my life once again came to
have significance. I had to neglect my family to some extent;
nevertheless, I was satisfied. My very family had to admit I was
a changed man. Our meetings now held a very special attraction:
we were once again "among men" as we had been at the front.
As I review my past life, I now see that my entire life has been
motivated by two relatively brief periods: my service at the front,
and my membership in the National Socialist party before it came
to power. During both of these periods the high ideals we strove
for were closely connected with our conscious manhood and the
sense of fellowship.

The following declaration of faith likewise bears out this
idea:

[3.7.4.] National Socialism was conceived in the experiences
of the trenches. It can only be understood in terms of these front-
line experiences.

The ideology of the Nazi movement thus appealed to those
who deplored the internal disunity of the German people.

They interpreted the idea of *Gemeinschaft* in terms of their front-line experiences, and saw in the movement the—

[3.3.4.] . . . uncompromising will to stamp out the class struggle, snobberies of caste, and party hatreds. The movement bore the true message of socialism to the German workingman. That the German worker, particularly the onetime fighter, promptly espoused the cause of National .Socialism, may be readily understood in view of the fact that by its very ideology the National Socialist doctrine appealed most to those who had borne the greatest burden of suffering both during the war and afterwards.

It will be seen therefore that two powerful currents that existed independently of the Hitler movement found in it an anchorage and a promise of fulfillment: a strong patriotic feeling which demanded the unity of the German people and a desire for social justice, which opposed the class struggle and class divisions. Evidently, then, the movement derived its strength from combining nationalism with socialism in its name and program.

2. National Socialism

There were nationalists in Germany to whom socialism had been anathema. There were, on the other hand, socialists who saw in nationalism a handicap to the realization of social justice, for they identified it with adherence to the old regime and the privileges of the upper classes. These people respectively constituted the Conservative and Socialist and Communist parties. But these extremists were in the minority in Germany. The majority of Germans, the bulk of the workers and the lower middle class, were responsive to nationalism but rejected it when it was advocated without consideration of the social question. While they favored the reforms advocated by the socialists, they were reluctant to adopt the Marxist program of internationalism. To this majority group the combination of nationalism and socialism within a single party program appealed as a welcome solution of a dilemma.

The following report illustrates this idea:

[2.3.2.] In the factory I became acquainted with workingmen and saw their sufferings. I discovered that Marxism to them was not so much a matter of philosophy as their daily bread. To it they looked for an improvement of their own condition as well as a decent future for their children.

I was deeply distressed to see the shabby treatment these men, who throughout the war had done their duty to the last, and who continued in the van of the struggle for Germany, received from our government. The latter did nothing to relieve the sad plight of these workers. The ruthless expansion of capitalism was in no way curbed. And so I became a socialist for a purely moral reason; for it seemed to me no more than proper that anyone who had unstintingly devoted himself to the Fatherland should be entitled to share its wealth.

And then I studied the history of our people. What did I find? The division of German provinces, together with the selfishness of our princes, had made it possible for covetous French kings to set back our borders, which in the Middle Ages extended to Sedan far beyond the borders of what now constitutes France, further and further to the East. During the Thirty Years' War, at the time of the struggle against the Turks around Vienna, whenever Germany was hard pressed, France appropriated a slice of German soil. Despite the bloody sacrifices of our people, we could not preserve our territorial integrity.

As a result of the lessons of history and my own experiences both during and after the war, I became a nationalist. The suffering and privations of wide strata of our people, on the other hand, made me a socialist.

In 1925 the Army of Occupation lifted the ban against the National Socialist party in my home town. I attended the initial meetings, and found that the Party subscribed to the very aims and purposes I cherished. I joined the movement, and have been one of its active workers ever since.

The concept of National Socialism was not an invention of Hitler. In 1896 Friedrich Naumann, one of the great political leaders and economists of the Wilhelmian era, attempted to organize a party to which he gave the name *National-Sozial*. The German Workers' Party of Austria, led by Schoener and

Jung, changed its name to the German National Socialist Party
of Austria in May 1918. According to Heiden [2] the name was
originally suggested at a party meeting as far back as 1913. It
might also be pointed out, as in Schumann's [3] work, that the
idea, if not the name, of National Socialism can be traced back
to the German Romantic movement, the idea of the Prussian
state propounded by Frederick the Great, the socialism of Las-
salle, and so forth.

Thus neither the name nor the idea of National Socialism
was a novelty. But the fact that a mass movement was created
in its name is an original accomplishment. Hitler succeeded
where Naumann, Jung and others failed. The timeliness of the
idea, in view of prevalent conditions, favored his effort and in
part accounts for his success. More important was the fact that
the speechmaking of Hitler and his lieutenants endowed the
idea with a powerful emotional content. What was previously
an academic theory, the name of a debating society, or a minor
political party, became at once a faith capable of inducing in its
adherents a fervor bordering on fanaticism. It became a cause
for which people were willing to sacrifice their lives.

[3.7.2.] We acted as if under compulsion. Even had we wished
to, we could not have been untrue to the movement without having our hearts torn out of our breasts. Unshakable faith and unselfish devotion to the hallowed cause were our weapons against
apparently invincible opponents, armed with the power of the
state, and the determination to use it at any cost to curb the achievement of our aims. Many an honorable opponent had to admit,
albeit unwillingly, the readiness of the National Socialists to sacrifice everything for the cause; this despite the fact that the leaders
of the opposition did nothing without first considering what they
would get out of it. What fellowship was there among the men
who left their wives, families and parents, preferring the sacred

---

[2] Heiden, Konrad, *Geschichte des National-Sozialismus.* Berlin:
Rohwolt, 1932, p. 33.

[3] Schumann, F. L., *The Nazi Dictatorship.* New York: A. H.
Knopf, 1935, pp. 95-96, 116-117.

sign of the swastika to their means of livelihood! They mocked Hell, death, and the Devil in their faith in a just cause. What joy and honor to be allowed to fight side by side with such comrades!

Other writers strike a similar note.

[3.3.3.] The joy of fighting for Hitler's principle gave my life a new meaning. The philosophy of the movement endowed my hitherto aimless life with a meaning and a purpose.

The above are a few samples of the typical response of our contributors to National Socialism. Most of them explain that this response was due primarily to the fact that the movement appealed to their obligation toward the common good, demanding sacrifices rather than making promises for the benefit of individuals.

[3.3.3.] I was attracted to the National Socialist party because it did not indulge in the high promises other parties made in their campaign literature. On the contrary, we were told that we must suffer and sacrifice; that the end of our striving must be a greater Germany rather than personal aggrandizement.

As in war propaganda, therefore, the National Socialists made an emotional issue of their aims, embellishing them with the symbols and feelings which lie at the basis of group loyalty. The secret of their success is identical with the appeal of war propaganda.

War propaganda technique and powerful popular sentiment therefore raised the *Gemeinschaft* concept to be the rallying point of a movement. A third factor in the promotion of the *Gemeinschaft* idea was the principle of leadership; lastly, there was the concept of blood relationship, as its assumed realistic basis. Both these principles require some elucidation.

3. *The Principle of Leadership*

The concept of the nation as a *Gemeinschaft* is, in the last analysis, utopian. Accordingly, those who advocated it insisted upon a "change of heart" and even the need of breeding a new species of human being to make its realization possible.[4]

As more and more people flocked to the Nazi movement, the National Socialists felt that the "change of heart" was taking place of its own accord. But what was to follow? How should national life be organized, in order to best insure the maintenance and proper function of the desired *Gemeinschaft?* In what political form could National Socialism become the basis of a new social order?

The National Socialists had ready answers to all these questions. There could be no *Gemeinschaft,* they argued, unless the members of a community could be restrained from pursuing activities unfavorable to the common good. Who was to prescribe this restraint? A single leader to whom unquestioned obedience could be given, one who could be trusted to make his decisions solely in the interest of the community. Submission to a leader acting for the common good would weld the nation into a unit, eliminate injustices and internal strife. Only such recognition of supreme authority, under which the individual would have to obey commands rather than follow the dictates of self-interest, could insure the maintenance of *Gemeinschaft.*

The National Socialists derived the leadership principle from the organization of the Prussian army. Hitler writes in his memoirs: "The underlying principle of our proposed state is the same as that which not so long ago made the Prussian army the most wonderful instrument of the German people." [5]

The principle is that of hierarchy: "authority from the top down, responsibility from the bottom up." Leaders are selected on the basis of merit and personal qualifications. They command their inferiors and, by the same token, obey their superiors. They are personally responsible for all their decisions.

This chain of ranks is secured at one end by popular sub-

---

[4] For example, Mannheim, Karl, *Mensch und Gesellschaft im Zeitalter des Umbaus.* Leiden: A. W. Zijthoff, 1935, particularly Chapter III.

[5] *Mein Kampf,* p. 501.

mission to the hierarchy of leaders and at the other end by the supreme commander, in whom is vested the highest authority and the greatest responsibility. The supreme leader lays down the plan of action, which is then worked out in detail and executed by his subordinates. He may have expert counsel, but the final decision and sole responsibility are his alone. There is no collective body, no parliament to censor his decisions or serve as a scapegoat for his failures. His responsibility is directly to the people who gave him the mandate to rule, and to the followers who have given him their allegiance. This, the National Socialists argue, is true democracy: not majority rule, which leads to irresponsibility, but a plebiscite that passes upon the trustworthiness of those to whom power to make decisions has been delegated.

This concept of the state, organized in military fashion, the National Socialists set forth and elaborated in their speeches as the means of securing permanent unity, and the fulfillment of the common good. The ultimate goal of the movement was the militaristic or totalitarian state as it is now called, in which all citizens, without regard for parties or classes, were to be political soldiers under the leadership of executive officers. Pending accession to power, this pattern of organization existed in embryonic form within the movement itself. Hitler himself looked upon the movement as the future German State, the Third Reich in miniature.[6]

The autobiographies show that those who joined the Hitler movement were well aware of the meaning and implications of the proposed new social order. Furthermore, they not only approved it, but also believed in it as the means of bringing about the desired *Gemeinschaft*.

We have seen that a widespread dissatisfaction existed with republican institutions. A person or group profoundly dissatisfied with something can easily be persuaded to favor its

---

[6] *Ibid.*, p. 503: *Die Bewegung in sich selbst traegt schon den kommenden Staat.*

opposite. The National Socialist platform advocated item by item the opposite of everything to which the public, rightly or wrongly, attributed their troubles. If parliamentarianism was blamed, the National Socialists advocated a dictatorship; with class privilege as the point at issue, the National Socialists advocated merit and achievement as the sole basis of advancement. The general indignation against a policy of conciliation in international affairs was offset by the promise of the National Socialists to wield a strong hand in dealing with the victors of Versailles. The calamitous multiplicity of parties was to be eliminated by a one-party system.

Additional factors supported the popular inclination toward a militaristic state. Among these was the fact that of all the radical proposals for improvement then advocated in Germany, the National Socialist plan alone left the existing economic system virtually intact. Hitler's dictum, "Economics is a secondary matter," appealed to the middle class, anxious to maintain its rights of ownership. The idea of rigid control under a militaristic state led the employer to believe that the demands of labor would be effectively curtailed. By the same token the employee saw in the principle of leadership a means of checking exploitation. Under the influence of Gottfried Federer, to be sure, the National Socialists at one time were keen for economic reform. But these reforms, despite the fact that they had been incorporated in the official party platform, were soon forgotten. Undoubtedly Hitler's campaign to win the support of industrialists and landowners which began in 1927 [7] accounts for the fact that from that year on the economic program was hardly ever mentioned by National Socialist speakers. Any break in the general obscurity surrounding economic reform was interpreted as referring to the alien owner and capitalist alone, that is, to the Jewish entrepreneur.

Another important factor in influencing public opinion was

[7] Ganzer, K. R., *Vom Ringen Hitlers um das Reich*. Berlin: Zeitgeschichte Verlag, 1935, p. 67.

the conformity of the militaristic state to the traditions in which most Germans had been reared. Our contributors repeatedly stress the shock they experienced upon realizing that they had to participate in government, choose a party, and pass judgment upon political matters. They were used to an autocratic government, and army service had inculcated in them a strong sense of discipline, and willingness to submit to a leader. Hence the average German was not opposed to the return of a system involving submission and decisions made by trusted leaders. The difficulty and intricacy of the problems of government in Germany contributed to the willingness of people to leave the burden of responsibility to others.

It is the combination of these factors that accounts to a large extent for the favorable response to the principle of leadership. One thing, however, it leaves unexplained. According to the theory of the militaristic state, the supreme commander, *der Fuehrer,* makes his decisions solely in the interest of the nation. Furthermore, he is directly responsible to the people for his actions. What assurance is there in the proposed scheme of government that the Fuehrer will act for the common good? What means are provided for the execution of the public will against a refractory leader? On these two vital points the theory of the militaristic state is silent.

Why didn't this seemingly obvious weakness deter the followers of the movement? Why weren't they suspicious of the scheme? The possible answer lies in the attitude the adherents of National Socialism took toward Hitler. Hitler was *the* Fuehrer, and was to be supreme commander of the future German state. The loyalty and devotion, the esteem and admiration he inspired in his followers, made it impossible to imagine that he might not act for the common good, or that the need of removing him might ever arise. Consequently, the weakness of the theory escaped notice. Equally irrelevant, because it was a matter of the distant future, was the question of the successor to Hitler. The principle of leadership was impregnable as long as Hitler was leader.

The reverence with which his followers regarded Hitler was the outstanding feature of the movement. What light do the autobiographies throw upon this phenomenon?

It is a matter of common observation that a prolonged, severe crisis favors the rise of a leader. Pained, bewildered people wish for a savior to lead them out of their difficulties. They readily acknowledge any strong, aggressive individual who proposes a definite course of action and is able to inspire people with confidence and hope.

The post-war period of German history was one continuous crisis, at its severest during the days of the revolution, 1918 to 1920, and during the depression of 1930 to 1933. The wish for a leader is frequently echoed in the autobiographies. For example, a high school teacher writes:

[4.7.4.] Around 1923 I reached the conclusion that no party, but a single man alone could save Germany. This opinion was shared by others, for when the cornerstone of a monument was laid in my home town, the following lines were inscribed on it: "Descendants who read these words, know ye that we eagerly await the coming of the man whose strong hand may restore order."

An East Prussian businessman reports:

[4.5.4.] Communism was rampant in East Prussia from 1921 to 1923. Those were sad years, made sadder by the inflation. As a cattle dealer, I had ample opportunity to observe the reactions of people. Practically everyone rejected the idea of a return to the monarchy; none but a few great landowners took it at all seriously. But the call for a second Bismarck resounded throughout East Prussia. The desire for a leader was evident in every political manifestation of East Prussians. They could not abide the unholy treaty of peace, the occupation of the Rhineland. They could not understand why a great leader had not arisen to scatter Marxism to the four winds and give Germany a new lease on life.

During a crisis, numerous individuals invariably try to make use of the opportunity for leadership offered by unsettled conditions. A number of our contributors were engaged in initiating and managing counter-revolutionary groups before they joined the Hitler movement. In general, the life histories of these early leaders show the presence of three background factors. First, there was usually a powerful emotional experience, such as a frustration experienced in childhood or the period of adolescence—mistreatment, and so forth, that became a dominant and absorbing drive to the exclusion of other interests. In all such cases there is a strong desire to overcome a handicap or to be avenged. Second, a general lack of ties—familial, occupational, or any other—that impose responsibilities is to be noted. Most frequently we find among the first counter-revolutionary groups individuals who have not yet settled down, established a family, or become tied up with some business enterprise. They were mostly young people; however, there were some older men, too, whose lives had been uprooted by the war and who had nothing to lose through some new venture. Third, these men had acquired confidence in their ability to induce obedience or to influence others.

Under ordinary circumstances such men would have little chance to assert their ambitions. A crisis, however, introduces new evaluations of personalities, and individuals with initiative, daring, and self-confidence are frequently able to win recognition. This does not mean that anyone who aspires to leadership can become a leader. People must see more than self-assertion in a person before they become his willing followers. What are these added qualifications? We can answer this question with regard to the reaction to Hitler.

Foremost is the impression produced by his oratory:

[2.8.4.] What impressed me most about Hitler was the courage with which the wartime corporal attacked all evil. I felt the urge once more to be a soldier.

[2.8.2.] I heard Hitler in Bonn, in 1926. What he said, in clear, concise phrases, had long since agitated the feelings of every good German. The German soul spoke to German manhood in his words. From that day on I could never violate my allegiance to Hitler. I saw his illimitable faith in his people and the desire to set them free. His conviction upheld us, whenever we weakened amidst our trials; we leaned upon him in our weariness.

[2.7.4.] His never-to-be-forgotten speech affected me as the words of a prophet.

[4.8.4.] I first saw Hitler at an *S.A.* meeting at Gera in September 1931. The experience was a revelation to us, and we should have rushed blindly anywhere Hitler commanded us to go. The sun shone all the time Hitler was there, in proverbial "Hitler weather." Before his arrival and after he left, it rained so hard we were drenched. Yet to have seen and heard Hitler was ample reward. We had travelled in mufti all the way to the Thuringian border, since brown shirts were once again taboo in Prussia. Afterwards an old comrade, who had for years been out of work, confided to me with tears in his eyes that Hitler had looked straight at him. The fact is, Hitler looks every man in the eye. His looks wander from one trooper to the other as the *S.A.* marches by.

We, oldtime National Socialists, did not join the *S.A.* for reasons of self-interest. Our feelings led us to Hitler. There was a tremendous surge in our hearts, a something that said: "Hitler, you are our man. You speak as a soldier of the front and as a man; you know the grind, you have yourself been a working man. You have lain in the mud, even as we—no big shot, but an unknown soldier. You have given your whole being, all your warm heart, to German manhood, for the well-being of Germany rather than your personal advancement or self-seeking. For your innermost being will not let you do otherwise."

No one who has ever looked Hitler in the eye and heard him speak can ever break away from him.

Numerous contributors comment on the magnetic power of Hitler's personality.

[3.3.2.] I made the personal acquaintance of Hitler, and discovered that he emanates a power that draws everybody to him.

[3.7.3.] When the Fuehrer administered our oath at Weimar and we marched past him, we felt that all our sacrifices had been amply rewarded by this experience. As the Fuehrer addressed us, his eyes became like hands that gripped men never to let go again.

These quotations are typical of the major reactions to

Hitler. They indicate that the factors that attracted his followers were the ability to cast a spell, his dramatic oratory, startling performances (such as accurate predictions), and fortunate decisions under difficult circumstances, the sincerity of his convictions, unbounded faith in a cause—in general, the attributes of a prophet.

The last qualification is particularly important. Leopold has shown [8] that people recognize prestige in others when they are aware of their own inability to compete with or imitate them. But prestige is not sufficient to make anyone a great leader. A man must be able to induce in others the feeling that he is called upon to fulfill a mission, that he possesses a superhuman endowment and can exercise authority that "resolves all doubt and hesitations," before they will give him their unquestioned allegiance. Hitler succeeded in impressing people in just that way. And the forces that brought about his recognitions as *der Fuehrer* were the very ones operative throughout history in creating charismatic leaders.

4. *Anti-Semitism*

Equal in importance to the principle of leadership as a quasi-realistic underpinning of the ideology of the movement was the racial doctrine advocated by the National Socialist. Next to attacks on the government, it was probably the most frequently discussed theme of the propagandists of the movement.

The racial doctrine of the National Socialists consisted, in the main, of three tenets: first, the belief in the biological superiority of the "germanic" race to which were attributed all human achievements in culture and civilization; second, the opinion that racial purity is the basis of national health and survival and that intermixture of races is the source of all social decay; and finally, what we may call the anti-Semitic clause of the doctrine, the claim that the Jews are an inferior

---

[8] Leopold, L., *Prestige*. London: T. F. Unwin, 1913.

race and that their influence on the economic, political, and cultural life of Germany, past and present, is responsible for all that was and is evil.[9] The National Socialists assigned an important place in their ideology to the racial doctrine because they believed that race consciousness and awareness of blood affinity provide the bond that would hold the nation together as a *Gemeinschaft.* Behind this assumption is an argument by analogy; just as the unity of the family and the *we*-feeling of its members is based upon kinship, so a nation also could be expected to act and feel as one great family if the people who compose it be conscious of blood relationship. That the German people were of common blood was not questioned by the National Socialists.[10] Neither did they doubt that to this "blood" adheres a quality which makes its bearers willing to sacrifice self-interest for the common good.[11] The lack of unity of the German people on vital questions affecting the national interest was attributed to a weakened race consciousness. And they saw the symptom thereof in a general indifference toward the race problem, as shown particularly in the neglect on the part of past governments to preserve the racial purity of the German nation.[12] To the National Socialists the achievement of national unity was predicated, therefore, upon making the German people race conscious, and this they hoped to accomplish by converting people to their racial doctrine.

The autobiographies show that the racial doctrine attracted many people to the Hitler movement. But there is no indication that it was the preaching of Aryan superiority and of the mysterious force of blood affinity that impressed them. The data reveals that the propaganda value of the racial doctrine rested almost exclusively upon its anti-Semitic clause.

---

[9] For an elaboration of these tenets, see Hitler's *Mein Kampf,* Chapter XI. For the best attempt to refute the racial doctrine, see Huxley, J. S., and Haddon, A. C., *We Europeans.* London: J. Cape, 1935; and Valentin, H., *Anti-Semitism.* New York: Viking Press, 1936.

[10] *Cf.* Hitler, *op. cit.,* p. 78.

[11] *Ibid.,* pp. 326-7.

[12] *Ibid.,* p. 359.

Invariably the involved and obscure talk about race was trans-
lated by the followers of the movement into the simple dictum:
"Destroy the power of the Jews in Germany." Or, as the
popular slogan brutally expressed it: *"Juda verrecke."*

This they understood; of this they approved. There was
nothing to prevent such an interpretation. On the contrary,
by preaching violent anti-Semitism and attacking the Jews on
all occasions, the National Socialists did all in their power to
encourage it. And apparently the racial doctrine, especially
its anti-Semitic emphasis, has struck a popular note and in doing so contributed to a considerable extent to the success of
the movement.

Anti-Semitism was a prevalent sentiment in Germany after
the World War. It first manifested itself in numerous bodily
attacks perpetrated on Jews by mobs in cities like Berlin and
Munich during the days of the revolution. Later it showed
itself in the many anti-Semitic clubs and associations that were
organized all over Germany. The autobiographies give us an
opportunity to see some of the main sources of this sentiment.

The following quotations are taken from the life-histories
of those who were anti-Semitic before they joined the movement and who were attracted to it by its stand against the Jews.

The most frequently occurring source of anti-Semitism was
the interpretation given to personal experiences arising from
contacts with Jews.

Some of these experiences occurred during the war.

[4.7.3.] On August 2, 1914, I took charge of the business end
of the supply division of district headquarters number eleven in
Berlin. Almost at the same time as the families of the first of our
fallen heroes reported for aid, the first staff of men on furlough
were assigned to my department. My helpers, I recognized, were
largely of Jewish faith.

As early as 1914 these people had found a way to make the best
of the war. With their own people on hand as physicians, they
readily obtained medical certificates, which in turn enabled them
to get suitable clerical work. Quartered at home as they were, they

were thus able to attend to their business, our own hours from eight to four.

As the end of 1918 approached, I had a staff of 128 men, approximately forty of them Jews, ranking from private to sergeant. Having been a soldier from the time I was eighteen, I had no idea of politics and forms of government. As the fortunes of war turned more and more against us, my Jewish subordinates frequently "enlightened" me regarding the things that went on in our Fatherland. In the course of my steadfast opposition to these machinations, I became aware of certain developments, designed to undermine our military power, which were ordinarily discussed only behind closed doors in party caucuses. I was thus able to estimate the extent of the power wielded by these people. As early as May 1918, a certain Jewish publisher, employed as a clerk in my office, declared that the war would end in revolution by the end of 1918. The strike of the munition workers was the event that presaged this conclusion.

Early in November 1918 all my Jews found some threadbare excuse to stay away from the office, and when the armistice had been signed, they were all active once more as hawks of the revolution. The time had come when Germany was to be sold out and destroyed. The war had been a business deal for these creatures; human life and suffering were immaterial.

[4.5.5.] A brief period of my World War experience also calls for mention here. The year was 1918. That spring I had been wounded for the second time, and I was laid up in a hospital at Kissingen, Bavaria, to cure my wound as well as my stomach, ruined by trench fare. It was there I made a discovery that predisposed me toward National Socialism. I became an anti-Semite.

The picture that confronted us daily was as follows: There was the broad resort walk, shaded by two rows of trees, flanked by benches on either side. On one side there was a sign, "For soldiers only." On the other side the sign read, "For resort guests." That in turn presented this picture: on the one side there were miserable undernourished wounded soldiers, in their old deloused uniforms. Most of them were so weak from their wounds and lack of food (hospital fare at that time being much too inadequate for healthy people, let alone wounded men) that they just about managed, half unconsciously, to get along. At the same time the other side presented the picture of gay laughing guests, talking and munching fruits and delicacies, beautifully dressed ladies, their hands and fat necks decked out with diamonds, conducting themselves in loud, un-German fashion and altogether carrying on in a manner totally unsuited to those hard times. The gentlemen of this select community were well-fed specimens, who each morning carried their bags of snow-white flour to the baker and who devoted their time to discussions of business and stock exchange quotations. Indeed the financial pages of the *Berliner Tageblatt,* which was feverishly awaited every evening, were the main topic of conversation. Briefly, a more striking contrast could not be imagined than this, between two utterly different worlds of thought and being. The bloody irony was inescapable! Of all shades and classes yet in the last analysis very much alike in their manner and behavior. It was disgusting! The fate of Germany seemed a matter of indifference to these international allied parasites thriving on the people. It was a lasting burden to us front-line soldiers to have to put up with this ignominy day by day. At that I wish to emphasize that I had not, up to that time, been subjected to any anti-Semitic influences or attitudes, though as a German I had at all times had an almost unconscious aversion to Jews.

[3.7.3.] Here in the bank, during the war, we learned to know the Jew as he really is. My work in one of the most important departments of the bank often brought me in contact with Jews of all the central European countries, and I had listened in on many a conversation that gave me food for thought. My loyalty to the bank prevented me from mentioning these things that at the time appeared incomprehensible to me. Thus here was an extremely wealthy Jew, an officer in the Rumanian army, who had been captured by the Austrians. This man frequently went on extended trips for the bank. At the time I couldn't understand why a prisoner of war, who should have been locked up, was allowed to go about his business unhampered. I was equally puzzled by a number of other obvious irregularities which today, on the basis of my subsequent experience, are to me clear indications of the fact that the Jews of all nations were secretly allied, that they attended to their business and lived like lords at the same time that German manhood bled at the front, and we at home had not enough to eat.

A similar idea, that the Jews have a hidden plan directed against Germany, was the interpretation given by one of our informants to the following experience which he claims has made him anti-Semitic.

[2.1.2.] After my graduation from agricultural school in 1919, I worked on my father's lands. In 1921 my father was joined by another volunteer from Hamburg, who, as we later discovered, was of the Jewish race. This Jew owned to me that he didn't want to become a tiller of the soil. He was a Communist, and he sought to learn about agriculture because he hoped to be state commissar of collective farms in the German Communist state. One day as we were working together, the postman came and brought a newspaper with the headline, "Walter Rathenau Appointed Chancellor." Upon reading this, the Jew whooped, and cried "Hurrah!" I asked why he was so pleased, since he was a Communist, and Rathenau a Democrat. He answered that all that didn't matter; Rathenau was one of his people. It struck me, then, that these Jews made use of different parties to divide the German people against each other, while their leaders all subscribed to the same hidden purpose: namely, the exploitation of German workers.

Disadvantageous business deals also are mentioned frequently as the personal experiences which resulted in anti-Semitism.

[3.2.5.] The bourgeois camp of the German National party suited me. Ever since I had become an executive I suffered no material or spiritual want. I had a family; I was doing well; indeed, I could wish for nothing better. I found little time to think about the misery of the workers, though I myself had experienced it for years. My own well-being loomed big in my mind. I voted at the elections and felt that I thus performed my civic duty to the full. From time to time I helped some poor family whose misery had come to my notice. My own ego was thus satisfied; everything else seemed immaterial. I listened to populist speakers and read their writings without any inner sense of community.

One day my brother visited me and told me that despite all diligence and frugality could do, my parents' homestead became more heavily indebted each year. It was then, when our plot of native soil seemed in danger, that I roused myself from my middle-class complacency. I had to forestall the catastrophe that threatened our homestead. My sisters wanted to marry, but they had no dowries. Consequently my father proceeded to mortgage the farm. At first he found the money lenders willing and ready to help him out at the rate of 10 per cent or more interest. The instant he was unable to pay the interest and amortisation debts, however, it would be all over for him. The Jew threatened to drive him from the soil his ancestors had tilled for over 300 years. I was struck by the terrible realization that the government sought to seize all farms through the granting of credit. The Jew at the bottom of it all had to tame the farmer in order to achieve his plans. After this shocking realization it occurred to me that these facts had long been exposed by the preachers of National Socialism without my having paid any attention to them. I went to ask the advice of my party leaders. But their shrugs and discouraging attitude taught me that no rescue could be expected from that quarter. I ascertained how certain men who called themselves Nationalists and Christians always blessed themselves before everyone else and even misused their Christianity and nationalism for their own advancement. I then tried to contribute as much as I could out of my modest income, in order to avert the worst. In 1930 I turned my back on the *Deutschnationale Volkspartei* and after attending National Socialist party meetings regularly, I was won over to National Socialism.

Another source of anti-Semitic feelings was the influence exerted by the reading of anti-Semitic literature, which was particularly voluminous in Germany.

[3.0.1.] After the assassination of Rathenau I began a searching inquiry into the Jewish question. I read a great deal, and it became increasingly clear to me that international Marxism and the Jewish problem are closely bound together. In this fact I recognized the cause of the political, moral, and cultural decay of my Fatherland. I studied the solutions proposed by various parties, and I convinced myself that the National Socialist program is not only thoroughly justified, but absolutely necessary for the rebirth of Germany.

[4.3.2.] At the beginning of 1925, my wife introduced me to a young student of architecture whose entire conversation consisted of a song of hate against the Jews. He maintained that the Jews were to a large extent responsible for the misfortunes of the Fatherland. He even asserted that next to the vindictiveness of the French, the vengeance of Juda held the lion's share for the outbreak of the war, since the Jews could only accomplish their aim of world rule upon the downfall of the Aryan race. This trend of thought was new to me. I examined these charges, and upon reading the appropriate literature I found that both my studies and my own experience forced me to conclude that these charges were, at least in part, well founded. Consequently I became an anti-Semite.

These were the people whose strong hatred of the Jews led them to commit acts of violence after they joined the storm troops. Several of our informants reported frankly how they "beat up some Jews," "threw them out the window after raiding one of their meetings," "played 'pranks' on Jewish-looking passersby in the streets," "demolished the show windows of Jewish shops," and so forth.

The tendency to interpret personal experiences in a fashion that made the Jew the culprit, the prevalence of anti-Semitic literature in Germany, the acts of violence perpetrated on Jews, have for their background a tradition which is at least a thousand years old. The popularity of anti-Semitism after the war, which the National Socialists adroitly utilized as a means of propagating their movement, was merely one of many similar outbursts that have occurred from time to time throughout the course of German history since the establishment of the Carolingian Empire. The story of the Middle Ages is a sequence of mass-murder, burning of Jewish settlements, wholesale expulsion, exploitation and acts of discrimination (such as the confinement of Jews to the Ghetto in the fourteenth century, the obligation to wear discriminating marks, and so forth). In some cases the persecutions were local in character, restricted to a town or a province. But sometimes they were nation-wide, as during the first crusade (1096), at the end of the thirteenth century (1298), and again in 1335 (the peasant crusade against the Jews), in 1348 (during the pestilence that ravaged the continent when the Jews were accused of poisoning the wells), and the destruction of Jews under the leadership of Capistrano in 1453. The persecutions on these occasions were so savage that thousands of Jews, in order to escape it, committed suicide collectively by killing each other or throwing themselves into burning buildings.

In every case the nation-wide persecutions were associated with a critical time in German history, and the general dissatisfaction unloaded itself upon the Jews. Usually some accusation such as that of ritual murder, or of desecration of the Host, served as a pretext for collective action. During the Middle Ages, supposed commission of the latter crime never failed to incite mob action.

Modern times have changed the tactics of persecution. Defamation, scoffing in speech and writing, throwing of stones, and beating took the place of mass murder and arson. But the strategy remained the same. Whenever there was a crisis and the concomitant widespread dissatisfaction, some group or individual is always to be found to start a wave of anti-Semitism. This was the case, for example, after the trying times of the Napoleonic invasion, and particularly between 1873 and 1893, the period following the Franco-Prussian War when the nation was shaken by a severe business crisis and disturbed by the political struggle between the liberals and the conservatives. New pretexts, like the accusations of intended political domination with evil designs on the German nation (Grattauer, 1819), of interfering with the racial mission of the German people (Marr, Duehring, Chamberlain in the 'eighties and 'nineties), took the place of the religious pretexts of the Middle Ages.[13]

The anti-Semitic waves during the critical times immediately after the World War and during the severe depression of the 'thirties were simply the recurrences of a process that has became traditional, the rekindling of sentiments deeply rooted

---

[13] For a history of the Jews in Germany, see Elbogen, I., *Die Geschichte der Juden in Deutschland*. Berlin: Erich Lichtenstein, 1935; also the scholarly work by Baron, S. W., *A Social and Religious History of the Jews*. New York: Columbia University Press, 1937, in three volumes.

in the past. Because of their inferior and precarious social position in the structure of German society, because they are the strangers and often the pariahs, the Jews are more vulnerable to attack and less capable of defense than any other social group. Furthermore the rise of individual Jews into prominence in professions and in the economic and political sphere has often been too sudden and not sufficiently diffused and has made their position easily exposed to criticism. Whenever times are critical the brunt of dissatisfaction is therefore directed against them, and they become the object of concerted attacks. The pretexts employed by the post-war anti-Semitic agitators were mainly those which the previous wave of anti-Jewish aggression had created. The arguments of men like Marr and Ahrand, who led the Jew-baiters in the 'eighties, were repeated, often *verbatim*. But the National Socialists introduced at least one novelty: the accusation that the Jews were trying deliberately to degrade the morals of the German nation. Puritanical indignation is a frequently expressed sentiment in the life-histories. For example:

[4.6.2.] Those we found at home (after return from the front) were no longer our honest people. All the great virtues of the German people seemed to have been swept away by the dismal flood. All that had been great and beautiful was trod in the dust and spit upon, while immorality, shamelessness and dishonesty were enthroned. My observations convinced me that our honest and upstanding people had been poisoned to the marrow by alien Jews. Jewish literature and the Jewish press raged with impunity and dragged everything in the mud. Not even the most sacred feelings were spared. What did they make of the theater, films, art, and literature? A caricature, a stinking sewer filled the German land with pestilence. They corrupted the youth. In the tents of the youth organizations there were Jewish "leaders" who slept with golden-haired girls. This they declared was "freedom of the individual," but they quickly vanished if children resulted.

While anti-Semitism always was a popular issue in Germany, not all Germans were anti-Semitic. The Jews had many protagonists in Germany who did not hesitate to oppose discrimination and persecution, or who, like the great writer G. E. Lessing, actively advocated tolerance and the recognition of Jews as equals.

This fact also is reflected in the autobiographies. Sixty per cent of the contributors make no reference whatsoever to indicate that they harbored anti-Semitic feelings.[14]

Even if we assume that a number of our contributors did not find it necessary to refer to their support of the racial doctrine of the movement, avoiding even the mentioning of the word Jew, because membership in the National Socialist party implied that they opposed the Jews, still the total must be regarded as surprisingly high. That there were many among the members of the movement who were not only indifferent to anti-Semitism but opposed to it is shown by the fact that nearly 4 per cent did not hesitate to express their disapproval of anti-Semitism, although they were members of the Party. For example, one of our contributors explains why he was so late joining the National Socialist party. He writes:

[4.7.4.] In 1922 I read a National Socialist pamphlet that repelled me. I got the impression that they incited to war and I resented their blind hatred of the Jews. Even after I joined the party I did not see eye to eye with it on the Jewish question.

Equally frank is the statement of another contributor:

[2.3.4.] I was greatly impressed by the first meeting I attended. It quickened my pulse to hear about the Fatherland, unity and the

---

[14] Anti-Semitic sentiments are most frequently recorded in the life-histories of the older generation (forty years and over). Thus 50 per cent of this generation, against 26 per cent of the younger men (twenty to forty) expressed antagonism against the Jews. Anti-Semitism also is more frequent in towns and cities than in rural districts (40 against 23 per cent) and more frequent among the middle and upper classes than among workers (47 against 29 per cent). Correspondingly, the number of anti-Semites is higher among those occupied in government service, clerical jobs, professions and trade than among those engaged in industry and agriculture (48 against 29 per cent). Finally, anti-Semitism is less frequent among those who had only a public school education than among those who went to high school and attended a university (32 against 46 per cent).

need for a supreme leader. I felt that I belonged to these people. Only their statements about the Jews I could not swallow. They gave me a headache even after I had joined the Party.

The last quotation clearly shows the need of discriminating the relative significance of the ideological aspects of the movement. I have tried to show in this chapter why the main ingredients of the ideology—the idea of National Socialism, the principle of leadership, and the racial doctrine—exercised an appeal and therefore contributed to its growth. But how much weight should we give to the ideology in the complexity of factors that influenced this movement? To this question we shall turn our attention in the next chapter.

Chapter VIII

The Why of the Hitler Movement

THE PREVIOUS CHAPTERS have portrayed the development of the Hitler movement in the words of those who participated in it. Four general factors have been named which may be said to have molded the character, and thus have a bearing on the ultimate success, of National Socialism:

1. The prevalence of discontent with the existing social order.

2. The particular ideology and program for social transformation adopted by the Nazis.

3. The National Socialist organizational and promotional technique.

4. The presence of charismatic leadership.

The adequacy and relative importance of these explanations will be examined in this chapter.

1. The Function of Discontent

The social unrest which was prevalent in post-war Germany had its source in many and divergent events. The outcome of the war deeply affected two groups of the population: first, those who were in power before and during the war—the military, the conservatives, the big land owners and industrialists, and all those who indirectly drew sustenance from the exalted position which these groups occupied in the social structure of Germany; and second, nationalists. The revolution following the armistice brought about far-reaching changes in the alignment of power. Even so it had its source in despair and confusion rather than in a genuine desire for a radical transformation of the social order. The adherents of the old regime were suddenly and precipitously thrown down from their seats of power, while the socialists, the workers' and soldiers' councils, and the trade unions dominated the stage. The deposed groups went into hiding but did not resign themselves to their fate. Their vital interests were affected and they were determined to stage a come-back, by force if necessary. Thus they were actively opposed to the republic not only because they harbored a grievance against the perpetrators of the revolution, but also because they realized that the continuation of the regime was an obstacle to return to power.

The second group included those whose national pride was deeply affected by the peace conditions imposed upon Germany by the Allies. The republican regime committed the grievous mistake of deluding itself and the German people with the hope that the establishment of a democratic government would enable them to obtain a "just peace." The patriots blamed the government for failure to negotiate a better peace and for putting its signature upon the Versailles Treaty. A strong social motive for opposition to the republican order was thus added to the private motives of the dispossessed. Discontent ceased to be an issue merely of the formerly privileged class and became an attitude shared by members of all classes of the German population.

The passage of time, the return to the routine of daily living after the hectic post-war days, failed to develop a conciliatory attitude and a resignation to the inevitable. On the contrary, the number of people who opposed the government was constantly increasing as post-war developments in the political and economic life of Germany were experienced by many, as threats to their personal and social values, and brought forth new grounds for discontent. Among the added reasons for opposition was ineptitude in the handling of affairs of government by a parliamentary system that lacked democratic traditions. There was a hopeless deadlock owing to the multiplicity of parties which alternately warred with each other and engaged in horse-trading, apparently more interested in self-maintenance than in the nation's welfare. Furthermore, the inability of the government to maintain the order and discipline which Germans have learned to regard as the *sine qua non* of government, and its ineptitude in the handling of foreign affairs, which kept the issue of German humiliation constantly in the foreground, were noted and resented. Finally, the government was held responsible for economic chaos —first, the disastrous inflation, later, from 1929 on, the stagnation of business enterprise, the mounting rate of unemployment, and the hopelessness of the outlook for improvement under existing conditions. The businessman who suffered deficits, the worker who lacked security of employment, the youth who saw little to encourage his hope for a career in the future, all augmented the army of the discontented.

The social unrest that was prevalent in Germany had two important features which made it a potential basis of a social movement. First, it was persistent and continuous. The passage of time did not assuage it but intensified it. While the causes of the discontent varied in the course of time, they followed each other in close succession and prevented a relaxation of the persistent tension. Secondly, discontent was focused upon a single object: the post-war political and social system. Despite the fact that the reasons for dissatisfaction varied for different individuals and different groups, almost all blamed the government for their troubles and turned their attacks against it. The existence of a common focus for many oppositions was a potential rallying point which made concerted action on a large scale possible.

Attempts to organize the discontented for collective action against the government began shortly after the end of the World War. Mainly through the initiative of disgrunted officers, small groups were formed all over Germany which were animated by a desire for a speedy counter-revolution that would restore the old regime. Political developments gave these groups a chance for action sooner than they expected. The government was hard pressed by Communist uprisings in the cities and had to appeal to the military for help. The makeshift alliance ended with the defeat of the common foe. The adherents of the old regime had regained a foothold in Germany and felt sufficiently encouraged to go ahead with their plans. They soon launched a concerted campaign against the government by instigating *Putsch*es, assassinating republican leaders and organizing subversive and secret military units. They drew their supporters mainly from the former military caste, the upper class, and those members of the middle class who, motivated by patriotic feelings, were willing to compromise with their opposition to a restoration of the old order, hoping that a defeat of the republican government might start a campaign for regaining the losses which the nation suffered as a result of the Versailles Treaty.

But the counter-revolutionary efforts were unsuccessful. They lacked the support of the masses, which the counter-revolutionists, counting upon a *coup d'état* as a short cut to success, did not endeavor to win. In the course of time the hot-heads pressing for immediate military action were replaced by the politicians, who decided to pursue different tactics. They instituted a long-range plan of propaganda and agitation aiming to defeat the government by a majority vote of the German population. Furthermore, they turned their backs on the unpopular issue of the restoration of the old regime and in its stead advocated a new social order, anti-republican as well as anti-monarchical in character. A number of political parties were formed on that basis. Among them was the National Socialist German Workers' party, which became the promotion group of the Hitler movement.

At first the party represented the counter-revolutionary sentiment, inasmuch as it drew its main support from the groups that were interested in the restoration of the old regime. It even went as far as to instigate a *coup d'état* of its own, the so-called Hitler *Putsch* of 1923, which failed. But from the very beginning the National Socialist party pursued a definite plan of winning the support of the masses by developing an ideology of its own that was broad enough to appeal to all classes, and in particular to the German workers. It was ultimately the advocacy of a new social order which saved the Hitler movement from the fate that befell other counter-revolutionary groups. A defeat like that of 1923 would have been a death blow to any other group. Such a blow was averted, however, because counter-revolution was not the only aim of the Hitler movement and because its other aims had the support of the discontented among *all* classes of the population. It was able to perpetuate itself by breaking counter-revolutionary ties after the *Putsch* and by shifting its emphasis to the single-minded advocacy of a new social order. It not only retained most of its following, but gained new adherents in ever-increasing numbers by proclaiming solutions for all the issues that had become a source of widespread discontent throughout the post-war history of Germany.[1]

The evidence points to the fact that discontent was of fundamental importance in the development of the Hitler movement. The main items of this evidence are first the

---

[1] The life histories show that dissatisfaction with the regime was a constant factor in relation to the year of joining the movement. Thus we find that for every year between 1920 and 1933 the percentage of those who gave dissatisfaction with the regime as the main reason for joining is practically the same (40 to 42 per cent of the total number of cases for each year).

fact of a prevailing dissatisfaction with existing conditions and the consequent opposition to the government, which led people to seek an outlet in concerted action. Secondly, the fact shown by the life-history data that discontent on the part of individuals had a direct effect upon their subsequent joining of the Hitler movement. General consideration, furthermore, supports the contention as to the vital importance of discontent in accounting for the movement. All observations of human behavior point to the significance of problem experiences as a source of action. We also know that when individuals realize that they are unable to solve a problem through their own effort, they seek the help and support of others in order to accomplish a solution through concerted action. Insofar, then, as the basic conditions for the kind of concerted action represented by the Hitler movement were like problem experiences of many individuals caused by factors which no individual alone could control, discontent must be regarded as a necessary factor in the origin as well as the growth of the movement. Without it the movement would not have been possible. In fact, it is difficult to see how any movement can arise without a basis of widespread discontent. We should add, however, that in order to become an effective source of a movement, discontent must be persistent and continuous and capable of being focused upon a common object of opposition.

Although the evidence leads us to the recognition of discontent as a necessary factor in the Hitler movement, it would be fallacious to regard it as a sufficient explanation of what happened in Germany. Discontent accounts for the origin and the growth of a movement insofar as it explains why people were impelled to join groups and support collective efforts directed toward a change of the existing order. It does not, however, account for the reasons why a movement of a particular kind developed and why it, rather than another, based upon the same discontent, succeeded in realizing its aim. The function of discontent in regard to a social movement is, therefore, limited. It sets the conditions which make a movement possible, but it does not at the same time determine its special features, nor does it by itself determine its success.

2. *The Functions of Ideology*

The special features which distinguish the Hitler movement from other movements are expressed in its ideology. We have seen that the ideology of the Hitler movement comprised, in the main, three ideas: first, the idea of National Socialism with its implications of national unity and the abolition of classes, and the reintegration of national life into a *Gemein-schaft;* second, the principle of leadership, the idea of an hierarchical organization of society according to accomplishment which was to be the means for the realization of the *Gemein-schaft;* third, the racial doctrine, the idea that common blood binds individuals into a *Gemeinschaft* and that racial intermixture is the cause of disunity as well as the deterioration of the native stock. Other aspects of the ideology are merely corollaries of these three basic ideas. The anti-liberalism of the Hitler movement, for example, derives from the National Socialist idea that common interest comes before self-interest, which is dominant in a parliamentary system where many parties compete for ascendancy. The anti-intellectual attitude of the Hitler movement is conditioned by its romantic conception of the mystical qualities of "Blood and Soil." The idea of the totalitarian state is derived from the principle of leadership, and so forth.

Trends that were current in German history as well as the creative imagination of its founders wrought the pattern of the ideology of the Hitler movement. But in the last analysis the acid test of public approval determined its special features, since those doctrines which appealed most were selected for emphasis. We have seen that the ideology of the movement attracted people because it was in accord with prevalent sentiments. It appealed to a strong national feeling and reinforced this appeal by linking it with another powerful sentiment directed against class and caste privilege. The synthesis of what were in Germany opposites—nationalism, on the one hand, regarded as the monopoly of the conservative-aristocratic party, and socialism, on the other, as the doctrine of the internationally minded Marxist—was a stroke of genius. It gave to the Hitler movement the broadest possible basis of appeal to the German public, which was composed, for the most part, of nationalists who for social reasons refused to identify themselves with the privilege-seeking conservative party, and of socialists who for national reasons were opposed to the international doctrine of the Marxists.

In turn, the principle of leadership appealed to a strong sentiment for the disciplinarian Prussian state ideal which most Germans considered the epitome of law and order. The mores of the majority of the German people favored submission to a supreme commander in charge of the affairs of the nation as against a parliamentary form of government.

The racial doctrine appealed to a prevalent feeling of anti-Semitism which, as we have indicated, was a common popular reaction in Germany in times of crises since the period of the Crusades.

The force of the combined appeal to different sentiments that were shared by many enabled the National Socialist party to far outdistance the other promotion groups which were competing with it for public support. The support that it gained was ultimately due to the fact that, among.the many programs of change advocated in Germany at the time, the Nazi program promised the realization of the sentiments that were most vital and, at the same time, threatened the least number of personal and social values held by the German people. It was in accord with traditions, although radical in nature. Near the end of the struggle for power, only the Communist party was left as a serious challenger. The Communists also appealed strongly to the idealism of youth. and found

many adherents to their cause. But they were handicapped
by their subservience to Moscow and by their emphasis upon
internationalism and the curtailment of private property. These
aspects of Communism run counter to deeply rooted traditions
and, in consequence, failed to attract the masses of the German
people. The National Socialists were quick to turn the handicaps of the Communists to their advantage. They made the
challenge of Communism to their own aspirations a challenge
to the nation as a whole by presenting it as a threat to national
integrity. The civil war which dominated the German scene
in the years 1930 to 1933 helped materially to sustain this claim.

Our analysis of the role played by the ideology of the Hitler
movement points to the fact that its importance as a determi-
nant is at least equal to that of the general discontent which
existed at the time. The National Socialist party voiced in a
determined fashion the prevailing dissatisfaction with the existing order and thus appealed for the support of the discontented. It was not this appeal by itself, but the ideology which
induced the decision on the part of the discontented to throw
in their lot with the Hitler movement. The function of the
ideology, therefore, was to provide an incentive to join the
movement. To fulfill this function adequately, it had to appeal
to prevalent sentiments and be sufficiently diversified to encompass divergent interests and individual predilections without involving itself in contradictions. As we have seen, the
ideology of the Hitler movement met these conditions. It
appealed to nationalists and socialists, to workers and employers, to the idealizers of the Prussian state and to the youths who
were in favor of radical changes. In consequence, it found
supporters among all classes and all age groups of the population. Those who were repelled by this or that feature of the
ideology found sufficient compensation in other features to
induce them to join the movement. At the same time, all the
elements of the Nazi ideology were in some fashion or other
related to the idea of *Gemeinschaft*. Thus, built around a cen-

tral concept, the features of the ideology, in spite of their diversity, were sufficiently integrated to give the appearance of logical consistency to the ideology as a whole.

In spite of the great importance which, in view of the evidence we must assign to the ideology as a factor in determining the success of the National Socialist movement, it cannot be regarded as the sole cause. While it served many as the *justification* for joining the movement, there were others who joined although they were indifferent to the ideology, or even objected to it on intellectual grounds.

But the main reason why the ideology has only a limited causal significance is the fact that it represents only a declaration of faith and intention. A declaration of that sort by itself is ineffective unless it is backed up by adequate promotion activities and by a belief in the possibility of victory. It is for this reason that tactics and strategy were important factors in determining the growth of the Hitler movement.

3. *The Function of Tactics and Strategy*

Given favorable external conditions and receptivity on the part of the masses to the proposals advocated by its leaders, the spread of the Nazi movement depended largely upon adequate promotion. The task confronting the promotion group of a movement is twofold: it must win adherents and supporters, and it must hold the allegiance of those who have been won over.

The winning of adherents is largely a matter of propaganda. We had occasion, in the historical section of this study, to describe the kind of propaganda that was carried on by the local groups of the Party. The Nazi propaganda machine was notable for its shrewd and daring use of modern advertising psychology and for its mass effect. Even more remarkable, however, was the sheer bulk of its effort. Proselytizing went on unceasingly, regardless of physical or man-made obstacles. Moreover, the Party "covered" Germany with a thoroughness that made its doctrines known in almost every home, in city and countryside alike.[2]

In the propaganda of all other German parties, these features were either totally lacking or insufficiently developed. For this reason, the National Socialist party had a decided advantage over the other parties in reaching the attention of the German public.

Adherents, however cannot be won for a promotion scheme by effective propaganda methods alone. Many people might succumb temporarily to alluring promises or to a persuasive sales talk for a cause. But in the long run even the best-directed verbal barrage cannot have a lasting effect unless backed up by more substantial assurances. The individual who joins a movement must first be convinced of its probable success as well as of the desirability of its objectives. Expectation of success is predicated upon *confidence* in the ability of the leaders of the movement to get what they want eventually. The people who supported Hitler, although animated by sentiment, were primarily influenced by the belief that they were backing a winning contender. The life histories show that this confidence was engendered by several tangible factors, chief of which was the superiority of the National Socialist organization over that of other parties. Its ramifications were more detailed and its sphere of influence more extensive than that of any other party. It also was better coördinated and disciplined and showed greater vitality and driving power. Its military, aggressive nature appealed to many.

[4.5.4.] I attended the meetings, and I always felt happy to see the little groups of brown-clad soldiers march through the city with rhythmic strides and straightforward mien, unlike the Communists, who shambled through the city streets like so many robbers. As an old soldier, I was pleased to see Hitler's fighters march in this disciplined fashion.

---

[2] *Cf.* Nelson, R. B., "Hitler's Propaganda Machine," *Current History*, June 1933, Vol. XXXIII, pp. 287-300.

[4.6.4.] The more I saw of these strong battle-hardened men, the more I came to believe that some day Hitler would take over the power of government for the good of our nation.

[3.7.3.] The Communists were the only ones who had the energy and the strength to back up their demands with the proper show of power, in that they got out on the streets and asserted themselves through brute force whenever necessary. On the other side was no one but the National Socialist party, ready to fight the Marxists with their own weapons.

[3.0.3.] Throughout 1928 I followed the work of the Nazis through the press, and it became evident to me that even the sympathizers with the movement were ready to die for Hitler's ideas. Consequently it wasn't difficult for me to make up my mind.

Many others were impressed by the aggressive character of the National Socialist organization in the pursuit of its goal, the fearless way it handled its opponents, its policy of no compromise with other parties. All these factors impressed the follower of the movement as indicating the kind of strength and endurance which carries with it the promise of success.

The dynamic nature of the movement also inspired confidence. Its very growth helped the Party to gather greater momentum by attracting people to whom evidence of growth was a prognosis of ultimate success. This was true particularly in the period after the election of 1930. Once the Party had shown its ability to get votes, its spectacular gain in voting strength became an incentive for many to throw in their lot with the movement.

In consequence of this fact, a certain portion of the support that was given to the movement came from people who were acting from the familiar motive of "getting on the band wagon." They wanted a change and even favored the social order which the National Socialists advocated. But they were motivated by expediency rather than by fanatical belief in and devotion to the cause and willingness for sacrifice which animated many adherents of the movement who joined before the 1930 election. The existence of these two kinds of membership is stated clearly in some life histories. The following two quotations illustrate the point.

[3.8.2.] At the beginning of November 1930 I became the leader of my cell. I still like to think of the party comrades who paid their dues promptly and were ready for any service on behalf of the leader. The lukewarm ones who looked on without doing a thing and only paid their dues after repeated reminders considerably added to the difficulties of my work. The curious thing is that these party members are the very ones who now act as if *they* and no others had borne the Fuehrer's colors to victory, and seem greatly offended whenever their "services" are not sufficiently honored. On the other hand, I have discovered that the most loyal fighters who made the greatest sacrifices in those days are modestly withdrawing at this time, at a loss to understand the others' mad hunt for advancement. They were and are idealists, while the others have looked upon National Socialism merely as a stepping stone. These people are a standing threat to the movement and our people. If they succeed in satisfying their materialism and thirst for power, they'll never distinguish between the cause and their own benefit, and so continue to injure the cause of our Leader.

[5.0.3.] Great rejoicing and a deluge of new members followed the election of 1930. Our own "Mommsen" local also received a number of new recruits. On the whole these new members were very decent comrades of all walks of life who promptly became valued collaborators; there were, however, those whom district leader Dr. Goebbels aptly dubbed "Septemberlings." It soon became evident that the latter had joined only to secure a certain amount of attention for their sacred egos. They made it appear as though the National Socialist movement had only achieved standing through their delayed support, and held lengthy and decidedly inferior discourses at the meetings of local groups. These giddy comrades, however, soon became less noisy at the prospect of jobs on behalf of the Party, offered them by their local group leaders, which demanded self-sacrifice.

The party congress was the foremost device by which the interest and loyalty of the members was maintained. These congresses were large annual assemblies attended since 1927 by many thousands of party members. Every local group of the Party either attended in full or sent its representatives, so that, in the course of time, the bulk of the membership attended at least one of these annual rallies. Designed to impress the members with the strength and unity of the Party and to show the confidence and determination of the leaders, the party congresses were an important agency in maintaining the evangelistic fervor of the movement and in enhancing the morale of the members. This point is frequently emphasized in the life histories.

[2.1.2.] We returned from the party meeting in Nürnberg strengthened in our belief in the Leader and his mission and determined to redouble our efforts for the movement. Position, family, every other consideration must be forgotten for the sake of our cause.

A strong feeling of comradeship was induced by the "frontline" character of the National Socialist party, especially in the storm troop units.

[2.7.2.] In those days the *S.A.* represented a unity of purpose such as has never been achieved, nor shall be hereafter. We were united by the terrorism raging around us every hour of the day. It was natural for everyone to take the part of his comrade, and the fellowship thus cultivated was in itself a great experience. Yet the ideal we defended rose above our fellowship. Day by day we covered the environs and each of us became a bearer of its tidings.

[1.0.5.] We had to be careful at that, as the police were hard on us if we did anything forbidden. Nevertheless we managed to put a thing or two over on them. We had to pay for all the expenses thus incurred out of our own pockets, as the movement had no money. My apprenticeship over, the economic crisis precipitated me into the ranks of the unemployed. From that time on I lived solely for the movement. Day after day, night after night, we were on the go, enlightening the people about the corruption of the red-black governments since 1918. At the same time, we steeled our bodies through exercise and cultivated comradely relations. We were reared in a spirit of constructive social thought: our last piece of bread, our sole remaining cigarette were always shared with our fellows. This comradeship was indeed a condition of survival in the face of Red mobs that ruled the streets, as well as other opponents. Unlike other factions, however, we did not look upon our opponents as scoundrels, but rather as misled fellow Germans.

[2.3.1.] During my training for *S.A.* service in 1929, I was shot in the abdomen by a Communist. As a result, I was laid up for six months. During my illness many of my comrades came to see me, and brought me all manner of little presents. One day I received something like forty bouquets of roses which were distributed throughout the hospital. In the same ward with me were some Communists who marveled at our cordial comraderie. Indeed it was this very comraderie that attracted many members, particularly among young men. I was particularly pleased when the erstwhile Berlin district leader (at this time Propaganda Minister) Dr. Goebbels came to see me and stayed about an hour at my bedside.

[4.2.5.] In the Nazi party I recovered the exhilarating sense of comraderie I had known in the army. There were fine, battle-hardened human beings here, united in their love for race and Fatherland, stubbornly holding out for an overwhelming ideal, unswerving in their faith in the future of Germany.

[2.0.2.] During my *S.A.* service I was in Storm Troop Thirty-three. Our storm leaders, Fritz Hahn, Maiko, and Appelt, were the right men to usher us into the new age. Our storm headquarters in the Hebbelstrasse near Reisig *became our second home.* The hours I passed there were too beautiful, and perhaps too difficult, to be described here.

4. *The Function of Charismatic Leadership*

The knowledge which we gained from our study of National Socialism gives convincing evidence of the influence which Hitler has had on the movement. His function was a twofold one. On the one hand, he was the chief executive, the planner and organizer. On the other hand, he played the role of the prophet of the movement. Recognized as such by most of the members and supporters, he commanded their unquestioned allegiance to his person and through this personal allegiance inspired them with loyalty and devotion to the movement itself. The combination of these two functions of chief executive and prophet is found among all the leaders of the past who have captained the actions of the masses. They are interdependent to a high degree, for the position of chief executive depends largely upon the ability to command personal allegiance. And in turn, the recognition of leadership depends upon superior executive ability and extraordinary accomplishments of planning and organization.

Hitler was a strong-willed, dauntless executive. LeBon has found that an indomitable will "to which everything succumbs and which nothing can resist, which asserts itself in spite of insurmountable obstacles" characterized the founders of religious and political movements and pioneers like Columbus and DeLesseps, the builder of the Suez Canal. Such rare determination is usually associated with an unshakable belief in oneself or one's mission, a quality which Hitler showed to a marked degree. Like other leaders of the masses, Hitler had the qualifications which make a good executive: organizing ability, a realistic sense for the implications of the conditions with which he was confronted, and authority in dealing with his associates. Hitler himself was the driving power and the directing genius of the movement.

The second function which Hitler fulfilled is revealed in the attitudes of our contributors toward him. Many of them were followers in the true sense of the word, submitting themselves to him willingly and unquestionably. To them he was a prophet whose pronouncements were taken as oracles. In their eyes he was a hero whom they naïvely trusted to perform the impossible if it were necessary. He was endowed by them with that highest degree of prestige which emanates not merely from the recognition of one's own inability to imitate or compete with such a person, but from the belief that he possesses an out-of-the-ordinary, superhuman power, that a special star is guiding his destiny. In all cases of mass leadership, this belief has been present to a greater or lesser degree. It is the basis of what Max Weber has called charismatic leadership.

What induces this worship of a person as a prophet and a hero? A satisfactory answer to this question would have to account for the peculiar influence which Peter of Amiens, Luther, Napoleon, Lenin, and scores of others have exercised upon masses of people. No scientific explanation of the phenomenon of charismatic leadership has been given so far. A discussion which could do justice to this problem is beyond the scope of this book. I will answer the question merely by restating the clues, with regard to Hitler's charismatic leadership, which we obtained from the life histories, without entertaining any claims that the example of Hitler is commensurate with that of other charismatic leaders.

These clues are: (1) A widespread, abject desire on the part of the people of Germany for a leader—an attitude often observed in a period of crisis when people who are seeking a way out realize that only collective action can solve their individual problems. (2) The impression which Hitler's performance and personality produced upon the people—the spell which he cast as an orator, the contagion of the faith which he had in himself, the "fascination" which he was able to evoke in many people who came into face-to-face contact with him, the success of his undertakings. (3) The legend which was built around him, often deliberately fostered by his associates, which perpetuated and rekindled a feeling of the unusual and made Hitler a man of mystery by emphasizing his "prophetic insight," "asceticism," "prodigious power of endurance," and so forth.

From the rôle which Hitler played in National Socialism, we can infer the function which charismatic leadership fulfills in a movement. Personal allegiance to Hitler was the common bond which united the supporters of National Socialism and counteracted the disruptive effect of divergent opinions and aims. Charismatic leadership may be said, therefore, to be an integrating factor of great importance. Furthermore, Hitler was to his followers the symbol of the movement.

[4.6.3.] Hitler alone is the true nationalist. The rest of us must try to emulate him as far as possible. Our young men and women will one day be the better for it! The first step toward becoming a National Socialist is to cease believing that one already is one.

[3.0.4.] I felt that Hitler personified all my desires for a new Germany.

[4.6.4.] A high political leader of the Nazi party once said of the oath of allegiance: "Anyone who takes the oath to Adolf Hitler can call nothing his own."

Because of his Messiah-like rôle, Hitler was sedulously imitated. His fanaticism and his belief in ultimate victory were incorporated into the personality patterns of many of his followers. Charismatic leadership may thus act to stabilize a social movement.

In view of the evident importance of charismatic leadership as a determining factor in the Hitler movement, the conclusion can be drawn that it represents probably an indispensable factor in the success of any movement. A movement which possesses charismatic leadership has a decided advantage over a collective effort under diffused leadership or one that is run in the main by a bureaucratic organization. It would follow, therefore, that between two movements operating upon the same basis of discontent, whose ideologies have mass appeal, and who employ similar tactics, the one which, in addition, has a charismatic leader will win out against the other. In the period between 1930 and 1933 in Germany there was no other political leader who in any way approximated the exalted position which Hitler occupied in the eyes of his followers. If there had been no other reason, this fact alone would account for the inability of Communism to compete with National Socialism.

5. Conclusion

In short, the Nazi movement may be explained as follows. Various events simultaneously threatened the personal and social values of many individuals, resulting in discontent and attempts to find methods of collective action. The solution offered by Hitler's group appealed to many because the flexible ideology of that group embodied a large number of popular views. Finally, the energy and resourcefulness of the party organization, buttressed by popular trust in Hitler's charismatic leadership, led large numbers of people to enroll as National Socialists, confident in the ultimate success of their cause.

This conclusion is valid only if the qualifying conditions incident to any summary are kept in mind. "Discontent," "ideology," "tactics," and "charisma" are abstractions that have meaning only with reference to the concrete instances of behavior which constitute the "Hitler movement," typical illustrations of which have been already reported.

Therefore, the first qualifying condition is that the account of the origin as well as of the success of the Hitler movement be contained in the study *taken as a whole.*[3]

Another condition is equally important. We can not understand the function of the four factors which we have stressed as determinants unless we view them with reference to the milieu in which they operated. This milieu is the realistic background of the movement: the economic and political conditions in Germany, the traditions and habits of thought of its population, the international situation. These factors are determinants of the success of the movement only in so far as they operated in close interaction with the milieu and derived their specific character and content through adaptation to existing conditions.

A final qualification must be made with regard to the causal character of the factors mentioned. They may be considered as causes which explain the Hitler movement only if we realize that they are not in themselves agents, but are general terms which give us the clues to the forces that made and

---

[3] By "Success" I mean here not the gaining of political power but the maintenance of a "going concern," which was able to attract and hold the allegiance of thousands of followers and to outdistance its competitors.

sustained the movement. These forces are the specific motives, the concrete actions, and the personal experiences and decisions of individuals.

These are the only *real* causes of the Hitler movement. The general terms employed in our analysis are merely reductions of the multiplicity and diversity of these causes to the meaning and characteristic features that they have in common.

With these three qualifying conditions in mind, we can now discuss briefly the question of the relative significance of the four factors as determinants of the movement. The result of our analysis points to the unavoidable conclusion that the growth and success of the Hitler movement was an outcome of their *combined* effect in such manner that none of the factors considered separately can be said to have played a greater or lesser rôle. Discontent created the condition which made large scale collective action possible. The winning of adherents by a promotion group operating on the basis of this discontent depended upon the appeal of its ideology. In turn, the continued support of the movement by its adherents was conditioned upon the strategy and tactics by which the affairs of the movement were conducted. Charismatic leadership provided the needed integration and stabilization of the movement and conditioned the devotion of its followers and their confidence. The four factors were dependent upon and supported each other in such fashion that the absence or deficiency of any one factor would have fatally disabled the movement. For this reason, its growth and success never could be accounted for in terms of a single factor. Thus, it would be futile to see the Hitler movement merely as the result of the dissatisfaction of a class, or of economic adversity, or of the Versailles Treaty, and so forth. Equally futile would be the attempt to account for it in terms of the content of its propaganda or the methods of promotion. Nor can the movement be attributed solely to the presence of charismatic leadership.

The Hitler movement must be viewed as the resultant of factors which operated not as independent "forces" but functioned as a pattern in which none of the component parts was more significant than the others. Without the full development of this pattern, the Hitler movement as we know it would not have been possible. On the other hand, the development of the movement was inevitable once a pattern had developed in which widespread and persistent discontent, purposes that appealed to prevalent sentiments, efficient organization and propaganda, and charismatic leadership had made their appearance and had become coördinated in their effect.[4]

6. *Critique of Other Interpretations*

The literature on the Hitler movement contains several interpretations which vary from my analysis. Among these, the psychoanalytical and the Marxist interpretations are of special importance. They postulate the determining influence of factors other than those disclosed by the life history material and, therefore, question indirectly the adequacy of our findings. For this reason, it is important to estimate the validity of these interpretations.

a. *The psychoanalytical interpretation*

The most comprehensive and far-reaching attempt to apply the psychoanalytical approach to the Hitler movement is that of Frederick L. Schuman, in his book *The Nazi Dictatorship.*[5]

According to Schuman, National Socialism is a symptom of a psychological malady with which the post-war middle class in Germany as a group was affected. There was maladjustment among all classes of the population, but "fundamentally the

---

[4] *Cf.* Abel, T., "The Pattern of a Successful Political Movement," *American Sociological Review,* Vol. II, 1937.

[5] New York: 1935. The quotations from this book are reprinted by permission of and special arrangements with Alfred A. Knopf, Inc., authorized publishers. Page references to this book appear in parentheses. (Italics mine.)

psychic disorder was a disease of the *Kleinbürgertum* (the lower middle class). This group suffered from acute paranoia, with all its typical delusions of persecution and systematic hallucinations of grandeur. In Hitler it found at last an articulate voice. In the *Weltanschauung* of the Nazi party it found solace for all its woes, forgiveness for all sins, justification for all its hatreds, scapegoats for all its misfortunes, and a millennial vision of all its hopes" (p. 109). Elucidating in detail the manifestations of this collective neurosis, Schuman utilizes most of the psychoanalytical concepts which have been developed in the course of the clinical investigations of such men as Freud. The discontent among the lower middle class is explained as owing to a "denial of the normal and satisfying expression of the *id-drives*" (p. 106). The aggressiveness of the National Socialists is attributed to a weakened *super-ego,* as a result of which "sin became fashionable. But the puritan conscience of Lutheranism and Prussianism rebelled. Its unconscious protest against the violation of its imperatives was the stronger because its audible voice was stilled. These indulgences, therefore, brought no healthy animal satisfactions, no surcease from anxiety, no reintegration of personality on a new level of freedom, but only dark guilt-feelings engendering new anxieties and demanding punishment: *masochistic self-punishment* and *sadistic punishment of others* as scapegoats. And as so frequently happens in neuroses, the psychic satisfactions derived from punishing sin became an *unconscious motive for sinning*. Moral offenses had to be committed in order that they might be expiated by self-torture or by the torture of others" (p. 106).

The nationalistic feeling which animated the supporters of the Hitler movement is traced by Schuman to a *castration phobia* arising out of the World War, which brought about "the amputation of various parts of the Fatherland and the reduction of the Fatherland to impotence" (p. 107).

The opposition to the republican regime is explained by the

fact that "it offered to patriotic infantilism neither adequate *mother symbols* nor adequate *father symbols*" (p. 108). The conciliatory policy of the regime toward the Allies was distasteful to the lower middle class because, "to a patriotism which was impotent and castrated, the *phallic symbol* of the bloody sword was necessarily an emblem of salvation and recovered strength. The *Kleinbürgertum* yearned for what was hard, well armored, even brutal, to disguise and forget its own weakness" (p. 108). Furthermore, there was also "in the turgid depths of the German soul" a strong desire for militarism. War experiences had left a lasting mark on its participants. "The forbidden but sanctified pleasures of mass murder were too keenly relished. Death-fears and guilt-feelings were transmuted into a highly enjoyable cult of 'heroism' and admiration for that which has furnished opportunities for permissible sins and crimes" (p. 108). This feeling extended, according to Schuman, to the post-war generation. It was "nourished on war-dream fantasies. Its members aspired to the stature of the brave front fighters who were fathers and brothers. Here was the psychological genesis of the *Freikorps,* the *Kampfbünde,* the Feme murders, the military fanfare, the hero-reverence of a nation deprived of an opportunity to be heroic" (p. 108).

Anti-Semitism was a pathological phenomenon, a persecution of victims "to appease the unconscious guilt-feelings of the persecutors and to afford a convenient discharge for aggression in a direction relatively harmless to the established order" (p. 112). The idea of *Gemeinschaft* had a strong appeal because its advocacy was associated with "assaults on impersonal monsters and fiends conjured up out of diseased imaginations" (p. 119) that made the attack on the forces disrupting national unity most effective.

Finally the principle of leadership and the recognition of Hitler as charismatic leader are interpreted by Schuman as the most complete expressions of "the pathological *regressions to infantilism* of the *Kleinbürgertum*" (p. 123). "The citizens of the new Germany were to be safely nestled in the all-embracing arms of a deliverer. If the neurotic burgher could not quite return to the dark unconsciousness and the complete security of the unborn foetus in the womb, he could at least become once more a little child. His whole life would be controlled for him by a stern but loving father . . ." (p. 123).

From this seemingly convincing interpretation of National Socialism in terms of psychoanalytic concepts (complexes, phobias, regressions, sublimations, projections, and so forth), Schuman concludes that at the bottom of the Hitler movement was a collective neurosis, a psychological malady of the *Kleinbürgertum*. The aspects of the Hitler movement considered in this study would appear to be merely superficial. The mainspring of the movement is imbedded in the "unconscious," in the disorganized and pathological personality of a whole class of the German population.

Schuman's thesis is based upon a deceptive argument. Its sole support is the apparent facility with which psychoanalytical concepts may be applied to behavior manifested in the Hitler movement. Although we may fit a given action to a concept, it does not follow that the concept explains the action. The fit might be the result of reasoning by analogy and therefore be purely fictitious.

Psychoanalytical concepts, in particular, lend themselves readily to such deceptive reasoning. In clinical use they are related to well-defined symptoms of psychic disorders. The diagnosis of a patient's mental illness is made after a careful and prolonged study of the case has established the unmistakable presence of these symptoms. To such concepts, for example, as "regression to infantilism" and "castration complex," correspond specific clinical pictures to which the use of these terms is restricted. Outside of the clinic, however, this restriction is frequently disregarded. The amateur analyst is tempted by the verbal meaning of such terms and uses them as synonyms in describing behavior even when a corresponding clinical picture does not exist or is not ascertained.

The psychoanalytical interpretations of Schuman are excellent examples of such reasoning by analogy. A patriotic German is emotionally aroused by the fact that valuable provinces have been severed or cut off from the Reich by the Versailles Treaty. "Castration" is analogous to "severed" and "cut off." There is nothing which indicates the presence of the characteristic symptoms of "castration phobia" in this emotional reaction. In ascribing the national feeling which animated many Germans of the middle class to a castration phobia, Schuman uses the term merely as a verbal substitute. His "interpretation," therefore, has no real significance and is little more than a play of words.

The same kind of criticism applies to all other "interpretations" made by Schuman in support of his thesis of a collective neurosis of the middle class. For example, by analogy the wish for a leader shared by many Germans can be described as a desire "to nestle in the all-embracing arms of a deliverer." In turn, "nestling in somebody's arms" suggests the analogy to a little child seeking the protection of its mother. The word "child" suggests the word "infant!" Unless we are aware of the deceptive nature of reasoning by means of successive verbal substitutions, we can easily draw the erroneous conclusion that the wish for a leader is, as Schuman claims, a pathological "regression to infantilism."

The amateur analyst who applies psychoanalytical concepts in this fashion tends to disregard, also, another restriction imposed upon their use. The theory of unconscious motives has been developed to account for behavior which cannot be explained as the result of rational considerations, manifest emotions, or conformity to tradition. The continual washing of clean hands, or the unfounded belief that one is being persecuted are examples of such irrational behavior. This act lacks adequate motivation; there is no meaningful relation between some manifest mental content (purpose, feeling, and so forth) and the circumstances or situation in which the individual finds himself. We do not understand this behavior unless we assume the operation of unconscious motives, or the existence of a problem, hidden from view, to which the individual is adjusting. But where the actions of individuals conform to common experience or are rationally motivated, a description of the situation in which they occur offers a sufficient explanation of the behavior. Where we understand the behavior already, instead of giving us better insights, a psychoanalytic interpretation is most likely to put us on the wrong track.

Schuman has failed to conform to this implied restriction on the use of psychoanalytical concepts. Most of his interpretations are superfluous, since the behavior in question can be understood without recourse to unconscious motives or processes. Thus it is not necessary to speak of "frustrated id-drives" in order to explain the widespread discontent that prevailed in Germany. A description of the actual state of affairs in the economic and political life of the nation suffices for the understanding of the discontent of those who suffered under it. We can understand the opposition to the government on the ground that it failed to cope effectively with the severe crisis, economic and political, which beset Germany. We do not understand this opposition any better by attributing it also to "the absence of adequate father and mother symbols" in the Weimar republic. Finally, we understand sufficiently why two groups that are in bitter conflict over vital issues will take drastic measures against each other without having to assume that the fighters are "compensating for guilt-feelings," are "nourishing war-dream fantasies," or expressing "sadistic and masochistic tendencies." In these and similar instances, psychoanalytical interpretations are nothing more than superfluous adumbrations except, of course, to the dogmatist who assumes arbitrarily that all our behavior is dominated by the "unconscious" and that any explanation is superficial that does not employ psychoanalytical terms.[a]

Reasoning by analogy and superfluity, however, are not the only defects of Schuman's thesis. It presupposes the existence of a collective personality, a psychological structure underlying a social group or class as a whole. This structure is assumed to be identical with that of individual personality, and, therefore, capable of being described in terms of individual personality disorders. There is no valid reason for such an assumption. Besides, the postulation of collective personality as an entity has an unmistakable kinship to "group mind," "group self-consciousness," "*Volkgeist*" and similar discredited fictions of the older school of social psychology.

While Schuman accepts the assumption of a collective personality (p. 99), he is aware, at the same time, of its odious implications. He attempts to avoid them by asserting that a collective neurosis is merely an aggregation of individual neuroses. In support of this assertion he gives an ingenious explanation of the process by which a collective neurosis emerges. In a community in which a large number of individuals are neurotic, the solution of maladjustments may take a collective form. Thus "the various individuals comprising the group may reintegrate their disordered personalities not through individual behavior judged to be insane but through collective behavior judged to be quite sane by all the others similarly afflicted. In this case, adjustment takes the form of identification with group symbols which evoke the requisite integrating emotional responses among large numbers of people, thereby promoting cohesion in the group as a whole and at the same time affording to each individual in the group an opportunity for the emotional re-orientation demanded by his own psychic

---

[a] It should be said, in fairness to Schuman, that, although he seems to make obeisance to a fashionable trend in the social sciences, according to which an interpretation is not complete unless it is couched in Freudian terms, the merit of his book is by no means contingent upon the validity of his "neurosis theory."

difficulties. Collective delusions and collective persecution of scapegoats play the rôle of individualized hallucinations. Here the private personality disorders are expressed and in part resolved by the mechanism of public symbols. When such symbols are born of private neuroses many times multiplied in a given society and are used by manipulators to produce collective behavior . . . the result may not inaccurately be described as collective political insanity. This process suggests in brief the social and psychological dynamics of National Socialism. . . ." (p. 100).

On closer inspection, we find that this interpretation raises more questions than it answers. But even if we grant that it describes a possible process by which such a thing as a "collective insanity" emerges, it is clear that the plausibility of the reasoning cannot be taken as proof of the validity of the conclusion with regard to National Socialism. For this reasoning involves the basic assumption that most, if not all, of the members of the middle class, at any rate, millions of people in Germany, were individually "insane," had "disordered personalities," "psychic difficulties," suffered with "private neuroses." Here we have a question of facts, and no reasoning, no matter how plausible it may seem, can circumvent the necessity of proving their existence.

This proof Schuman fails to give and it is on this score, primarily, that his thesis of a collective neurosis and with it, the psycho-analytical interpretation of the Hitler movement falls down. Individual case studies might have furnished the proof. The absence of documentary evidence might be excused on the ground that the task of undertaking such cast studies would involve a prodigious amount of labor. However, there is nothing in the vast literature on conditions in Germany, or in the statements of competent observers of German life which even remotely suggests the possibility of finding such evidence. We may add that the life histories of our contributors, at least with regard to the sample of followers of the Hitler movement which they represent, provide positive evidence against the assumption of a wide-spread "insanity" in Germany. A careful study of the material has failed to show any indications of the presence of "private neuroses." On the contrary, they provide, in most instances, clear cases of adequate motivation for joining the Hitler movement and, therefore, direct support of our contention that the psychoanalytical interpretation is superfluous.

b. *The Marxist interpretation*

In contrast to the psychoanalysts, the Marxists view the Hitler movement as a result of conscious and rational motives, the calculated and deliberated planning on the part of Germany's "economic royalists." In the most uncompromising form, this view has been expressed by John Strachey in his book *The Menace of Fascism.*[7]

The point of departure of Strachey, and of the Marxists in general, is the dogma that economic forces determine historical processes. At the bottom of contemporary historical occurrences lies the fact that Western civilization is dominated by a death struggle between two forces in the economic sphere. On the one hand is the trend toward economic planning necessitated by technological developments. The problem of distributing the mass of goods which our machinery is capable of producing in abundance cannot be solved unless the profit system is abolished and a world organization created that will destroy the unsound political division of mankind into independent states. The full utilization of our technological accomplishments, the elimination of economic depressions and of imperialistic wars are not possible as long as the means of production are privately owned and competition for world markets continues. If Western civilization is to survive, the privileged and property-owning classes must be destroyed and a planned

---

[7] New York: Covici Friede, 1933. Page references to this book appear in parentheses.

economy established in which the means of production are pooled under the ownership of the community.

Opposed to this inexorable trend is the effort of the beneficiaries of the present capitalistic system, the industrialists, landowners and bankers, who are determined to retain their position of power at all costs and are combating with all the means at their disposal any attempts to change the *status quo*.

According to Strachey, all contemporary political events are merely aspects of this struggle between an inevitable progressive trend and the opposition of vested interests. "The incompatibility of modern methods of production with Capitalism," he exclaims, "is the one hypothesis which will give order and coherence to the otherwise baffling complexities of the present situation. It is the key to the puzzle, and until we have grasped this key, the other pieces—the deterioration of the economic situation, the decay of the progressive parties, the appearance of Fascism, the onset of a new war—will not fit into place" (p. 115).

The "key" explains also the Hitler movement. National Socialism, which Strachey views as the German form of Fascism, is a symptom of the profound historical process which is hidden from the eyes of the uninitiated. Therefore, to explain the Hitler movement in terms which do not take cognizance of this fact is to ignore what is essential. National Socialism, according to Strachey, is in essence nothing more or less than a movement "for the preservation by violence, and at all costs, of the private ownership of the means of production. . . . Fascism kills, tortures, and terrorizes in defense of the right of the capitalists to keep the fields, factories and mines of the world as their private property" (p. 124).

How did the Hitler movement come about? A big banker or landowner does not fight his own class battles by himself. Indeed he creates a mass organization composed of members of the lower middle classes and of peasants who do the fighting for him. To Strachey, the creation of such a mass organization is simplicity itself. The people can easily be fooled by adroit propaganda. Their eyes can be kept from seeing the truth that they are merely "the militant arm of the largest property owners" and, instead, made to "suppose genuinely that they are part of a progressive movement" (p. 125). The plotters dupe them by catering to their illusions and by simulating a more or less idealistic nationalism. As a result, the middle class and the peasants fail to realize "that they are being used as hired mercenaries for the defence of the ownership of the factories, fields and mines of the capitalists" (p. 125). Strachey takes for granted the gullibility of the masses of the German people and the craftiness and uncanny capacity for deep and large scale plotting of their "masters." It is obvious, therefore, to him that from the very beginning National Socialism was "a movement owned and controlled by the very richest and biggest capitalists who used the middle class and the peasants as their indispensable instruments for the destruction of the working class" (p. 128).

Strachey's evidence that the Hitler movement was a sinister, calculating plot of the German "economic royalists" is very scanty. No documentary proof of the necessary ingredients of a plot is given, such as general agreement among the industrialists, bankers and landowners, an organization for the planning and supervising of the plot the means by which it was carried out and so forth. Strachey contents himself with a reference to the fact that some industrialists and bankers were among the contributors to the Party's campaign funds, and with an assertion pertaining to the "actual history" of the way in which the National Socialists have come to power. According to Strachey, "it must be obvious to all that Hitler did not seize power. On the contrary, the Nazi movement was, during the autumn of 1932, in evident and admitted decline. And then President von Hindenburg and his advisers suddenly handed over the power of the state to Hitler—without even the pretence of a struggle" (p. 130).

Why should this have happened? Strachey argues that while the capitalists from the beginning had in fact owned and controlled the movement, "they had undoubtedly preferred to keep control of the government for themselves, and to let the Fascists do the dirty work in the street for them. But such considerations became merely trivial when it was apparent that if the Fascists were not given power, the Fascist movement would disintegrate and the capitalists would lose their last basis of mass support" (p. 208). "At this moment," writes Strachey, "a question of fearful urgency came into the minds of the German ruling class. If the Fascist movement was to disintegrate, what would then be left to protect the capitalist ownership?" And thereupon the fertile imagination of Strachey envisages a dramatic scene. "Papen looked at Schleicher, and Hugenberg looked at Papen. They saw only blankness and dismay in each other's eyes. If the eyes of the senile Hindenburg could still see anything, they could see this—that if the Fascist movement was allowed to disintegrate, nothing, literally nothing, stood between them and the workers' revolution" (p. 207). So Hindenburg, "who had been made president by the Social Democrats simply and solely to keep out Hitler, nine months later sent for Hitler and made him Dictator of Germany" (p. 208).

It is hardly necessary to point out that such isolated facts as contributions by capitalists and the sudden appointment of Hitler to the chancellorship in no way demonstrate the sweeping contention of Strachey that the Hitler movement was a capitalistic plot from beginning to end. Actually, the inferences which Strachey draws from the facts presuppose the very thing which he intends to prove. That some industrialists, bankers and possibly owners of large estates contributed funds to the movement does not imply necessarily that the capitalists created, owned and controlled it. Unless the existence of a plot is assumed, these contributions do not signify more than the plain fact that private individuals of means supported the movement for what it stood for or for the sake of personal advantages which they hoped to gain from its success.

Likewise the interpretation of the events which preceded the rise of Hitler to power are meaningful only on the presupposition that the movement was a tool in the hands of the plotters who were at liberty to decide what should happen to it. Actually, the opposite interpretation comes closer to the facts in the case.[8]

The decision of Hindenburg was forced in part by a political deadlock, largely due to the fact that the National Socialists were kept out of the government although their numerical strength in parliament had entitled them since 1930 to ministerial posts. Brüning, von Papen, and Schleicher, who acted as semi-dictators, failed to control the political situation. Their decisions were hampered by the National Socialists. In the meantime, the economic situation became more desperate and required drastic measures. Lacking the confidence of the people, no party in power and no presidential appointee would dare to put the needed measures across. Furthermore, in spite of all efforts the National Socialists could not be suppressed. They were clamoring for power. A virtual state of civil war existed. The set-back of the Nazi party in the September elections, largely owing to the secession of Strasser, failed to dim the fervent hopes of the adherents of the movement. In addition, the election to the Landtag at Schaumburg Lippe in January 1933, in which the National Socialist party regained most of its losses of the previous election, showed that the set-back was, at best, only temporary and that there was no basis for the hopes of Schleicher *et al.* that the movement would disintegrate. The appointment of Hitler was an adequate way out of the dilemma that was threatening to disrupt the country and submerge it in civil war. Hindenburg had to give in reluctantly and only after he was assured that satisfactory safeguards

---

[8] Detailed description of the events of January 1933 are available in the books by Heiden and Schuman referred to above. The situation was full of intricate complications and was by no means as simple an affair as Strachey makes it appear.

were taken to insure that Hitler would be merely a figurehead. And indeed, Hitler had to stage a *coup d'état,* precipitated by the Reichstag fire, before National Socialism became the ruling power in Germany.

Behind the theory, then, that the Hitler movement was a capitalistic plot stands nothing except the assertion that there was one. Strachey argues as a typical dogmatist. To him the Marxist doctrine of history is an axiom. There is no need to study the Hitler movement in detail. Since it follows from the doctrine that National Socialism should be a capitalistic plot, it therefore is one. The simplified history of Strachey recognizes only a pro-capitalistic and an anti-capitalistic motive; there is no room for the expression of other sentiments in mass behavior. National or religious sentiments, reform ideas, any ideology all are to him only facades which hide the real issue—the class struggle as Marx saw it.

The plot idea in a modified form has recently been revived by Robert E. Brady.[9]

He says that about 1928 the Junkers and the large industrialists and financial interests "saw the use to which the Nazi party could be put. The specific content of its program did not matter so far as they were concerned. . . . The real significance of the Nazi party lay in the fact that it had a certain following amongst the amorphous and hesitant masses. . . . Ideal for the purposes to which it was to be put, there was a plank in the Nazi platform to meet the prejudices of nearly every group to be appealed to. . . . Whenever need called for it, and at the proper time, anything one desired could be made out of the program. For the right, the set-up was perfect" (p. 206).

There is little left here of Strachey's idea that the National Socialists are "the capitalists and their dupes in fancy dress." Instead, the genuineness of the movement is recognized. It is assumed, however, that the reactionaries have supported the

[9] *The Spirit and Structure of German Fascism.* New York: The Viking Press, 1937.

movement in order to utilize it after it came into power. Brady's whole book is an effort to prove this contention by showing how the measures undertaken by the National Socialists after they came to power have played into the hands of the industrialists, bankers and landowners.

A discussion of Brady's thesis would lead us beyond the scope of our study, which closes with the events of January 1933. It would require another study of similar nature to do justice to a subject of such magnitude as is the fate of a movement after it comes into power.[10]

It is clear, however, that the validity of my findings on the determining factors in the growth and development of the Hitler movement is not affected by the possibility that the movement may have become the victim of a plot *after* Hitler was made chancellor. We need to be concerned only with the claim that the movement itself was the result of a plot. On the face of it, the plot theory appears to be highly improbable, since the assumption of well-nigh super-human powers on the part of the plotters is required to account for the creation, maintenance, and growth of a mass movement by deception. Therefore, extensive documentary proof in support of the theory is necessary. Such proof has not been given. Instead, we have found that the adherents of the plot theory rest their case, in the main, upon faith in a philosophic doctrine. Belief in the correctness of Marx's philosophy of history is hardly sufficient, however, to offset the improbability inherent in the plot theory. We are forced, therefore, to reject the Marxian interpretation of the Hitler movement on the ground of inadequacy.[11]

---

[10] For different interpretations of events in Germany since 1933, see Luedecke, K. G. W., *I Knew Hitler*. New York: Scribner's, 1937; and particularly Lichtenberger, H., *The Third Reich*. New York: Greystone Press, 1937.

[11] In the light of our discussion of the nature and role of discontent among the adherents of the Hitler movement, it should be clear that our rejection of the Marxist interpretation does not imply that, among others, economic motives and class antagonisms were not involved in the movement.

PART III

Selected Life Histories

Chapter IX

Six Life Histories

Introduction

In the preceding sections of this study I dealt with the historical development of the Hitler movement and analyzed the factors that determined its growth and success. The results of my investigations were derived from life histories of adherents of the movement. So far, however, I have referred to the first-hand material only through quotations and isolated passages.

The reproduction here of selected complete autobiographies is designed to show, in unified, more realistic form, patterns of National Socialist experience separately analyzed in previous chapters. These accounts are a sample of the material on which the analytical section of this book is based.

The autobiographies reproduced in this section were chosen for the following reasons: first, story value and richness of content; second, usefulness in enriching points previously raised; third, portrayal of typical personality traits and mental reactions.

My comments are restricted to passages that presuppose knowledge of German background.

1. *The Story of a Worker*

My father was a factory worker in the Friedrich-Alfred foundry in Rheinhausen. With thousands and thousands of other laborers he pursued his tasks in this factory, which is known far beyond the boundaries of Germany, day after day and week after week. I can still remember that we children did not see him at home any too often. Even when he was at home, there was nothing for him but work, and more work. In the evenings he worked together with my mother in the garden and on a piece of land we rented for farming. Each week he changed from the day shift to the night shift at the factory and then back again. On rare occasions he told stories in the intimate circle of his children. In these tales—although, of course, I realized this only much later—he revealed an enormous store of knowledge of good literature from almost all parts of the world. I feel convinced now that there was in these tales a longing for liberation from the eternal monotony and the harsh uniformity of his daily work. As we grew older, we children noticed more and more that he continually showed himself an ardent patriot in all his thinking and conduct; yet he seemed completely dissatisfied with his Fatherland. He must have been the victim of an inner conflict, seeking the right path.

Our mother was a worthy, honest, German housewife. She met all the experiences of life with an unfailing piety and faith in God. Nothing could disconcert her. Filled with burning love, she worked from four-thirty in the morning till late at night for her husband and children. If there ever was a woman whose thinking and conduct was purely German by reason of her feelings and blood, she was just that. Her soul was an inexhaustible storehouse for us children, from which we derived all knowledge, all our modes of thought and action. She never evaluated the Fatherland according to its social, political or civil institutions; to her the Germany she knew was the highest as it stood. Thus naturally a seed was sown in our childish hearts that was to grow into a pure love for our native land. Both our parents, our father and our mother, thus in their quiet and sincere way, were responsible for the awakening of a thirst for knowledge and pure ambition in us children.

In school the effect of this initial education soon asserted itself. We naturally had absolute faith in the authority of the teacher, together with a trusting belief in him as the one appointed to complete the work of father and mother. And another almost equally natural consequence was that I was considered one of the best in the class. In the street, in our games, it soon became apparent too that my comrades willingly subordinated themselves to me and let themselves be led. In addition to my respect for my teacher and all other things more highly placed than myself and my home surroundings, I also considered cleverer and better all people richer than we were. But in the course of time I frequently discovered that wealth and intelligence were not always found together, even among the children at school. I could not escape this fact, as my ambition for higher schooling and more knowledge could not be gratified because of my parents' poverty. Even as a child I inwardly tortured myself with the question of why that was so. As in all other matters, I sought advice on this point from my parents. Mother passed over the question with loving words of consolation. She said that was how things were; yet, even so, one could be happy and grow up to be a worthy and decent man. My father, too, tried to console me, but his explanation was different from mother's, and it seemed to me that the quiet longing in his heart shone more clearly through his eyes at such moments than at other times.

In school I was skipped and at the age of nine was promoted to a class shared by the upper grades. Thus I also heard the instruction of the older pupils, and my general knowledge was enlarged far beyond my grade. When I was ten years old, I developed blood poisoning in my right leg as a result of falling on a bottle while at play. This blood poisoning kept me confined to bed for almost two years. Secluded from my comrades, I was left to myself most of the time. My long sickness made me realize, as children on the whole are not apt to do, the self-sacrificing love of my parents. During many sleepless hours throughout my illness, I thought deeply about the words, precepts and actions of my parents. All this brooding, however, had but one result: a conviction that for me as a German boy there could be nothing higher on earth than my parents and my Fatherland.

I left the hospital on June 28, 1914. I was still unable to walk. At home I was again confined to my sick bed. Now the beginning of the war approached. Day after day I was feverishly eager for the newspapers. Together with my mother, who was full of enthusiasm, I read the first reports of victory. Outside the long lines of soldiers passed. My mother carried me in her arms so I might see how German men marched away to die for Germany, singing exultant songs. Hour after hour I sat at the railroad tracks. I could not move from the spot and so had enough time to carry away an indelible impression of all I saw. When they took me home and I lay still on my sick bed, I came to realize, despite my youth, that all those men were marching to their death, in the last analysis sacrificing their blood for German children. After all, we were Germany, and without us German children Germany could not survive. Thus, as I reflect today, I see that the greatest and most lasting lesson of my entire childhood was sown in my mother's hands and guarded by my father's eyes: There is nothing more sacred than an unselfish love of one's native land.

The year 1914 passed on to 1918. During the interim there was for us, the poor of Germany, need and hunger. I shall spare myself the pain of describing in detail the years of privations. Only one thing I must emphasize again and again, that often parental love went so far that parents would break down completely rather than share equally with their children. We lived through these years with open eyes. Though our parents had implanted in us an absolute honesty, and this honesty had grown and become mature, our eyes were critical enough to determine that the same honesty did not rule all life. On top of this discovery there came again the comparison of our own existence with that of others. If ever I had the wish to learn and accomplish more in life, it reasserted itself with greater forcefulness than ever in these first years of young manhood. As my life appeared to be headed at the time, no course seemed open to me other than to follow in my father's footsteps. Although I entered an office in the Friedrich-Alfred factory because of my injured leg, nevertheless, my career until old age was planned in advance. My illness had made my parents even poorer than before and now it was up to me to work and earn money. I had occasion to visit my father at his place of work. He was a worker at the smelting furnace. Even now I can see him standing there in his overalls, pulling the buckets of ore up and down. From morning to evening, day after day, week after week, year after year, always the same thing. I was seized with a horror of this eternal sameness, of the everlasting hardships of the German industrial worker. At the same time, however, I felt a holy respect for the vast, silent heroism of the German laborer. The first time I faced my father at his machine I felt that his expression became frightened, as though he wished to stop his child from seeing the longing in his soul. Then I became aware of the meaning of the quiet gleam in his eyes, as he used to tell us children stories. Gradually our hearts became attuned to the same need and the same longing. Among smelting furnaces, buckets of ore, and the howling of sirens, I made the first step toward becoming a revolutionary. I determined to become active politically and become a fighter for the German workman.

The overthrow came. Revolutionary speakers travelled through the country. They preached the liberation of the German workman. The German workman came to have a definite political orientation. Promises followed upon promises, proclamations on proclamations. The eight-hour day was introduced at the foundry as everywhere else. In youthful enthusiasm I rejoiced over this apparent liberation of the German working man. I fell back only too readily into the error of accepting men as honest in the sense of the word I had learned from my mother. The socialist speaker on the platform amid the masses of laborers took over the rôle once filled by my school teacher. I gave him my faith and confidence. I began to discuss politics with my father and my brother. Full of enthusiasm, we boys believed in the beginning of a new age. We did not see the accompanying phenomena as repellent to our being as they were irreconcilable with German nature. If the speaker spoke of socialism, we believed that he meant socialism as we pictured it. If he spoke of freedom or other things, we assumed his meaning to be the same as ours. Only our father said even then that socialism in the form of Marxism could never be the right precept for the German people. We did not believe him.

In 1920 I began practical work in the electrical shop of the Friedrich-Alfred foundry. In this workshop, at the time one of the most radical, I was given a systematic introduction to Marxism by my older fellow workers. Slowly but brutally they uprooted the teachings that my mother had implanted in me, which had once and for all been inscribed in my heart during the quiet hours of childhood. Where was the hallowed love of Fatherland, where the holy sacrifice of the soldiers at the front? Where was the faith in Germany? Away with those things! All that was said to have been deceit and mockery. Marxism had no use for these things. Bit by bit they were torn from my heart. My heart bled, for this tearing out of the gifts of a loving mother was painful. But class hatred had no interest in these. The wound was covered with a bandage of mottos, promises and other hollow things. And then one deceived oneself into believing it had healed. We were so eager to believe that freedom for workmen would come. One's expression as well as one's thoughts became hard. My conduct in my intimate family circle at home became constrained. My mother's eyes could see through all the false phrases and always looked straight into my heart. And those eyes could not be confused by Marxist theories. If now and then her son's words ran away with his heart and he championed the new doctrine with eager words and a burning head, she was probably pleased to see that her boy expounded the new doctrine with the old integrity, but her expression showed her fear of the new doctrine itself.

In the silence of the night, one lay in bed brooding. The battle began, a hard inner struggle. On the one hand there was the voice of our mother and the call of the blood; on the other hand, Marxism harshly and coldly demanded its rights. Again and again this battle was repeated, and Karl Marx was more and more often the victor. My heart, however, was all but bled dry by the struggle, and the bonds of family relationship were completely severed.

Salary demands were made in the factories. They were denied. Strikes were called. They would go on for three days, five days, eight days and longer. Negotiations began. The worker was strong. The worker won. New salary demands, more strikes, renewed victories. This was repeated at more or less regular intervals. We all helped along without regard for anything else. The end was inflation.

In the meanwhile had come the Belgian occupation. What did Karl Marx teach us? That the Belgians were the same as we. All human beings were equal. And yet there was a difference. The Belgians spoke differently, they acted differently, though they were no better than we—quite the contrary. In fact I shall spare myself the pain of speaking of the shame and disgrace inflicted on us by the Belgian garrison. I found my way to my Marxist teachers. Their answer to my direct question was that we Germans must lead with good examples. In time our enemies, too, would espouse the same philosophy and the international brotherhood would come. But somebody must set the good example, and Germany must be the one. All well and good. We took the rôle upon ourselves, we deceived ourselves, for we never again knew a heartfelt joy when German national feeling asserted itself against the disgrace of the occupation. Again and again the stirring German blood made itself felt under the dung heap of Marxism.

December 1923 came. The eight-hour day was taken from the German industrial worker by the so-called Berlin agreement. A wave of indignation swept over us. I recall how I marched past the smelting furnaces of the foundry with a fellow worker and tried to arouse a revolt against this agreement. Never before was the whole body of industrial workers so completely unified. Faith in the victory of the German workman was firm as a rock. I hastened from one conference to another and everywhere I found the same unity of purpose. Only one thing struck me and oppressed me. While we young people were sincerely worried over the fate of labor, the Marxist leaders acted so indifferently and frivolously that we could not understand their attitude.

At this time I experienced another inner struggle. Again and again I talked myself into believing that what was happening must be the right thing; and ever again there was a voice that warned me in a soft, scarcely audible whisper. Had I been quite honest with myself, I should have had to admit to myself that I could no longer find my bearings. I did not, however, want to be honest with myself; I did not want to give up my Communist faith as I had once given up my faith in nationalism.

And yet I had to surrender. The battle of the workers

failed. The men who led them were the traitors. The very people who should have advised them betrayed them. No International helped the German workman.

My senses dulled, I wandered about, a crushed soul. The thing my mother had implanted in me, my holy love for my people and Fatherland, had been uprooted. Marxist socialism, that had taken its place, collapsed of itself. What good was life? What meaning, what purpose did it have? The one thing that upheld me was a pride that prevented me from showing my inner bewilderment together with my love for my brother and sisters and my parents. Then came the elections of 1924. Despite the absence of any inward interest, I nevertheless approached the ballot box with an indescribable feeling of hope and voted the Communist ticket. My father, with whom I no longer had any political discussions, acted differently. When the tickets were published, among them the one headed by Adolf Hitler, father said to mother that that ticket alone deserved to be considered. Even in 1923, when the battle of Adolf Hitler penetrated to us in the lower Rhine valley, it was my father who more than once declared clearly and unequivocally in my presence that Hitler was the right man. At the time all that meant nothing to me. He knew quite well that my wounded heart must heal some time. He depended on his son's wholesome heart to some day find its way to Adolf Hitler, even as he had found the way through the hours of quiet thought and reflection.

Nineteen twenty-four came. One day my brother approached me with the invitation to visit a meeting of the *Völkisch-soziale Block*.[1] My reply that I would never go over to the men of the swastika made absolutely no impression on him. On the contrary, after a few days he repeated his overtures, adding that after all I did not have to join but it would not harm me to hear them. The leader of the local group of

[1] A political party founded after the dissolution of the National Socialist party following the *Putsch* of November 9, 1923.

the national party in Rheinhausen at that time was the director of the electrical power plant, Herr Wilhelm Schönberger. Schönberger was held in the highest esteem in labor circles because he was a just man, one of the few intellectuals without any class prejudice or bias. In the last analysis, this was probably the reason I went to a meeting. At the first meeting, comprised of about fifteen people, a Herr Fuchs spoke about the treason of Marxism. I listened in silence and digested everything he said. Inwardly, however, I was completely disturbed. When I compared the speakers words with what had happened, I was forced again and again to conclude that what I heard was the truth. Two weeks later I went to another meeting. A Dr. Goebbels of Elberfeld spoke on the theme: "What does Adolf Hitler want?" The attendance was not much larger. I followed every word of the speaker. I felt as though he were addressing me personally. My heart grew light, something in my breast arose. I felt as if bit by bit something within me were being rebuilt. Dr. Goebbels did not complete his theme that evening. He promised to come back in two weeks and finish his lecture. I passed those fourteen days as if in delirium. I could hardly wait for the day of the meeting. I was there punctually, and at the close of the meeting I silently went home. I plunged into the little existing literature on the subject. I read Hitler's speeches, studied the program of the National Socialist party, and gradually I was politically reborn. Filled with a pure joy I realized that what my mother had once said was true after all—that it was a hallowed act to give up one's life for Germany as the soldiers at the front had done. At the same time, my father's lifelong yearning for a German socialism was tenable. I became a National Socialist. No voice protested against it; my heart was not full of fear at the thought of National Socialism; there was only a joyous acknowledgment, a bright enthusiasm, a pure faith in Adolf Hitler and Germany.

Now I proceeded to active coöperation. The first large

meeting I attended was in Dortmund in the Fredenbaum Hall. Because of the French garrison in Rheinhausen, we did not then officially belong to the National Socialist party nor could we form local *S.A.* units. So we went to Dortmund as inconspicuous civilians. At the station in Dortmund we had our first experience of the treatment meted out to *S.A.* men. The police took every *S.A.* member's cane away, prohibited our marching in a group, and showed in all sorts of petty ways that no *S.A.* member could count on friendly consideration. On the way to the Fredenbaum a procession of Marxists marched parallel to the *S.A.*, who had to separate. Provocative cries, despicable insults, jeers and shouts came to us from the crowd of Marxists. Now and then several would jump on an *S.A.* man and beat or stab him. The *S.A.* men without weapons—even their walking sticks had been taken away—had to protect themselves with their fists. At such moments, however, the mounted police came and struck out at the *S.A.* with their sticks. Defenseless, they had to make their way as best they could to the Fredenbaum. When we arrived at the Fredenbaum Hall, the wounded were carried or led in one after another. The number of the injured was announced before the opening of the meeting. As nearly as I can remember, there were nine serious casualties, while sixty-three suffered minor injuries. Adolf Hitler was to speak at the meeting that evening. Despite the fact that this was to be a closed meeting, he was not allowed to speak, since he was barred from the public platform throughout Prussia. Julius Streicher spoke in his place. We left the meeting full of enthusiasm and courage for the fight, only to experience the same attacks as previously, on the way back to the station. I remember an *S.A.* member standing at the station, who was being provoked by a mob of Marxists. The *S.A.* man did not react to the provocation with any word or gesture. Near by stood a policeman who entertained absolutely no idea of interfering with the Marxists. Suddenly a Marxist approached the *S.A.* man and tore his cap from his head amid the loud laughter of the others. The *S.A.* man turned around quite calmly, and dealt the Marxist a resounding blow. At that moment the officer came up and led the *S.A.* man away. For us Rheinhausen men the whole experience in Dortmund was a spur to the uttermost activity. We began to work with genuine zeal.

A few months later Adolf Hitler addressed a closed meeting at the Association Hall in Essen. Membership cards were examined with exacting care by several police officials before we were permitted to enter the hall. It is impossible to describe the experience of seeing and hearing the Leader for the first time. One thing is certain: from that day on I had no other purpose than to fight for him until the victory was won.

It would take too long for me to describe here all my personal experiences in the movement from 1925 to 1933. From the end of 1926 on I was active as a speaker for the movement. I shall confine myself to describing a few incidents that occured during this time.

I was assigned to speak in a small industrial community on the lower Rhine. The leader of the local group informed me on my arrival that a converted Communist wished to speak before me. I consented to this, but asked first whether the *S.A.* had sufficient protection for the hall. The unsuspecting leader said that up to that time nothing had happened and probably nothing would happen. My experiences in the field, however, had taught me differently. A glance at the audience sitting about in the inn showed me immediately that there were many Communists present and that their intention was to break up the meeting. A second glance into the hall where the *S.A.* were showed me that they were in absolutely no position to resist the intended attack. I demanded that the leader ask for reinforcements, which he did by telephone. We could no longer postpone the meeting, and I was confident that I would be able to keep it going until the reinforcements came. The meeting began; I had the floor. The converted Communist was to speak after me, when there was stronger protection. Interruption after interruption followed. To keep the meeting going I had to answer every interruption. It was a matter of thinking with lightning rapidity and answering just as fast. First, one had to give a serious reply, next make the heckler appear ridiculous, according to what he looked like and the extent to which his own comrades took him seriously. This demanded terrific concentration. You must appreciate that this meeting took place during an election campaign when my appearance on the speaker's platform was required evening after evening. Every night one slept in a different bed. In the morning one took the first train to one's next assignment. Directly one's work was done, one entrained for the next meeting.

With much effort I thus succeeded in keeping the meeting going until the arrival of reinforcements. The moment they entered, a number of Communists leaped to their feet and grabbed chairs. The Wesel *S.S.* Guard leaped into the fray with their straps. The policemen present also took courage now, and quiet was quickly restored. The Communists heard the lecture to the end, without joining in the discussion, and left the hall without singing the *Internationale*. Later that evening the leader of the local group was shot at by Communists on his way home.

In Krefeld one Sunday there was to be an *S.A.* parade. The banner bearer of the *S.A.* informed us that the parade was permitted. The *S.A.* formed ranks and marched away. On the way policemen came and led the procession away from the intended route back to the street from which it had started. When the entire *S.A.* was in the street, suddenly a larger detachment of policemen appeared at both ends and ruthlessly struck out with their sticks. The Vereinsstrasse, where this took place, has no side streets, being flanked on both sides by rows of houses. The *S.A.* men at the head now pressed backward, and those at the rear pressed forward, driven by the blows of the police. Driven together, they were beaten like a herd of cattle. Any *S.A.* man who dared to take on the police was immediately arrested and transferred to the police wagon. Those arrested would call from the patrol wagon in defiance of the entire police force, *"Hitler Heil."* At every cry of *"Heil"* they received blows on the head with policemen's billies until they finally collapsed, unconscious. Again an *S.A.* man would throw himself on the police, only to be overtaken by the fate of his comrades before him. When the mass of the *S.A.* was pressed together as far as possible, at the end where I was standing a row of *S.A.* men linked arms and advanced a few steps toward the police with the words, "You can't come any farther without first beating us to death." Thereupon the police drew their revolvers and stood waiting. An *S.A.* man, overwrought by the affair, suddenly broke through the chain of his comrades from behind, sprang upon an officer and struck him in the face with his shoulder belt. Then he tore open his shirt and stood before the pistol barrels, his chest uncovered crying, "Now shoot me; then you'll have what you want." A few of our leaders then asked very energetically to speak to the responsible commander of the police, pointing out that it was impossible to go on this way. Our emphatic demands finally got us permission to retire to a hall. An officer who dared enter the place beating about with his stick was beaten with beer glasses by the over-excited *S.A.,* and thrown out.

One fine day there was a large farmers' meeting in Krefeld, called by the National German party. A fellow party member, at the time the only National Socialist farmer in the district of Mörs, accompanied me. The hall was filled with about 800 people. Four or five National German Reichstag representatives spoke. Discussion was announced. Before the meeting, lists of those present were distributed. After the National German speakers had finished, I went to the speaker's table and asked for the floor. I mounted the platform, and spoke first about the general needs of the farmers, going on to the causes and coming finally to National Socialism. Up to that point everyone had listened to me attentively, even applauded now and then. At that point, however, the officers began to cry "Stop, stop." I continued to speak. Again they called "Stop!" Then I turned to the officer's table and spoke as follows, "Gentlemen, among you the principle of leadership is not maintained, so I suppose I may turn to the audience and ask them whether or not I should continue to speak." Then I turned to the public and asked, "What shall I do?" The farmers were surprised and remained silent. Only my fellow party member yelled from his corner, "Keep on speaking, keep on speaking." I thereupon turned again to the official table and said, "Gentlemen, you have heard that the people want me to continue speaking. They could find no solution but to place the final speaker for the National German party on the speaker's platform right in front of me, where he spoke at the same time as I. Under these circumstances nothing could be heard and the farmers slowly rose and left. I then did the same. My comrade had meanwhile collected a group from the attendance lists that had been distributed by the National Germans. We took these home and supplied the farmers with propaganda material.

Some years later I managed by close stinting to buy myself a light motorcycle. I needed the motorcycle to be able to keep up my numerous appearances throughout that large province. The Rheinhausen Communists were well acquainted with the license number, model and sound of this motorcycle. I had found out that they were planning an attack on me. As I was wearily on my way home, between twelve and one at night, I had to focus all my attention on avoiding these fellows. Stopping suddenly, I would light up the entire region with my searchlight; more than once I had to disappear at full speed. Often I could not go home for weeks because the whole neighborhood was besieged by Communists. Sometimes, too, I was pleasantly surprised when *S.A.* in mufti blocked the streets and received me with cheers.

It would be impossible in this brief autobiography to describe all we suffered in the battle for the elevation of our German Fatherland. Icy cold, fiercest heat, wind and storms, rain and hail—nothing could prevent us from continuing on our way. We bore many a comrade to his grave, shot or stabbed to death by the Communist mobs. Many a comrade we accompanied to prison and called for at the prison later. Faith was the one thing that always led us on, faith in Germany, faith in the purity of our nation and faith in our leader. Holy was our battle and holy our victory. We know that we must build up again what has been destroyed in Germany during all those years, and we must use the same energy and stubbornness which we drew during the tireless battle. Some day the world will recognize that the Reich we established with blood and sacrifice is destined to bring peace and blessing to the world.

2. *The Story of an Anti-Semite*

The fifth son of a gardener, I was born on August 17, 1890, at Dittersbach, Kreis Lüben, in Lower Silesia. As the youngest in the family—my brothers and sisters had died before my birth—I was brought up mainly by my grandmother, who lived with my parents. My mother as well as my father had to work on the land from early in morning until late at night. Although both of them worked very hard, we had just enough for the most necessary things. Nevertheless a small, very modest part of their earnings was laid aside weekly for their old age. From my sixth year I attended the public school, which had only two teachers for all the classes. At the age of eight, like all children of that age whose parents worked the fields, I had to work in the afternoons. In addition, during school time the more gifted children were called upon by the teacher for his own agricultural work. Because of circumstances beyond their control, my parents often changed their place of work and thus also their residence. As a result, I attended five different public schools. My parents as well as I were intent on quick learning. For that reason I did not learn a trade nor become a teacher, as my parents had been advised; that would have required a longer attendance at school.

I would probably have remained on the estate as a worker if the pay had been better. In the city, which was only five miles away, I could earn three times as much as a piece-worker. Consequently I became a laborer in a paper factory. There, with my otherwise modest demands, I had enough money left to gratify my passion for books. As I had no advisers, I bought several Indian, robber, and detective books. My love of adventure was aroused, and in the first three and one-half years I changed my position about sixteen or eighteen times; to be sure in this way I became acquainted with many different people and cities. Even then, it struck me that in spite of good earnings there was seldom a satisfied person to be found in the city. At the age of seventeen and a half I learned to be a servant, because after a brief apprenticeship one was supposed to be able to earn much money. In this way my wish to learn to know the world was partially fulfilled. The view of laborers that rich people were happy was not confirmed by my experience. Probably then for the first time I put the question to myself, "What meaning does life have anyhow?" In almost all the people with whom I became acquainted the impulse to earn as much money as possible was present. In the so-called higher classes of society that I learned to know as a servant, the urge for still more possessions was strongly in evidence. One of my employers, a member of an old noble family, put his extensive library at my disposal. After two years I had with its aid formed my own opinion of life. Unconsciously I had become a revolutionist. Why did the higher classes of society have so many privileges? Why was the workman or subordinate treated so condescendingly? Why was one ashamed to sit down at a table with laborers? Why did the rich man say to his children, "You must not play with the children of workmen. They are too dirty and naughty?" Why did the master converse in a comradely tone when alone with the servant and why, when another "gentleman" was present, did he make the difference of rank so grossly evident? Up to this time I had seldom read any newspaper, the political part not at all. "Politics spoil the character," they said in bourgeois circles, and I wanted someday to become a member of the middle class, so as not to be despised as heretofore. Nevertheless I now read the newspaper of my master, the *Deutsche Tageszeitung*.[1] Through this, class differences were brought more and more to my consciousness. Occasionally, I bought myself a labor newspaper in the city. The things printed there were facts that I daily witnessed myself and that gradually made me the enemy of the higher class of society. Naturally I dared not let my opinion be noticed; a servant must be a "nationalist." But why must a servant be a "nationalist?" Wherein did the expression of the national feeling of the higher classes consist? I could not answer this question. Nor did I find anyone who might have given me an answer.

It was a matter of course for me that I must some day become a soldier, and so after the second inspection I enlisted in the cavalry. It was with great pride that I went on leave at Christmas, 1911, in my beautiful uniform. My parents were just as proud of their son. My father who before had always voted for the National German party, had in recent time become an adherent of social democracy. He believed that his interests were better fostered there, and I supported this opinion. As a soldier, I did not bother with politics, and like all my other comrades I was happy when mobilization was announced. The enthusiasm was apparently shared by all classes of the population. My comrades like myself were firmly convinced that we had to defend our native land. When the war lasted longer than we had expected we naturally continued to do our duty. The exuberant enthusiasm of the first few weeks had ripened into a serious but confident mood. The scarcity of provisions was comprehensible to us, as we knew that we

---

[1] A conservative daily.

were cut off from all importations. When I married in July 1915, receiving for that purpose my first leave of absence of four days, I found a different state of mind from that at the beginning of the war, yet there was nothing disquieting about it.

In 1916 and 1917, we heard much about injustice in the distribution of food at home. Whoever had money could buy everything. The young people in the munition factories and army work shops received high salaries and as a result were able to live in abundance. The soldiers returning from leave were glad to be back in the trenches, for there there were no distinctions; there a glorious spirit of comradeship prevailed and one man could depend upon the other. We only laughed at the handbills thrown down by enemy fliers. We were indignant about the strike of the munition workmen and were all of the opinion that those scoundrels earned too much money. At the end of 1917 rumors spread that we could long ago have had peace if only the Kaiser and the higher officers had wanted it. These rumors made no impression on the old soldiers. The breakdown of Russia completely dispelled our doubts that the war would end with victory. In our opinion the great offensive of the spring of 1918 would have to bring the war to a victorious end despite the poor spirit at home. In September 1918 I was again on leave in Berlin. By that time there was much open agitation. In restaurants frequented mainly by workmen the soldiers were publicly called upon not to return to the front. Many a soldier boasted of having already overstayed his leave. I was astounded, for that was desertion, and should have been punished by death. As for me, despite the fact that I had my son, born during the war, and my dear wife, I longed to return to my comrades at the front. In the Ukraine, where my regiment was situated at that time, the mood was quite normal, and we were preparing for winter. However, the officers expressed the view that the worst must be feared if the government at home should not soon take severe measures. On October 24, 1918, the officer whose orderly I was was transferred to Rumania. I followed with the horses. In upper Silesia at the Austrian border the transport train was not allowed to pass, for reasons unknown to me. My inquiries at the office of the commander received the reply that I must return to the Ukraine. This order, which I considered senseless, together with the rumors of the impending breakdown of all the fronts, made us fear the worst. In Warsaw I read in a German newspaper that the English fleet was mutinying and had hoisted the red flag. English and German sailors were said to have fraternized. The reserve battalion in a small city east of Warsaw was on the point of surrendering its army to the Poles when we arrived. The officers were disarmed and a soldiers' council was formed. I heard that this was done following the notice of the British mutiny in the German newspaper. While our transport waited for hours at the station, a horde of young Poles suddenly stormed the train, armed with German guns, and demanded our weapons too. This lawless mob had already attracted attention to itself at some distance by a wild firing of guns. The decision of the small escort of the train to defend us could not be carried out, as some had already thrown away their guns and declared they wanted to go home. Then we lost not only our weapons but also the horses and all our equipment. The soldiers' council negotiated with the Poles in the city for transportation to Germany. After many hours we were cooped up in cattle cars like herrings. At almost every station the Poles forced their way in and searched us for weapons. It was not long before every last one of us noticed that the surrender of the guns had been criminal stupidity. Then, as we were shot at and a number of us were wounded, the spirit of resistance was aroused even in those who wanted to see the war ended at any price. At the border we were received by young fellows with red arm bands whose first demand was that we remove the cockades from our hats and our shoulder straps. In the

light of the unpleasant experiences we had undergone, some
obeyed the demand, but most refused sharply. To some it
must slowly have become clear what direction this revolution
was taking. My efforts to obtain information as to where I
must turn now were in vain. The general word was: home.
An express to Berlin without equipment was made use of. The
arrival in Berlin was on schedule; discipline was still strong in
the bones of the railroad officials. We arrived at seven-thirty
A.M. The streets seemed to be dead, with an uncanny silence
brooding over everything. Now and then a shot rang out
somewhere. Sneaking figures of suspicious characters slinking
along the houses did not help to improve my spirits. Every step
of my hob-nailed boots resounded along the street. A policeman asked where I was headed, and advised me to keep close
to the houses as the shooting was still on. The day before a
severe battle with the Spartakists had taken place. Only after
I had knocked for a long time did my wife open the door, and
naturally she was overjoyed to have me at home.

This, then, was the happy return of the victorious warrior!
For years we had pictured this return and hoped to be present
at the procession through the Brandenburg Gate. This contrast
now was too great to be easily forgotten. Hungry, dirty, and
exhausted as I was, my wife succeeded in convincing me that
my report to the reserve forces could wait until the next day.

In the barracks of the Elisabether in Charlottenburg everything was topsy-turvy. The scum of the metropolis had almost
completely plundered the supply rooms during the first days.
The soldiers' council had watched, inactive, or perhaps even
participated. There were daily deliberations in the morning
in the yard of the barracks in which all persons present in the
barracks took part. The outcome of these always remained a
riddle to me. Gradually, then, the rioters also came to the conclusion that one could not completely do without order and
discipline. After a few days volunteers were sought for guards,
but since only a few could be found it was decided to pay one

mark per hour to each man. Despite the high pay the time of rest was also paid, for enough people were found only when the food cards were withdrawn.

The sudden demand for guards for all parts of the city during the day and night, while one never knew who the enemy actually was, strengthened my wish to see circumstances restored to normal. On December 3 I received my discharge. Meanwhile some measure of order had been established. Everyone discharged was supposed to receive 50 marks and a suit of military cloth. I received the money but not the suit, as there was nothing left. After a few days the money also was all gone. The employment office in Gorrmannstrasse to which I turned was overcrowded. There seemed to be no prospect of receiving work there. On the second day, however, I noticed that those seeking work almost without exception demanded impossible salaries. Most of the positions could therefore not be filled; if someone really reported, he was prevented by the others, from accepting. There were naturally no openings in my profession of servant. I was only able to get a position as handyman in a stucco firm by reporting to the man in charge outside of the employment office. I received a regular salary and was the only workman outside of two journeymen. The firm had closed up during the war and was now beginning anew. Both journeymen, one of whom had likewise just been discharged from the army, treated me with suspicion. Only gradually did I realize that both of them were Social Democrats, but dissatisfied with the present set up. The work we had to complete was urgent but they did not dare ask me to work overtime. The Social Democrats had proclaimed the eight-hour day and both had certainly joined in the demonstrations for this purpose. After I had expressed my willingness to work longer and was ready if necessary to work overtime we worked from four to six hours longer a day. On Sundays we likewise worked until one o'clock. I earned up to 100 marks per week. The work was very difficult, and we were constantly in fear of being reported. After three weeks, my former employer surprised me with a visit at Christmas time. He had just come from the field and needed a dependable servant. Conditions in Berlin were still not regulated; strikes followed upon riots and parades. My acquaintances persuaded me to accept. In the country in the backwoods of Pomerania everything seemed to be in best of order. To be sure there was even less dissatisfaction than ever before.

I had still not bothered with politics. One day I went to Köslin to shop with my brother-in-law from Berlin, who had returned from captivity and was visiting me. It was during the time when government officials also claimed the right to strike. There was talk of an intended strike of the railroad men. And then in the evening the strike had come and we could not return. We remained in the hope of getting away the next day by some sort of conveyance. To kill time, we went that evening to a meeting called by the *Schutz- und Trutzbund,*[2] of which we had read on posters. The hall was overcrowded; we could find seats only in the front row by the stage. We perceived from conversation that some were indignant, that people dared to hold a meeting directed against the Jews. A retired Captain Schmidt of Stettin made the speech, which lasted one and a half hours. During the first quarter of an hour he was often interrupted. Then he succeeded in fixing everyone's attention. It seemed to me as though scales had fallen from my eyes. There were no more interruptions; at last even those who had come with the purpose of breaking up the meeting seemed to be enthusiastic. Representatives of nine parties had applied for discussion. The first eight said things that were of no account. The last to speak was a rabbi who was received with laughter. At first he was not taken seriously at all; after a quarter of an hour he had the audience on his side. I too was once more tormented by doubts. Yet there was something in me that struggled against the Jew despite his

---

[2] An anti-Semitic organization.

convincingly uttered remarks. At last not a soul in the hall seemed to have a different opinion from the Jew. The applause grew louder and louder. Fortunately, probably inspired by the applause, he became impudent, and inveighed against Hindenburg, Ludendorff, and our two million dead. Now the ban was broken. Everyone cried: "Out with the Jew!" More quickly than he had come he was outside again. A final talk by the main speaker restored my inner balance. That evening had shown to me the danger of the Jewish intelligence. When one considered now that public opinion was created almost exclusively by Jews, one was filled with horror. Every honest German artisan was of the firm conviction that everything printed in a newspaper is true. If it were not true, the state would have to take a hand. From this evening on I occupied myself with the Jewish problem, and the more I understood it, the greater opponent of the Jews did I become. In this connection I also began to occupy myself with politics. Unfortunately I found only too soon that none of the existing parties paid any attention to the Jewish problem. Through enlightening books I found confirmation of the fact that in Germany everything in politics and economics at that time depended on Jews. I saw no way to change these conditions. For the second time I asked myself the question, "What is the meaning of life, anyhow?" Was it the will of a higher order to leave to the Jews the domination of the world? The study of the history of the Jewish people, however, convinced me that it could not possibly be God's will. Otherwise humanity would inevitably perish. I was struck by the thought, had not the Jewish people purposely been put into the world by our maker in order to force the other nations to battle so that they should be ennobled and perfected by this battle? From this thought, which was a revelation to me, there could be only one deduction: fight against the Jew by all means, as the embodiment of wickedness and evil. It was therefore important, first, to become strong oneself and firm in the belief in the victory of the true and the good, and then to stir up all the others—the weak and the lukewarm, the despairing and the despondent—and incite them to defense. But where could one hope to find the same understanding; in what camp did it exist? Class arrogance and the class struggle prevented the people in all camps, even though they had the good will, from coming together. The following example will show how great was the class difference. On the occasion of an election in 1920, my employer commissioned me to distribute to the farm workers an election appeal of the *Deutschnationale Volkspartei*[3] with the Rütli oath.[4] One of these workmen called this bait for the stupid and asked, among other things, "What would the captain say if I wanted to designate him my brother and treat him as such?" According to my own feelings this man was right, and I expressed this opinion to my employer. Indignant, the latter said that these were communistic views. My objection that according to blood, we belonged together, we were parts of one people, and, therefore, must form one large family, as the election appeal said, met with imperious rejection. His point of view was that the broad masses have to follow but dare not put themselves on one plane with the leading group. In the leading group he counted his own class and the leading personalities in industry. In the further discussion the difference between our views came to light more and more clearly. I had now become firmly convinced that the middle class parties would never be in a position to draw our nation back from the threatening abyss. In my isolation in the country I unfortunately had no opportunity to discuss these things with anyone. In general, the workman took too little interest. The Kapp *Putsch* brought new hope for middle-class circles. Among the working classes, too, there was joy in the country about its quick failure. The general opinion was that, had it

---

[3] The party of the conservatives.
[4] The oath to drive out the oppressors, allegedly sworn by William Tell at Rütli, Switzerland.

succeeded, economic pressure and class arrogance would have become greater than ever.

In view of the knowledge I had gained of that time I could not rejoice. The inflation was driving people ever closer to despair. More and more often one heard the question, "Why must we have been born at such an unfortunate time?" Is there still any sense in worrying about the future of one's children? The mad race for material possessions had taken hold of even the last decent person. The estrangement from religion became greater and greater. In 1922 I accidently got hold of a copy of the *Deutsche Tageblatt,* published by Wulle. I immediately became a regular subscriber. Wulle, Graefe-Goldebee, and Kube had founded the *Deutsch-Völkische Freiheitspartei*[5] at about that time. The aims of these men seemed to me to be the only right ones for the salvation of our fatherland. Above all I was drawn to them because they fought the Jews. In the meanwhile I had also grasped the necessity of our being national, but did not know exactly how to harmonize this with my socialist feelings. The *Deutsch-Völkische Freiheitspartei* seemed to offer a solution. About this time I read for the first time of an apparently local movement in Munich which was said to be mainly socialistic. I looked upon its adherents as a group that had split off from the Social Democrats, because of its anti-Semitical inclinations. The leader was said to be a certain Hitler, with whom, strangely enough, Ludendorff was in sympathy. I myself had no opportunity of joining. My membership in the *Schutz- und Trutzbund* was likewise without results, as I hardly had an opportunity to coöperate in the city from which I was about seventeen miles away. From my relatives in Berlin I heard that a certain Knüppel-Kunze,[6] who expressed opposition to the Jews, had many adherents there. Thus it seemed that everywhere men

[5] A short-lived anti-Semitic political party.
[6] Founder of the German Social party, which was absorbed by the National Socialist party. *Knüppel* means "stick," an allusion to the aggressive tactics of Kunze.

conscious of being Germans were working for Germany in her need, and I only regretted that I could not do my part. By my solicitation I had succeeded in securing a few subscribers for the *Deutsche Tageblatt* but they stopped after a while because the newspaper abused the Jews too much. Through the inflation everyone was even more interested in purely material things than before. Everyone thought only of himself, without considering that he could not live without the others. The poison instilled in the people for decades, with the help of the Jewish press, supported by the class arrogance of the leading classes, showed ruinous effects.

In June 1923 I changed my position because I could no longer agree with my employer, and I went to Neumark as a servant and chauffeur. In the very first week I became acquainted with the chairman of the *Deutsch-Völkische Freiheitspartei* in Fuerstenfelde. Fuerstenfelde was a small town with eleven hundred voters. The chairman was the youngest teacher in the town and still retained much enthusiasm and youthful fire. Each week a gathering of the members with guests took place in a small tavern.

There were about ten members, consisting of artisans and workmen. At first party decrees were announced and opinions heard. Then the chairman read aloud out of German books, and discussion followed. I was very much disappointed at first; not much battle spirit was evident in the debate. The following week, however, I was again impelled to go there. At any event one could express one's inward feelings. The participants were always asked at the close to bring a guest along. The number was seldom greater; to be sure new ones came, but the old were missing. After months of meetings there were hardly more members than at the time I entered. The payment of dues was a sorry chapter; warnings and reminders were always necessary. Probably in the majority of cases the impulse to join the party was not actuated by idealism but by the hope for the improvement of one's own economic condition. There were only few who never lost heart, and were always ready for great sacrifices. The chairman, especially, was untiring, and contributed his entire salary except for the modest share necessary for his own support. In the winter of 1923 we attempted the first public meeting. There were 150 present who showed great enthusiasm at the close of a lecture by a speaker from Königsberg. The two speakers in the discussion, to be sure, proved to be totally incapable. The influence of this meeting in other respects, however, was favorable. We had several new members and, besides a successful collection, several new subscribers for our newspaper. In addition we had become better known and people at last talked about us. The silver swastika pin peculiar to the party was unfortunately worn only by a few, as the others feared material disadvantages. Gradually we went over to public discussion evenings when the teacher Abeling spoke. Through his iron energy and his faith in the national idea he had already developed into a very good speaker.

In time all the people of Fuerstenfelde came to know us. The circles of active collaborators had already become considerably greater. During the time of preparation for the May elections of 1924 we succeeded in getting the present provincial leader and president of Brandenburg, Herr Kube. His extraordinarily inspiring words, his fanatical adherence to the idea, brought us a huge success. Our consequent meetings far surpassed those of the other parties even in the number attending. The influx into our ranks became greater and greater. A German evening finally also brought us the larger farmers as guests and, with that, financial security. We were constantly to be found in opposition meetings; very often Abeling spoke in the discussion. By this time we were so well known as to be feared. On the occasion of the Social Democratic meeting, a member of an education council from Küstrin spoke. Abeling naturally was not allowed to oppose his superior in the discussion. I was commissioned to watch out for our interests and, if necessary, to speak. In addition to our chairman, we unfortunately

had no one who would have dared to speak publicly. Sitting
on the first bench and well known to the leader of the meeting,
we were the target of the very skillful speech of the Social
Democratic counsellor. My notes had probably caused the
speaker to believe that I would talk afterwards. I would have
loved to do it, if only I had not been afraid of speaking. I was
boiling inside at the thought of the inciting and slanderous
remarks. When in the intermission no one applied to speak,
we nationalists were marked as cowards. Among other things
the speaker said that Fuerstenfelde had been described to him
as a citadel of the nationalists and he would at least have expected enough courage for us to defend ourselves. The participants in the meeting supported the speaker, and all eyes
were directed to me. Blushing fiercely, I was driven by some
impulse within me to mount the stage. Laughter and noise
received me, and I had time to regulate my thoughts. After
the speaker, probably firmly convinced that I would make a
fool of myself and thus of our ideas, had somewhat quieted
the meeting, he gave me the floor with the following sentence:
"Now the substitute of the Count will speak." Naturally
laughter started anew. To my own surprise I did not become
even more uncertain, but was still with an icy calm. My
thoughts worked with lightning rapidity. It was clear to me
that with these words they wanted to put us nationalists in one
class with the conservatives, and also to make me appear a
traitor to workmen. Of course I was not allowed to make a
long speech, which I could not have done anyhow. Therefore
I declared from the start that I could not speak, arousing more
laughter, but immediately added that I would permit myself
a few questions and begged for their answers. Besides three
other question I asked for a reply to the question of when Tirpitz [7] had taken his leave. Immediately silence followed. For
the speaker had maintained that Tirpitz had given the command for sharper submarine warfare. In the beginning the

_____
[7] German Admiral, head of the navy during the World War.

speaker occupied himself with the questions that were not in precise form, losing himself in many words without touching upon the heart of the matter. But one could tell that the public was not satisfied. He tried to avoid the two main questions. A shout from me won the laughters over to my side. When he had to admit at my second shout that he had been mistaken, outcries like "cheat," and so forth, were already to be heard. When he still did not refer to my clearest question, I called out, "Tirpitz was discharged in 1915. Therefore he could not have been in the command at all." Apparently the speaker did not know when Tirpitz had gone, for only after a few words with the chairman of the meeting did he say that Tirpitz had at any rate been the spiritual prime mover. Soon thereafter he finished his final word, receiving much less applause than after his main speech. I was enormously proud, especially since several people at the meeting asked me when our next discussion evening would be. At the elections in May we turned out to be the third strongest party in town, far surpassing the average for the nation. Our untiring work had thus been abundantly rewarded. A solicitation of subscribers for the *Deutsche Tageblatt* had brought us more than a hundred new readers. I even received a prize of five reichsmarks for about thirty new subscribers. Unfortunately, after a few months all these dropped out again. After the election we remained the only party that held public meetings. We succeeded in getting as speakers (among others) the Reichstag representatives Wulle, Graefe-Goldebee, and Count Reventlow.

We always had a full hall; the number of members grew constantly. In the surrounding towns, on the other hand, we had not been able to gain a foothold. We therefore determined to carry a chain of meetings into the plains in the second election campaign. Fortunately my employer had just gone on a trip for eight weeks, so that I had free time in the afternoons. Twice every week the teacher Abeling and I now rode into the villages on our bicycles bearing packets of handbills.

In distributing the sheets to the individual houses we announced orally that a meeting would take place in the evening at the inn. At the door of the inn we had hoisted a similar announcement. The meetings were usually well attended; seldom did anyone speak in the discussion. I functioned as leader of the meetings and constantly spoke the words I had learned by heart before. In this way we went through all the villages in the neighborhood, and looked forward to a gigantic success in the election. In Fuerstenfelde itself we did not hold so many meetings as we had held for the May election, but were sure of our success, as we had in any case done more than our opponents. We already had hopes of moving up to the second position. In the meantime we attended meetings in Bärwalde, Königsberg, and Küstrin, riding on our bicycles. In Küstrin, Kube spoke with great success before an audience composed mainly of Communists. On election day at the counting of the votes almost all our members were represented.

Right at the beginning we experienced a great disappointment. While we had been far ahead of the Conservative party in the May election, it was now on the same plane as we. Then it came to a race between us. First we were a few votes ahead, only to fall behind the others again. In the end we were beaten by three votes. Instead of being in the second place we had slipped to the fourth. To be sure, we had lost only a few votes. Nevertheless our spirits sank. This time our hopes lay in the open country. Neumühl, where we had been the last party to hold a meeting two days before the election, interested us especially. We had had an audience of over two hundred there. In the May elections, only six votes had been cast for us there; this time, at the most conservative estimate, we could hope for thirty.

The next morning we learned to our horror that our party had sunk from thirty-four to fourteen representatives. Our disappointment was boundless. How was it possible? At noon we then heard that in Neumühl, too, only four votes were left of the former six. That was the hardest blow; there the fault must surely have been with us. Again and again we considered what mistakes we could have made. Our opponents in Fuerstenfelde—and those were the adherents of all parties— mocked at us publicly. That alone would not have disquieted us; the fact that a great mass flight away from us was beginning, including people whom we had reckoned among the most faithful, was the most difficult thing to bear. For the first time we occupied ourselves seriously with the Hitler movement, of which we had heard the most contradictory rumors. The *Deutsche Tageblatt* seldom wrote anything about it. I read with the keenest interest the report of the trial and excerpts of Hitler's great speech of defense. According to all that one heard, he seemed a man of great capacities.

In 1925 we noticed that things were no longer as they should be within our party. The obstacles we had to overcome, however, only made us the more stubborn and morose, as they always do in life. With a few loyal members we set out to reconstruct what remained to us. Our main task now was sale of the newspaper. It was a strange thing that a subscriber seldom remained faithful to us more than two months. When he was questioned, the opinion was usually expressed that we were inciting too much against the Jews. One did not love the Jew; indeed one even rejected him, but one considered the reporting of Jewish vileness persecution. The argument went like this; we condemned the lies and falsifications in the Marxist press, and therefore we must not likewise make use of such methods. In view of the German's feeling for justice, this attitude was comprehensible. The guileless German simply did not believe that anyone could consciously and systematically engage in persecution. Abeling and I now occupied ourselves more and more with the Jewish problem, which is the problem of all problems, and without the solution of which humanity cannot grow well. On our discussion evenings we occupied ourselves almost exclusively with the Old Testament, the Talmud, and *Schulchan-aruch*. The circle taking an interest in these matters soon increased, because we were going to the root of the matter. We ourselves studied it more and more, and came to see what was necessary. Fellow Germans, grow stronger in your German spirit than the Jew in his Judaism; then we will be the victors. In the course of a year we made good progress with our stubborn and persistent work. One day my employer, the Count, sent for me, and warned me in a fatherly fashion not to be so active in politics. In his opinion one needed the necessary rudiments for it, in the way of formal education and history.

As far as a knowledge of history is concerned, I am of the same opinion; only I demanded that practical use be made of the knowledge, which cannot be said for our professional politicians. The Count feared that if our philosophy were not explained adequately, the working classes might be driven to Communism. Besides he considered it a great mistake to draw nationalists to our cause, as it made the dissension in the nation even greater. My point of view was naturally different, as I knew only too well the sins of the so-called "nationalists." I hope that the Count has today changed to a different view, as a result of the mighty work of unification of our Leader. To his credit I must say, that had all of his class behaved as he did, Social Democracy would never have become such a powerful force in Germany. I was not hindered any further in my political work, but something had come between us, which prevented us from being on the old footing. The sale of the car in November 1925 suddenly forced me to change my position. I was sorry to part from my new friends and co-workers.

On December 1, 1925, I went to Kienberg near Nauen as a chauffeur on the estate. Much work prevented me from reporting to the party in Nauen. No transfer was made by the party, and so I lost my membership. However, I remained true to my newspaper and thus kept myself informed. Almost all the workers and employees on the estate belonged to the *Stahlhelm*. As the *Stahlhelm* set itself up to be anti-Semitic, I joined. Unfortunately it was only a club, like any other; in Kienberg it differed in no respect from a soldiers' club. I could seldom take part in the monthly meetings, as I was kept back by my work.

In January 1926 I had my first contact with National Socialists. Seven new carriers were taken on the estate, clad in brown shirts, and singing old soldiers' songs. These men staged propaganda marches on Sundays. Naturally I was vitally interested, and revealed myself to them as a nationalist. The leader made great efforts to persuade me to join the Party. The personal appearance of his colleagues unfortunately differed greatly from that of the leader, and therefore I found it difficult to convince myself. My acquaintances and even my own wife constantly impressed on me the impossibility of my project. From others I received the information that in case of my joining, I would probably lose my position. The carriers were of even lower rank than the laborers, and it was considered impossible to associate with them constantly. At that time my conduct was not yet clear to me, but today I know that it was only egoism and, in the final analysis, cowardice, that prevented me from joining. I myself had class arrogance, no matter how strange that may sound; I considered myself higher than those fellow-countrymen who were only carriers. And I, as a nationalist, had dared to reproach others with class arrogance. It is through this experience that I know how deeply rooted class arrogance is in the German people. Only he who has himself fought this battle can estimate what an enormous achievement our Leader has accomplished in his work of unification. I also know that it is not out of a lack of good will that some fellow-countryman cannot find the right tone even today.

The seven National Socialists disappeared as suddenly as they had appeared. They had been noticed because of their propaganda and had to leave because of pressure from the owner of the estate.

In 1927 I took an active part in the *Stahlhelm* rally in Berlin. Then doubts again arose in me whether the German workman could ever be won over to the nation. Hatred met us especially in the north, where there were not even humans any more; they acted like wild animals. As a reader of the *Deutsche Tageblatt* I had again been influenced to such an extent that in 1928 I once more voted for the *Völkische Block*. Aside from the three votes of my family there was only one other in the town. The remark of the estate inspector who was present at the election shows how little known we were by that time. His words, literally, were: "What kind of party is that anyway? What kind of idiots can they have been?"

In July 1928 I was discharged because there was no work for me. After long efforts I got a position in the west end of Berlin as housekeeper and garage keeper. There I had so much work the first year and a half that I hardly had time to read a newspaper. Every single day, Sundays as well as weekdays, my work began at three o'clock in the morning or earlier. From five P.M. it continued until nine P.M. In the locked house the door had to be opened from seven A.M. to eight P.M. The bad air in the cellar garage made the physical strain of washing the auto even greater. At the beginning of 1930 the work became somewhat lighter, as the economic situation became worse. I now became a reader of the *Völkische Beobachter* and the *Angriff*.[8] With astonishment I saw from these what progress National Socialism had already made. My passion for politics immediately awoke again and drove me to various meetings. Then, upon my return, I had to start in working at once to make up for what had been omitted during the evening.

I heard Dr. Goebbels for the first time in the Friedrichshain, when the Communist Heinz Neumann spoke in the discussion.

---

[8] The Berlin daily of the National Socialist party, edited by Goebbels.

From that time on I was completely devoted to him and to the National Socialist party.

On the way home I first became acquainted with the underhandedness of the disciples of Moscow. After the close of the meeting, during which, contrary to our expectations, there had not been a battle in the hall, the whole neighborhood rang with cries of *Rot-Front* and *Heil Moskau*. Crowds of people were blocking the way as far as the Königstor. I do not know whether the weak *S.A.* troop got home unharmed. I became involved in a political discussion with a passerby. By the questions he asked he appeared to me to be one who sympathized with us. He even wanted to know how one could join the Party. Unfortunately I could not give him any information. Engrossed in the conversation, we often stood still, and I was pleased when others stopped to listen. I had the feeling that I was convincing the people, and became more and more eager. Close to the Alexanderplatz, near the place where men were building, I noticed that I had imperceptibly been forced from the sidewalk into the road. A close circle of eight to ten men surrounded me and kept trying to push me farther off. Immediately it occurred to me that besides myself no one had said a word for a long time. As in a vision I realized what danger threatened me; the faces about me seemed to be contorted like masks. Suddenly I called out a name in a certain direction, which caused all heads to turn that way. At the same time I made room for myself with my hands and elbows. A great leap freed me from the circle. During the quick run that followed I noticed for the first time that the streets were already completely empty. Luckily a police patrol took notice and my pursuers stayed back. Threatening fists and imprecations assured me that I had not been the victim of a delusion. Those then were the people whom we wanted to convert with mental weapons. I only wished that every complacent citizen who thought only of his own comfort had once been in a similar position. His opinion about the noise-loving Nazis

would probably have changed quickly. The result of this experience was the firm conviction that I, too, must now become
a member. But my entrance was delayed by over three quarters
of a year. At every new attempt a new hindrance arose.
Other highlights of my activity outside the Party include my
participation in the demonstration against the film *All Quiet
on the Western Front.*

The Reichstag election in September 1930 was under the
star of the Nazis. Paint on the sidewalks was not spared. On
houses, street lamps, trees and telegraph poles notices were
stuck, pointing out the importance of the election. I was so
bold as to prophesy fifty to sixty seats for the *N.S.D.A.P.* in
the circle of my acquaintances. At the count of votes one could
tell by the glum looks of the Jewish and Social Democrat
watchers that they had not counted on so many National
Socialists. Listening in at home, probably like everyone else
in the world, we were astounded at the result. From twelve
representatives, we had leaped to 107! At first we could hardly
understand it. We were then and there in a position to govern.
Even the regret that I had not helped actively enough could
not lessen my joy. What enthusiasm must have reigned in the
halls belonging to the *S.A.*! The next day people spoke only of
the great victory. The Jews were broken-hearted; after the
first two days their usual impudence vanished.

On January 11, 1931 I succeeded at last in being accepted
in the Party. Every week a so-called educational evening was
called in a restaurant. I was received there with extraordinary
warmth. The spirit was one of pure comradeship, and from
the very first moment I felt at home. As I learned then, these
evenings were mainly for officers, but I was allowed to participate.

After that I did not miss an evening. No comparison could
be made with our evenings in the *Völkische Freiheitspartei.*
Here there was the strictest discipline, and yet there were only
open, frank faces. At first I could hardly believe that a janitor

was local group leader. Here, in the west end of Berlin, where 90 per cent of the population were intellectuals! Nevertheless, neither envy nor ill will could be perceived. This was how I had always imagined the true community of the people.

Unfortunately I fell ill in February and had to go to the hospital for five weeks. There I had the opportunity to study Adolf Hitler's *Mein Kampf* properly. Even at that time I was confirmed in the opinion that the book must be the Bible of all National Socialists. The more I became absorbed in it, the more was I gripped by the greatness of the thoughts expounded therein. I felt that I was eternally bound to this man. Only one thing oppressed me, the thought that I could not repeat these ideas with the same passion and fanatical conviction with which they must have been written. After my illness I was soon offered the office of local group leader, which I accepted with great pride. I fully realized the importance of this office. Every fellow German who enters the Party must first be made thoroughly familiar with the philosophy of Adolf Hitler. The group leader has this responsible task. The more deeply he himself has penetrated into the idea, the more quickly will the party comrades entrusted to him be prepared for voluntary coöperation. He must be the soul physician of every individual. When I had been confirmed in my position by the district office, I had to give a speech with the theme: "How does the local group leader build up his cell?" At the close of my remarks, the chief of propaganda expressed the opinion that I had the makings of a speaker. I had already had a similar idea, but I was still much afraid of making a public appearance. Nevertheless, I could not rid myself of the thought, and I set out to work out lectures and learn them by heart. I made the first attempts in cell meetings of from ten to fifteen men. These came out rather poorly, as I often lost the thread of my ideas. I made the attempt again and again, and soon noticed that at points where I could give free rein to my inner feelings my audience was also engrossed.

The year 1931 went by with educational evenings, membership and mass meetings. The number of members increased steadily. The two-months plan of Dr. Goebbels doubled the Party in Berlin. In the meantime we carried on propaganda with handbills and newspapers among our fellow-countrymen. Although it was the task of every party comrade to help, in most instances the work was left to the leader of the local group. In the first half year one could not expect such work of new members coming mainly from academic circles. It did not come hard to the working man, as he was used to menial jobs; he did not have to overcome any inhibitions. As a man who had up to then been considered inferior, he was used to humble work, such as throwing handbills into letter boxes. The college men who had joined us out of idealism were, to be sure, also ready for this after half a year. Anyone who admitted allegiance to National Socialism during the time of battle had by that fact alone accomplished a great deed. Anyone from the middle-class circles who devoted himself to all the small tasks was certainly a fine fellow. For we were almost all outlawed at that time; even in our own families sharp contrasts led to conflicts. Our bread and wages were very often at stake. My uniform, that is, the brown shirt, I could never put on in my own house before the assumption of power. I had to seek the homes of friends for this purpose. When we appeared in ranks at certain hours of the morning or evening, it was even more dangerous. Often the entire family had to keep watch so that we could get away and come back unrecognized. One of my happiest memories will always be that of a two-day march to Mecklenburg with the reserve *S.A.* To get leave, to be sure, I had to have a relative die. A Jew living in the house thought he recognized me on my return and reported it to my employer; but I convinced him that the informer must have been mistaken.

Meanwhile I made progress with my development as a speaker. From January 1932 to February 1933 I engaged in a correspondence course for speakers, conducted by the present secretary of state, Herr Reinhard. Through this course I obtained the rudiments of extemporaneous public speaking. On the occasion of a special invitation from the circles of the philistines, I was allowed to speak about the "Principles of the National Socialist Philosophy and Its Effects on a Workman." This speech gave me the greatest satisfaction of anything I have ever done. I had the opportunity to show the middle class in a matter of fact form, without any animosity, how seriously they had sinned against the German people in treating the workman as an inferior. I was especially happy that through this speech I won over a highly respected university man as a true friend and comrade.

The year 1932 saw us rushing from one election campaign to another. Every campaign brought us a new victory. Through battle to victory and to comradeship—that we can truly say of this year. Class arrogance had been completely eliminated among us in the Party. The inward contentment for which I had struggled through the years became a reality for me in 1932. On the other hand, how did things look among the people outside of our ranks? Class arrogance and hatred became even greater; still, in spite of all, the adherents of the bourgeois parties imagined that they were nationalists. People still thought that an emphasis on nationalism sufficed. They spoke of the people and meant the others; they approved of the state, meaning themselves. They claimed leadership for themselves, and demanded that the others follow. They worried about their own good and that of their own children, but thought nothing of the good of their followers. They were indignant that the others were men without a country, but did not stop to think that the leadership they claimed signified a duty toward their following. They held every man who possessed money and a good suit to be a worthy citizen. They judged according to certificates and examinations passed; they did not regard character. Thus it came about that every shrewd Jew who mangled the German language became a citizen. The honest, reliable, German workman stood aside and froze in a state of this type. Even today, class arrogance is the worst enemy of all enlightenment. Later on, therefore, as a leader responsible on a small scale, I preached the practical mode of life to my party comrades as the basis of our philosophy, and attempted to live up to it. Then in November 1932, when we apparently suffered a defeat in the election, the real fighters did not waver. We knew that our hour must come. Our fanatical belief in victory would have to weaken our opponents in time.

The assumption of power came as a surprise. The joy bursting out of hearts glowing with passion must have been gleaming in people's eyes. How often before had we been asked, with a lack of comprehension: "Well, what do you get out of all the work, the sacrifices and worries about the Party?" Now we could answer: "We have helped to win the Third Reich. We have washed away the shame of 1918, and we have marched in victory through the Brandenburg Arch. Some day we shall go down in history as the first champions and prophets of a new, better age."

To be sure, if some believed that the goal had been reached, they found they had been deceived. The work continued the next day and will go on to the end of our lives. Our Leader, Adolf Hitler, would not have had to shoulder so great a responsibility if creating order had been his whole aim. The state of the future will assert itself through the new philosophy in every sphere of life. The personality that is to support and lead the state must be steadily shaped and developed; unfortunately, only a minority of the present generation can be considered for this. But one thing we already know today: the battle carried on by international Judaism with the help of degenerate people in Germany will lead to the ruin of its perpetrators. The Jew Rathenau once said: "The history of the world would have lost its meaning if the German army had returned victorious from the battlefield." But we say: "The history of the world would have lost its meaning if Judaism, with its corroding spirit, the embodiment of all evil, were to win the victory over the true and the good encompassed in Adolf Hitler's idea."

My belief is that our Leader, Adolf Hitler, was given by fate to the German nation as our savior, bringing light into darkness.

3. *The Story of a Soldier*

The description of our lives presents a cross-section of German history. Anyone who realizes this consciously places himself in a relationship to the great event he has helped bring about, which determines his point of view with regard to his whole life, his responsibility toward himself, his family, his nation, the present and the future—in short, toward Germany.

To set down my life history means to justify myself. It also means to reflect on what I am, that I *am* a National Socialist, by birth rather than by conversion. It means admitting the consequence that I became and am an *S.S.* man, and that I want nothing better than to serve in a black Hitler regiment.

I always was a National Socialist. The name of the concept is immaterial. Today I know that I was a National Socialist before there was a name for that idea. Today, when the concept and the name have been established, I know that I am a National Socialist and will remain one. There was never any question of compulsion. No outward pressure was brought to bear on me; nor did reason dictate this necessity. My heart commanded it. Even as today the result of long experience is the longing for a free, strong Germany and love of my Leader. No genuflections, no knavery, but honesty, and calm loyalty in service to the man to whom I have bound myself by oath, and to whom I shall keep faith, God standing by me, whatever other doubts may assail me, whatever others may do.

All my contemporaries had witnessed an unprecedented historical development.

Such an abundance of fateful happenings were so compressed in our decades that hundreds of years cannot equal them for action and significance.

Thus I actually have not lived a single life. It was more nearly like three long, full lives. The fourth life came into being on June 30, 1934.[1] A world was extinguished in me when on that day guns were put into my hands and those of my comrades. And a new world came into existence; a new life was born. What became of glamour, rank, and externals? When avenging shots pierced the traitors, what remained of their might, their titles and honors? Towering high above them stood the simple loyalty of the black-garbed soldiers of Adolf Hitler, unadorned with rank and high-sounding names!

This view of things, together with the will to be the Leader's simple man for better or for worse, is worthy of the fourth life. Office, honors, and dignity pale beside it.

Three lives were closed on June 30, 1934. The first lasted up to the war; the second was taken up with the war; the third was filled with the misery of post-war times and lighted by hope, by joy in the battle and joy in the victory.

The first life

I was born in Pankow on November 10, 1886. My father was a mason, my mother a laundress. There were six of us brothers and sisters. Two died. When my brother was laid out in his coffin, people were shocked that I whistled in the streets. I did not then understand death, for my brother's blue eyes were not closed. Buttons had been laid on the dead stars, for no one could see these eyes that I looked at secretly to discover why they were said to be dead. I was four years old. My father carried the heavy burden, the little coffin, to the

---

[1] The day of the "purge," on which Roehm, Schleicher, and others were shot.

cemetery, with the straps over his shoulders. A carriage could not be considered.

I was baptized. That was no occurrence in a sated, middle-class life. Our life, however, was neither bourgeois nor sated. It was a life of misery, and threatened to sink completely into the world of the proletariat.

My father was an enemy of the church. I do not know whether my baptism took place with my father's consent. But my brothers and sisters were baptized secretly. My father was not allowed to know about it. When he found out, there were scenes I would rather not describe. But I draw quiet conclusions from them when I want to see clearly where lay the spiritual need of my parental home and of my youth, and when I try today to comprehend the outlook of some fellow countrymen.

Mother and children prayed, while our father sought to prevent us from doing so. All this is no discredit to my dead father. We did not understand him, and he probably did not know what an effect these conflicts had on our childish being. I learned to think more seriously than other children. I read socialist writings at an early age. Thus a conflict arose in me because of my own religious feelings, when clergymen and teachers filled up religious lessons with formulas and sayings. It annoyed me to have to learn the history of the people of Israel. I wanted to hear about the German people. And for many years, without denying God, I did not go to church. It is still painful to me to remember one experience that filled me with such a distaste for the church. My sister, so emaciated by consumption that she was hardly recognizable, lay on her death bed at the age of nineteen. My sister was a pious, believing child who knew that the gates of eternity were opening. She had asked for last spiritual consolation. My weeping mother begged the pastor who had christened us to administer the sacrament to the dying girl. But the clergyman refused, with the statement: "I cannot enter your house, for your husband is a Social Democrat and an unbeliever!"

The Lord took my sister to Himself with a smile, but for mother and us older brothers and sisters, something was broken that is not yet healed. My father, however, I now regarded differently, even though I could not follow him.

My father was a Social Democrat. I early learned what this meant. Very early I learned to judge causes, and to think justly while others only shook their heads over effects. The observation of these things could only lead to honest conclusions. I saw facts from the inside. Other people did not live in our narrow confines. All of us—parents and children—slept in one room. I saw what happened with wakeful eyes. Others did not see that. I saw—and in my mind's eyes still see—my father standing at the window, breathing on the frost on the window-panes. Those were cold winters that made one's hands freeze. Buildings were untouched and there were no earnings. There was no unemployment relief then. I remember how, at the birth of my youngest brother, my mother was given salt herring and potatoes to eat right after her confinement. I was forced to become acquainted with the contrasts existing not only between different social castes, but also in all classes of society. Even during my school days I felt this bitterly. We went to school barefoot. Though our clothes were clean and whole, the sons of middle-class families appeared with collars and shoes. Only too often I was made to feel that this gave them an advantage, though such superiority was not justified by achievements or capacities. I learned easily and remembered well, so that years later, on the occasion of an anniversary, my old principal expressed the opinion that in his long years in office no other boy so gifted had been entrusted to his guidance. The old gentleman remained a fatherly friend to me until his death, and I to this day remember him with emotion and warm gratitude.

I had to work from my ninth year on. Today I stop at

every bowling alley to watch the pin boy, because I know how badly his back hurts when midnight comes and the bowlers start one game after another, and how parched his throat is after being exposed to dust hour after hour. The teachers were out of luck as far as my homework was concerned. However, a quick perception came to my aid, so that I did not have to work nearly so hard as others who actually appeared with carefully plotted compositions and arithmetic problems, trying to be model boys. I never was a model boy. I received plenty of beatings for my pranks. Up to the time of my confirmation, I was employed by a merchant for whom I acted as house servant; actually, however, I played a lot in the streets. Thanks to this, I did not forget how to laugh while a child. I brooded about it more and more and found the solution as to why my father was such an ardent Social Democrat. I saw with my own eyes that now and then a demand for a raise was justified; and I also saw how bitterly one had to struggle for it. I saw only too often the honest working man being exploited by the supporters of capitalism. I felt most bitter about the way the puffed-up bourgeois passed by the fellow German, who was only a workman with matter of fact gestures. My own view of life and my own observations of life led me to see that the class struggle was not a condition brought about by the working group. The middle class created the prerequisites for it, while on the other side false prophets found it only too easy to drive the wedge so fatefully amid the German people.

We loved our father dearly, even though he had little time for us. Party activities engrossed him. I know that millions of workers had a holy faith in socialism at the time even if the concepts of liberty and fraternity were merely abstract notions. For no matter what was preached about them in the saloons and on pay evenings, they existed only in the family circle. Consequently, I came to realize at the early age of twelve or thirteen that a great gap existed between theories, as set forth, for example, in Bebel's *Woman and Socialism,* and the practical way of life among the comrades. If the cause itself was falsified here on purpose, realization of this was naturally also prevented, while those who were better clothed were only too anxious to keep up the disparity until it grew into psychical catastrophe for us. Thus we felt that we were young, good Germans and knew that our fathers and mothers were honest people who had been industrious, had cheated no one, and had had the best of intentions, but could not overcome class arrogance, which repeatedly set up new obstacles for them to hurdle.

In the evening when we sat around our father after he returned from work, we picked the hardened sprays of cement out of his woolen jacket. Even then I formed the resolution to do my part so that one day in Germany the German man would be judged on his own merit: that the judgment might not be formed according to his suit, but that it would be the *man* himself that counted—his courage, his decency and his honesty. Today that stage has been reached. In the framework of my activities, this youthful memory remains the basis of my deeds and my cares.

I was supposed to become a mason. The urging of my old teacher took effect, and I was sent into the office of a dye factory as an apprentice. At that time not so much value was placed on a diploma. The employers came to the principal of the public school and had him introduce boys whom they took into their business as apprentices. Those masters did not fare badly.

Those years of apprenticeship were times of ferment for me. More and more I felt the crippling effect of narrow limits, psychological as well as spatial. For example, I tormented myself unspeakably about always telling the truth under all circumstances. How often was I cruelly punished while others emerged unscathed under similar circumstances because they knew how to cheat. Working at the desk seemed too much for me. I just could not learn to sit still. Often when my seat behind the account books was empty, I was found in the stables, at play with puppies or in conversation with the sooty workmen behind their machines. I passed the stage of reading trashy literature long before my years of apprenticeship. There was no book of travel I had not read. I knew by heart how many inhabitants there were in each square mile of every state of the United States of America. My intention matured to emigrate as soon as possible, and in the quiet noonday hours when accounts rested, the apprentice stared out over the open fields, with a passionate longing in his heart for the blue flower of distance.

My whole nature had always been that of the soldier, and since running away was not possible, all my longings were turned toward becoming a soldier. Naturally I wanted to enlist. My father gave me permission to serve only two years, so that, if it could not be avoided, at least I would have the shortest possible time to wear the gay coat. I myself had this certificate stamped at the police station, but first had squeezed in between two lines: "or three years' voluntary service." So I deceived my father and because of my love for soldiering committed a real falsification of a document. With this certificate I reported to the regiment of the *Gardes du Corps* and strangely enough, was accepted. I say strangely, for the other volunteers were introduced by their fathers and were "stout peasants" *(dicke Bauern)* as it were. When my father learned with what regiment I was going to serve there were unbelievable scenes. My departure took place with words uttered about me and "my" Kaiser which I cannot repeat today.

I did not take this so tragically because, according to my expectations, now the sun of a fresh and gay cavalry life would rise. How sadly was I disappointed! The atmosphere of stable odors, horse smell and sweat and leather, the unrelenting stiffness and the lack of comradeship between the older and the younger generation horrified me. There was at that time a custom that those longer in service "bring their new comrades in line" with ropes and straps. Everything in me revolted, and I always defended myself to the last gasp from maltreatment, until, after proofs of my decision were presented, they left me completely in peace, because, in the opinion of my narrow-minded comrades, it was now established that I was a "Red." Then they called that "being a Red"; today I know that even as a young man I was a National Socialist. I came there with a warm heart, to serve my Kaiser and my Fatherland, but I did not find a teacher, a friend or an adviser among my superiors. To fit myself into my uniform and to accustom myself to it took a long time. Then, of course, I looked upon many things with different eyes, and I passed over much with a smile that before had appeared intolerable to me. I often tortured myself with brooding about how it might some time be changed, that "being a superior" should not depend on sequence or age. There were noncommissioned officers who did not treat me very cordially, yet I saw these same officers quarreling as to whose column I should be assigned to before we rode away to field practice. For I could remember and repeat the whole field-service lesson which the cavalry captain gave only once. When I became clerk for the squadron every thing suddenly changed for me: all the superiors were my friends. It was quite possible that the clerk could do them all a favor some time. The conclusion I later drew was that I had done the men an injustice. They probably all tried honestly, as well as they could, to do their duty, and it was not their fault that the education of the men was placed in the hands of the non-commissioned officers. The corps of officers, as I realized later, was primarily recruited from the very highest class of society. The burdens of the barracks were borne by the non-commissioned officers. The thought often passed through my mind what things would look like if some day we were struck by a severe blow of fate, and what kind of face this feudalism would present then. And as we later experienced and witnessed, it was easy to cry "Hosanna," it was easy always to swear new oaths of loyalty, always to promise renewed devotion, as long as times were good. But it was hard—and this test was but seldom passed—to devote oneself to one's leader to the end of changing the course of destiny through steadfastness until death. My thoughts were fulfilled in all too horrible a manner. Of the splendid suite, not one died for his imperial lord in November 1918. The heritage of this experience was put upon us as an obligation; with this heritage and its burden we rode into the war and—above all, with this heritage we returned home.

The second life began

Little by little the circumstances of my service at Potsdam changed. At first they were oppressive and brought with them the resultant disappointment, grimness, and inward conflict; the second half of my service gave me unlimited joy through its gayety. The whole gave me a feeling of strength and assurance. The old cherished plan of emigrating was now to become reality. Just standing on the spring-board of the world, however, my father lay down on his sick bed. I had to help my mother, and I had to renounce the distant lands. Nevertheless I could not stay at home either. So I once again enlisted as a soldier. I served with the Westphalian Regiment of Cuirassiers. I served with passionate interest and truly led no life of carousing. Out of my salary my mother also received support. There it was again, that ever renewed observation of contrasts. I knew what I could do. I saw what other men around me and above me achieved, and I was painfully aware of the impossibility of my ever becoming an officer, despite my suitability. Yes, it even pained me that a social distinction was visible between the lieutenant of the Cuirassier-Regiment and the lieutenant of the infantry. When after long, fateful years I was discharged as a lieutenant, I felt and still feel today deep sorrow that I did not receive that rank while the possibility still existed of making the most of it. I say this not out of presumption or arrogance, but out of the wish I had of meeting all the demands that were made on a field-lieutenant.

I did not indulge in self-pity either as a common soldier or as an officer. Had my attitude been different, I might have made many things more comfortable for myself. For me, service in arms was the supreme expression of manliness; to me it was an inexhaustible source of joy and strength. I clung to every capable officer with glowing veneration; for any other I was a thorn in the flesh. I was a very uncomfortable subordinate.

All considerations and observations and all comparisons disappeared when the people streamed to take up arms in August 1914. We did not bother about politics; the subject was completely strange to us. I saw only the flaming enthusiasm flaring up about our ride into the hostile lands. At last all Germany was behind us. At last everything was pointed toward the existence or non-existence of the unnamable, of that which we longed for with all our heart, of the holy thing! The word "Fatherland" is easily said. For me that was not all. Now things would come right, I thought and felt, for now the mason and the scholar marched side by side and there were no more distinctions. The man once called a Social Democrat now rode beside us through the flames. He did not exactly cheer; but he was there and that sufficed. At last my comrade, at last! And they were good comrades with whom life had dealt hard, at the vise and in the fire-spraying foundry and in the coal mines. They made an eve of settlement; the nation marched; the great revolution of the Germans began. My father, the old dyed-in-the-wool socialist, the enemy of the church and the Kaiser, later enlisted for service. That he was refused was due to his state of health. I was intoxicated with joy, but I was only a little non-commissioned officer, and I could not suspect how necessary was the capable stateman at the side of the capable soldier. I could not know how destructively incapable were those who seemed unreachable, even in our thoughts. The great thing that began to grow there was too great for the political leaders of Germany to master.

I marched through the war, saw battlefields that made cheerfulness die. At the front I observed the phases of the mighty struggle, and as we stood alone beneath the grenade tracks, ragged and dirty, embittered and defiant, with the mask of death under every steel helmet—then only did I begin to understand Germany. Thus the revolution rose out of the craters of the battlefield. We sat in trenches and heard of lost prisoners, and decaying homeland. We heard the shirkers laugh. But we were silent, because we could say nothing, and because there was no one there to whom we could have said anything. We saw the horror approaching, but we were helpless against it. We felt that the Frenchman and the Tommy were not our worst enemies, but that worse, poisonous things were being brewed in the witches' kitchens at home. And when in November 1918 we marched through Lüttich—I was with the Seventy-seventh Reserve Infantry Regiment at the time—under Red flags—my heart seemed to break.

Then we were told that English fleet had approached ours with Red flags waving. *Sancta simplicitas.* I believed it and said to my men: "Now the greatest thing in the history of the world since the life of Christ has happened: soldiers who fought this terrible war are ending it themselves, and the subterfuges of those who heard no whistle of bullets are at an end." I was ashamed when I learned that they had lied to us, ashamed not of myself but of the others, ashamed that they were Germans, just as I have at times since then been ashamed of Germans.

The march home was the bitterest experience I have ever had. My second life was coming to a close. I was a broken man, on the point of losing himself, who could no longer find

God. I have preserved a picture of those days. So that was how I looked! I cannot recognize myself. Out of fear and courage, out of storm, enthusiasm and defiance, out of blood and dirt, out of hope and misery I returned, still with love in my heart. But when we saw Germany, the ground sank under my feet. We soldiers of the front walked in a thick night, in boundless darkness. We shook hands for the last time and passed others by; they did not know us.

The third life

Many thousands had the experience. He who has the gift of letting things slide off is better off. I often asked myself the question whether I ought to envy them, or whether it is a favor, a distinction to have experiences go deeply and—as is the case with me—not to be able to rid oneself of them. I cannot rid myself of the pictures of the comrades whom we buried. I cannot free myself of the thought that they are calling. I cannot free myself of the idea that the work of the survivors is not yet at an end, until the strength of the fighter is exhausted forever. I was like one recovering slowly, very slowly. And when I again possessed a little strength, I was at it again. For a few weeks I was on the soldiers' council to try to avert the worst, but disgusted and injured, I sought other ways. I was there at the battle against the Spartakus. That was the best medicine fate had to dispense.

Then the longing for a wife began, with the thought of carrying a boy in my arms. It seemed as if professional soldiers faced nothingness. So I grasped at the least thing that was offered me. I became a gendarme, only for a few months. It was not so very difficult to get a position as a government employee; one was offered me by the community of Pankow. Slowly a new, different life began to unfold itself. I became an assistant city clerk on probation, and married a good German woman. Our first home was in a basement. I received several other offers of positions and perhaps with a different choice of profession I might have led a splendid life. We heard the guns directed at the building of the police department thundering away. But I was so sick of the whole business, so miserably sick that my surplus energy, as far as one can speak of such a thing, was devoted to the tilling of a bit of land. In my service I tasted to the full all the bitterness of being a beginner. Often the fact that I would not bow down threatened to break my hopes. I again became an uncomfortable subordinate.

Softly the curtain before my eyes disappeared. The inflation took my young wife's heritage, honestly earned savings that had been worked for, inherited from her brother who had fallen in battle. The party mismanagement shot high; it disgusted me. I tried various ways of finding manliness and manly action. Many a circle was open to me, but I found nothing but disappointment everywhere. Bearers of power in the Socialist party courted me. They promised me a tempting future. But when this became the subject of conversation I thought of the fairy tale of world brotherhood and of the lie of the waving red flags on the English battleships, and I saw the sea of flags in Lüttich. I heard the cries of my dead comrades. Gradually passivity became unbearable for me. I was a member of the "Association of Nationally Minded Soldiers." It was prohibited. The *"Jungdo"* [2] tempted me; the leadership could not make me enthusiastic. I became a member of the *Stahlhelm,* was soon a local group leader, increased the local group from some forty men to three hundred, became district group leader, and, when I left the *Stahlhelm,* left behind me twelve hundred comrades. That was something, the Red north of Berlin! The battle for Germany's fate and all that went wrong in spite of most sincere honest effort cast me on the sick bed. I had broken down completely and for months could not move a limb, yet it was a blissful condition. Even if my body failed me, I enjoyed myself like a child over every

---

[2] A nationalistic youth organization.

circle that the sun painted on the walls through the window panes. Progress was unspeakably slow. My old comrade in battle, Prince August Wilhelm, often sat at my bedside, to which no one else was admitted except my physician. Hardly was I back on my legs when I went head on, back into the foaming flood. An argument with the leaders of the *Stahlhelm* followed. It was my idea that a new party should be founded for which millions were hoping, in which soldiers set the pace and whose aim it should be to destroy the party disorder. The returned memorandum with the marginal remarks remains a valued souvenir, for me. I made a renewed assault and wanted to make the suggestion to the leader of the *Stahlhelm,* that he sit down at a table with Hitler. That first of all. The result would then probably be that two columns would march under Hitler's leadership, a grey one and a brown one. Then let them forbid one or the other. We could march separately, for the bulwarks we had to storm would be the same.

I was definitely snubbed. This led me to seek membership in the Hitler movement. My departure from the *Stahlhelm* was very painful, for I now had to leave my comrades to their own devices. I was not a rebel; therefore I persuaded no one to join me. Many an experience had welded me together with my comrades; again dead men stood between us and before us. The battle of Germany's freedom demanded a tribute of us too. All that, however, I left behind me, because I saw clearly that once again the existence or non-existence of Germany was at stake, and that there was only one solution: Hitler.

It was not difficult to see that the system of parties and liberalism which only embellished Marxism had to break down, if Germany itself was not to be plunged forever into the abyss of ruin. It was not hard to see and to draw conclusions from the fact that a moral basis was lacking among the men in power. They clung only to external power. They grew fat and satisfied, vain and arrogant. Every thinking man, when, like myself, he had learned to judge causes in order to comprehend future effects, could see that the foundation itself was decayed and therefore not capable of bearing weight. No nation can be built upon such ground. They wanted to force us to attend their constitutional celebrations. I resisted. They knew I was a National Socialist, but they could not get me. The indifferent crowd of my colleagues put on their top hats like good fellows and mimicked the citizens who agreed with the state. Like everyone in my circle of comrades, I waited. We old party comrades realized that the day would come when we could not save ourselves from being National Socialists. People would again put on their high hats, again go to celebrations like good fellows to express their agreement with the state. We knew it. This sort of person will always exist. They would also be there if the Red Front were in our place. They scream, but they accomplish nothing.

For me to become a member of the National Socialist party in 1930 meant to risk everything. As a government employee I had nothing to win but everything to lose. Years earlier I had founded secret cells of dependable persons, but for the sake of carefulness had made them such that only certain individuals knew me. Thus we were protected from betrayal. My own brother, however, I could not protect against fate. He was a member of my cell. Even if one could not prove anything against him except that in a sudden search of his house he had an additional insurance card in a different name, this sufficed to have him discharged in disciplinary proceedings. Those were bad days when the officials of the Intelligence Service came among us. My mother's health was seriously affected as a result. My brother was on the street for a year and a half. To get at me, the terrorism of the Red gentlemen had succeeded in having my sister discharged from her position in the employment bureau. My savings had shrunk to fifty marks. How often did I walk through the weekly market and consider what trade I was in a position to begin if destiny struck at me. It was close enough. The secret police were already on my heels. In my neighborhood inquiries were made as though it were a case of unmasking a serious criminal. Only they made the mistake of asking the doorman questions, too, since they certainly did not suspect that he was an *S.A.* comrade. So I was warned. Then there was no difference to speak of between party comrades and the *S.A.* Nevertheless I enlisted in the *S.S.*[3] And I must say that up to the present time I have not regretted it, for I found there what I had been seeking: the expression of steadfastness, manliness, honesty, simplicity, modesty. With that the danger of losing my source of support had increased considerably, though I was firmly convinced that my comrades of the *Schutzstaffel*-kept absolute secrecy. But that was not sufficient; in spite of our civilian clothing we were in daily danger of being caught. The Red Front did not need to know us personally. The Red scum recognized from our faces what sort of persons were before them. It was a bad time when one of us had to bring the other home. It was not so easy to see, on our return home during the night, how the rabble shunning the light hid in the gaps between houses and waited to get hold of our men. If they got him, he hardly could stand up again. More than once did I have to act as though I were a stranger and ride past my own house. The remaining hours of such a night I spent in the garden colony. The next day I had to go to work; then I was supposed to be an absolutely republican official. Originally I had good prospects of having a fine career. I had been entrusted with a position which was a focal point of the whole administration. But when the factional leader of the Social Democratic party expressed the opinion at a banquet: "We shall find ways and means of doing away with the Fascist," then my loyalty and service did not help me, and none of my capacities spoke in my favor. I disappeared into

---

[3] Abbreviation for *Schutz Staffel,* the special black guard troop of Hitler.

oblivion. The office superintendents one after another protested against having me as their assistant. They had at least
to create the appearance that they had nothing in common with
me. Today no one refers to that; today it is forgotten; today
they no longer remember how much they hurt me. Then my
colleagues came and wanted to hear from me. They did not
trust me, and when I had pinned them down, they got away
from the screws with some such remark as: "It's all very fine,
everything you say but your cursed war. If the brown shirts
get control, war will certainly come." There was another
who wanted to hear some details of the movement from me,
who pretended never to have heard anything of it. But to
him I pointed out the gigantic placards and also advised him
to visit the *Sportpalast* some time when Dr. Goebbels was speaking. . . . The following day he came to me and said: "National, good; socialists, rotten; German, of course; but laborers' party, no, Herr K. I am an official, not a laborer." That
is how things were among my group. But I did not stop, and
the result was that many a valuable man was won over to the
National Socialist movement.

In the *S.S.* I did not always have service at the front. What
I undertook in the interim cannot be revealed in this life history and thus made accessible to the public. This much, however, let me intimate: I was in the thick of things; I was among
men who studied the Red mob at its source, and I need not
emphasize how free they were with knives and pistols. As a
result, however, we had a better idea of how things really
stood with the criminal police. It was misery and a tragedy to
know in the afternoon that in the evening in a certain storm
troop and in a certain place one of our men would lose his
life, and to be powerless to prevent it. It was unbelievably ex-
citing to keep firm in spite of bloody sacrifices in our own
ranks, and to follow the command of the Leader to wait. This
waiting and these sacrifices were rewarded. There was little
ado. We were proud of doing our part quietly and modestly.

My comrades in the troop and I will remain as we always were. It did not impede us when at night snipers attacked us with shots. Nothing much was said about my being struck by a bullet. It came out all right; it might have been different. All that was a matter of course for us. But the next day we had to go to work again. That meant the office, and no one must be allowed to notice that I was one of those who had been attacked. I had to play, act, pretend that as a harmless stroller I had been hit by a stray bullet and bore away a shot as a memento. And when in 1931 my brother and another *S.A.* comrade and I traveled to the *S.A.* meeting in Brunswick, I asked for leave of absence to attend a regimental celebration. I was given leave but no one was so stupid as to think that I was in Münster, and they would have loved to know how I managed to get to Brunswick in such a short time without using the train. The Intelligence Service, however, knew it, for this ride was carefully noted in the charge against my brother.

It is superfluous to describe the sacrifices I made. They were nothing unusual. These sacrifices were made in the spirit of *Gemeinschaft*. But let me point out one thing without appearing presumptuous. My wife led a heroic life at my side. Yet I never saw her tremble; on the contrary, if weariness and disappointment overcame me, she stood beside me and pointed to Hitler to remind me that my worries were slight in comparison with that man's. It happened sometimes that when I awoke in the morning, comrades had been in our house for hours while my wife bandaged them. They had begged that I should not be awakened. And there was excitement when police appeared after midnight, or when a comrade who had stolen into the house scratched at the door softly to call for me. It a horrible task for my wife to care for her broken husband, who could not stand the slightest noise; because of the smallness of our apartment, she had to ask our boy to say his evening prayer in the toilet. It is martyrdom for a wife when her joy in her life companion's recovery of strength is lessened by the knowledge that the man goes his own secret ways again as soon as he is on his feet. Just as I remind you of my wife, let me recall the wives of all my comrades. All that will be forgotten some time, but our task would not have been accomplished had our wives not been so strong. Their heroism was that of those who have suffered.

On January 30, 1933, I remained at home, and reviewed my entire life. I thought how easily the masses cry "Hosanna" and how quickly they are on hand with their "crucify!" That gave me a duty that was a signpost for me. Honors and dignities do not matter. All that counts is that as soldiers of the front we keep our promise to Germany. We still have a piece of work to do. If we have been permitted to help Adolf Hitler erect the Third Reich, we have an obligation to help to preserve it. And as I learned to interpret the growing effect from the cause given, we saw June 30, 1934, coming. Again destiny has compressed the consciousness of life in one final formula: The Leader is calling, gun in hand! And everything else falls away.

The fourth life

"*S.S.* man, your honor is loyalty!"

4. *The Story of a Middle-Class Youth*

I know nothing of the World War from my personal experience, for the roar of cannons was far from my home on the Mosel, but even though I was only five or six years old, I realized that something was wrong. Twice we had to go into the cellar when airplanes flew over the Mosel valley. That was all. What was war, I asked my parents time and again?

I was the youngest of seven children. As a result of a childhood illness, my eyesight grew weak. I could no longer write. My sisters read my lessons to me.

I was eight years old when my youngest brother died. He

died at Bonn, after an operation unnecessarily undertaken by a Jewish head physician. I was particularly fond of this brother; consequently I felt a strong hatred for the head physician, which developed into a hatred of everything Jewish.

When I was nine years old my eyesight grew worse. I could no longer even play. My youngest sister was a good companion to me. When she left to go to boarding school I was alone a great deal of the time. Then I began to think. I knew we had had a Kaiser, that the termination of the war had not been favorable for us, and that new Germany was a republic. What was a "republic"? I heard my people say that Germany owed the world a great deal of money. Why was this? A large portrait on which was written *"Heil Kaiser Dir"* had to be taken down because the republican regime so decreed it. Did not the republic know anything about the Kaiser? Why could we no longer hoist our flag? Once I heard my father say to my mother, "If I can no longer fly our flag, then I will never show my colors, except the flags of the Church." Was the banner forbidden because we had lost our fight beneath it? I often asked myself this question.

When I was nine years old I visited my uncle, a teacher in Barmen. I went to elementary school there for the next three years. This was an important period for me, for after many operations on my eyes, I regained my full sight. How beautiful was nature! It fairly astounded me. Yet living in a large city was pleasant, too.

This was during the year 1923, the time of the inflation. I often saw people in the streets in large numbers. I remember the slogans on their banners. "Open the coal houses, for we are freezing!" was one. "Bread for the proletariat!" was the other. What was the proletariat? My teacher told us that these were people that would not work and wanted to make a mess of everything. My uncle told me that there were many poor people among them that I must respect, and also that I was to return home whenever I saw the Communists (also called Spartakists) in the streets. Once my uncle said that many of these people had entered his shop that day. He tried to get police protection, but they wrecked his telephone. Not one paid for his purchase.

Another time we went to the courthouse. In front of this building were a number of people. Many sang, some laughed, others whimpered and called out, "We are hungry!" My uncle told me that we could not go into the courthouse, for the streets were blocked. I had never seen anything of the sort, and I asked him to take me. Slowly he led me through the crowds. The *"Grüne"* (the uniform of the Barmen police was green) were there with weapons and shouted "Back!" That street was likewise blocked. My uncle quickly turned around. We had not gone 100 metres before we heard a loud report. Behind us there was a great deal of running, and if my uncle had not dragged me into a house entrance, I think we should have been trampled under foot.

"The cowardly bands!" my uncle said. Then there were more shots and soon a great confusion and clamor ensued. But the people wanted bread; why did they run away? If they were hungry they should not have run away. Was there no bread in the courthouse? My uncle thought the Communists wanted to seize the courthouse, so they could have the say in the entire city. It was all just like war—in our own native land. "This would not have been possible before the war," said my uncle, yet the same sort of thing was going on all over Germany at the time. Obviously the republic was not strong, since it could not stop the plunder and the killings. Often children came to classes without doing their lessons, because their parents had forbidden them to do them. Why were they hindered in this manner?

One of my uncle's acquaintances, a converted Jew, used to bring me sweets whenever he came. Today I cannot recall his name, but I know I never touched the candy. Such incidents during my youth suggested a number of questions to me. I wanted to clarify all of these confused thoughts. One Sunday in September 1923 my uncle, aunt, and I went for a walk. Toward evening we arrived at Elberfeld, where we heard the tramp of marching feet accompanied by a song. We waited, as did the other people. Uniformed men came, flanked by marching men.

The parade was preceded by one man who kept his right hand raised high. Then came a man carrying a large banner which was mostly red; in the middle was a black and white design. Two uniformed men walked at his side. It was quite a long line of men and they sang loudly. I did not quite understand the text, but the tune was known to all. Today I know the words:

"We are the army of the Hakenkreuz, and fly the red banner.
"We will lead the German working class to freedom."

I asked my uncle to let me accompany them, but he would not let me go, and we returned to Barmen. My uncle explained that these were the "Hitler men." What did that mean? Who were they? Who was Hitler? My uncle could tell me only that he was a man from the southern part of Germany who wanted to unite a number of young men, put them into uniform and start another revolution in order to gain power.

Naturally he could tell me only what he had heard in Barmen, a stronghold of the Reds. These men were quite different from those who had taken possession of the courthouse in Barmen, yet the latter had also wanted to obtain power, I said to myself. The Hitler group sang beautifully, and they marched equally well. I did not believe they wished anyone ill.

I stayed in Barmen until Easter 1925. I did not see any of the incidents of November 9, but I can remember hearing something at the time. I often heard people say yes, things had been quite different in time of peace, or "he is a man of the good old days before the war!" Why were things so different after the war? Had we lost everything because of the war?

I stayed for three more years in Barmen. Numerous clashes took place here. In 1924 they were a regular daily occurrence. Strong police patrols walked through the streets. Communists plundered the city, and there were many deaths, both among the policemen and among the Communists. I remember that at the burial of a Communist further clashes occurred and that day, too, many *"Grüne"* lost their lives.

So I soon drew the conclusion that matters were a great deal worse under the republic than they had been before the war. My three years of schooling at Barmen were over. I also decided that, apart from the fact that matters were so much worse since the war, the war did not in itself account for this fact. Then I remembered the "Hitler men" whom I had seen for the first time in Elberfeld.

In March 1925 I left Barmen forever. I stayed at home a short time and went to public school. Here in a small town, the picture was different from that in the large city. Every Saturday I went home. One day I found a swastika emblem in my brother's room. I recognized it even though I was not sure of its significance. I knew who bore this emblem, and that this had been the insignia of the men whom I had seen marching so proudly through Elberfeld. This was the first time I had seen a swastika at home. Was my brother one of them? I asked him at the next opportunity. He was overjoyed to find me interested; he told me all sorts of things about the cause and gave me an emblem.

I had to be careful so that our father would have no inkling of our alliance. One day I wore the swastika to school, and at first the teacher did not do anything about it. But two Jewish boys saw it and I had the first fist fight in my life. They both went after me, and I finally was the victor. As soon as one of them had a bloody nose, both withdrew.

Now I was truly proud to wear this emblem. My joy was short-lived, however, for now the teacher had to forbid my

wearing the emblem on account of the two Jews. Now they
were victorious. At that time there was a student at the school
called *"der Hitler"* because of the cap he wore. I always felt
drawn to him, but I did not have much opportunity to speak
to him alone. I made the best of every minute I had with him
alone. His parents had a barber shop, so that I often had a
chance to talk to him there. I must admit that these few hours
of conversation meant a great deal to me and helped me solve
many questions that puzzled me.

I must admit that at home the situation was no different
from that in most homes. There were frequent quarrels, which
often had disastrous results. The aforementioned brother, who
was the only other son at home, was drawn into these disputes.
When I returned home for vacation, I was often drawn into
the quarrels, and since I did not think I should oppose my
mother and sister, I tried to avoid taking sides. But in spite of
of this I could not help supporting my brother.

When I was sixteen years old my mother bought me some
brown trousers. If she had known the significance of this color,
she would never have bought them for me. I told her that
they pleased me, and she also got some for my brother. Now
I felt as though I were half a Nazi. At school my trousers
attracted a lot of attention. I told one of the teachers who had
forbidden them because of the color that I had had no idea
what they represented. I had to answer in this way to protect
my father.

In the August vacation of the same year, I took a fourteen-
day bicycle ride with my sister. It led us through Koblenz to
Köln. I saw the followers of Hitler marching for the second
time.

At school the National Socialists were opposed, but there
were a few comrades who opposed the teacher, a Social
Democrat. (Later I learned that the teacher was a Bolshevik.)
In our class there were also some members of the Catholic

party,[1] who got a great deal of support from our teachers. Our class carried on lengthy discussions, some of which went on for hours. Sometimes the discussions became so heated that the teacher had to remind us of his authority to maintain order. Undoubtedly I found these German classes most interesting.

A great change now came in my life, largely through my own fault. It was one of the worst blunders of my life when, over my father's opposition, I left school. I wanted to take up a practical business and earn money, for matters did not look too promising at home. My father threatened to put me to work in the vineyard. But school had become a constant annoyance to me. I left school on September 30, 1929.

My brother and I talked frequently about the Hitler party. On the first of November, All Saints Day, we took a two-day trip to Verdun, with its battlefields and German monument. That was quite an experience for me. There should be fewer cemeteries to remind people of the terrible fights. The monuments at Fort Douaumont and Vaux are huge witnesses of the dire tragedy. The *"Ossuaire de Douaumont"* was particularly impressive. In this memorial chapel I seemed to hear and feel the power of the unknown soldiers of our Fatherland resting in strange earth. These were precious minutes for me.

We stopped at Trier on the way home. Here I took part for the first time in a National Socialist demonstration. It was Sunday, the second of November, 1929. The district group of the Nazi party held a memorial service at the cemetery dedicated to World War soldiers. Dr. Ley, at that time leader in the Rhineland, made a brief, concise address. Then he left a wreath with a swastika emblem on it, and we marched to one of the city squares. Here Dr. Ley addressed the group again. The German national anthem was sung, and we raised our hands in allegiance to Germany and Adolf Hitler. Now I felt as though I were a National Socialist, for I had taken the oath. Many times I tried to join. These ideas were for me the ful-

---

[1] The so-called *Zentrum* (center) party.

fillment of an inner longing for clarity, and I realized for the first time how easy it was to act according to National Socialist ideas. This was clear to me the first time I publicly avowed them, for all stood as a symbol of a better Reich.

At home I took a three months' course in making wine. I took no part in politics during this time. At home things were not so quiet. Often fights ensued when we talked about National Socialism. At the end of February the first meetings were held in my small home town. My brother led them, and I was overjoyed to be able to attend them. I returned to school in Easter 1930. I could not find what I was looking for at home. I had not been gone from school for eight weeks, when I regretted my action. I then attended the higher trade school at Trier. My father forbade me to take any active part in politics during my school time. But the next meeting, held in the *Rathskeller,* lured me on. Soon I participated in various propaganda marches, and in the course of one of these, a classmate recognized me. With all possible speed he told my teacher. The latter took me aside and said that it was quite strange that a person who had come from such a good family should become interested in the Nazis and march with them. He said they had been badly brought up, and hardly ever so much as wore a collar. Another teacher said that National Socialism sought to mislead the workers. I often opposed such statements in class. In addition to these discussions there was much talk about the Catholic party.

Many nights I never went to bed, not because of any drunken orgies, but because I had joined a group of men who played jokes on the Separatists.

In the winter, when I could no longer take lengthy walks in the evening, I walked through the city. I wandered through the Communist district. I talked to the people there a number of times. I was allowed to come and go without molestation. My life suited me, for there was much to do and I was ever active. The more I was opposed at school the more actively I helped the cause both in school and outside. I grew strong through meetings and contacts with old party comrades. I was not dismissed from school, despite my open declarations. The only drawbacks were my father's letters and the fact that I did not want to obey his commands. The meetings I attended gave me courage, and if my father wrote me something like, "Don't bother with all this party rubbish," I made up my mind that I would have to choose between politics and family.

After the September elections, the National Socialists were regarded seriously in Trier for the first time. Our position was precarious. The Catholic prelate Kaas and his clique incited the Trier middle class against us. During the summer vacation I took a bicycle trip. On my return trip I joined a group of Duisburger *S.A.* at Godesberg. They had a swastika flag with them.

Koblenz was splendid. We lined up our bicycles and went to the monument. We sang the Horst Wessel song high up so that it would be heard afar. When the police came we went on to Bingen. We had a battle with the "Red Falcon," a Social Democratic organization. At Hunsruck, the goal of my comrades, I left them, for my vacation was at an end. On the return journey the fourteen *S.A.* men were able to spend three days at home. When they walked through our city on a propaganda march, the police entered our house and sought weapons. Naturally they found none, for there were none there.

Easter 1932 concluded my schooling at Trier. I left Trier, which had proved to me that I was on the right track, because of my various discussions with members of the Catholic party.

On April 21, 1932, a day after his birthday, Adolf Hitler spoke during the Prussian provincial election in Trier. This address made a great impression; to have a meeting so eagerly attended was unique in Trier. I saw the Fuehrer for the first time. Since the *S.A.* were forbidden at this time, the former *S.A.* men wore white armbands with the black inscription,

"Order!" Long before the Fuehrer came, we had blocked off one street leading to the entrance for him. Then suddenly we heard many voices shouting *"Heil,"* and shortly afterward the Fuehrer entered. First came the *S.S.* standard bearer, behind him the Fuehrer with some party members. In all the hall the greetings were heard continuously. Never before in Trier had any man been so joyfully received. The Fuehrer spoke a short time, for this was his third address that day. When he finished, the shouting continued and all were filled with inspiration and joy. At the beginning a child had given him a bouquet. The Fuehrer kept one flower, sending the rest to a wounded man. Then he left. I looked at him as he passed by and felt that he met my glance. All who have ever seen him must have felt the same way. The shouts of *"Heil Hitler"* continued. . . .

I stayed home for the next few months. I could now help my brother, who had become the political leader of his district. I accompanied him during his work and his meetings. It was a grand time for me. Then the wearing of the uniform of the *S.A.* was forbidden. All worked twice as hard as before. One propaganda march followed another. The work was not in vain, however, as shown is by the election of July 1932. I was in Saarbruecken. Since I often stayed with my sister, I soon came to know some local comrades. I spent many happy hours with them, and one of our greatest joys was to snoop around the Communist districts. We could not attend meetings, since open discussions were forbidden. Once we were searched for weapons. I hid my blackjack and then, after the search, took it with me again. Outside, the Communists greeted us with jeers, scorn, and stones (some windows were broken). The police tried to hold back the attackers and soon we walked through the city under police protection. When they left us, we waited until they were out of sight, and we began to sing again. Then what we had all been waiting for happened. The command to attack was given. We hid. Later we went through the streets of Altstadt, and because of the hour, the

Communists did not expect us. So we were not hindered in our march. Those were, all in all, interesting days in Saarbruecken. In 1932 the comrades in Saarbruecken took walks in the evening through the main street (Bahnhofstrasse was the name) either in pairs or with girls, who knew nothing of their purpose. They were guarding the business houses.

I returned home at the end of August 1932. In Saarbruecken I was offered a position in Naples with a German firm. We finally decided to leave on September 2. My sister accompanied me on this journey. We went to Frankfurt-am-Main, then to Nuremberg and thence on to Munich. There we found a great deal of mail awaiting us. In every letter were admonitions to return. We stayed in Munich three days. Naturally we visited the *"Braunes Haus."* [2] We went to the dining room to meet some comrades. We went to a place where a man and a woman sat. He said to me: "You are sitting in the place of our Fuehrer. He often takes his midday meal here." I was proud, and it was a shame that we did not see the Fuehrer; we learned that he was in Berlin.

Then we set out again and went to Starnberg, Garmisch-Partenkirchen, Mittenwald, and Seefeld on the way to Innsbruck. Here our fate awaited us, for matters were quite different from what we had anticipated. We learned that our mother had suffered a serious automobile accident and was in a hospital at Trier in a critical condition.

We decided to stay in Munich over night. We went to Iselberg, and there we made up our minds to go home. Love for our mother drew us. In just such a way the comradeship which we enjoyed in the National Socialist party was a concrete example of the loyalty we felt for each other, since we were all working for the same cause. . . .

In the *S.A.* homes we were all brothers in one large family. In Bavaria and Suabia I found National Socialist unions. This struggle for a unified land is the foundation of a strong free

---

[2] Name of party headquarters in Munich.

German Empire. Even though this journey of mine had not been completed, still it served its purpose in awakening in me a deeper sense of duty and brotherhood toward my people, and a willingness to renounce all that stood between it and me.

When we returned home and visited my mother in Trier, we found she was much better. The November elections entailed a great deal of work for us and we were busy day and night. I had no time to think of personal matters. The result of this election did not discourage us.

Then we learned that our Fuehrer had stated that he would not take the state by force, that he would proceed in a legal fashion. At Christmas we celebrated a National Socialist Christmas festival in our family. I shall never forget that. We regained our courage under the Christmas tree.

In the middle of January the Landtag[3] president, Herr Kerrl, spoke in Bernkastel. He explained briefly the psychological result of the November election. He called it a temporary impediment, and said that the Nazi cause was once again prepared and was ready to conquer. At the end of January my sister and I went to Saarbruecken. There I experienced the most wonderful moment of my life. As soon as my sister and I arrived we heard the extras shouting "Hitler made Reich Chancellor!" I could hardly believe it and could not quite be certain until I heard the news over the radio later on. How happy we all were. It was difficult to collect our thoughts. Now every day brought something new, the acts of the new Reich's regime. One of the first laws related to the encouragement of agricultural activities. I no longer had to return home, for the miracle had happened. We had power in Saarbruecken and were no longer suppressed in the region of the Saar. We no longer had to bow to the will of a strange people. But the fight here was a hard and bitter one nevertheless.

I was in Trier again at the elections in March 1933. The Communists had not been entirely suppressed there. All night

---

[3] Provincial diet.

long we were ready for emergency alarms. The Reichstag election turned out in favor of the Fuehrer. I was a volunteer in Trier for a few months. In June I took a long journey to East Prussia and spent about two months there before returning home.

This was an important trip for me, as I realized that under the new leadership National Socialism would actually achieve all that had been promised. The Fuehrer had always promised to do all things possible to bring freedom and food to the German people. At the end of the first half year of National Socialist rule East Prussia was no longer suffering from unemployment. Everywhere the employment situation was relieved. The peasants clung to the Fuehrer with reverence and love, and even in the larger cities the working class raised its hand in respect to him.

Everywhere in Germany there was a rebirth of life and courage and renewed hope. I returned home in October. There, too, much had changed. New interest and activity animated everything. In November all Germany was for the Fuehrer, and he won by a unanimous vote of "Yes." The people understood him. I went to see my brother in the middle of November. During my journey I learned a lesson: always remain natural and do not lose the way to your comrades!

I know now that our people can find the true way only through the unity of all: we will find strength in our Fuehrer, who arouses in us the slumbering ideals of Germanic freedom and heroism.

5. *The Story of a Bank Clerk*

The development of the younger generation, presupposing certain natural tendencies of character, will doubtlessly be strongly influenced by the events of the two past decades. The outward glamor of pre-war days, the outbreak of the war, the invasion of the Russians, our troops marching through to the East, the distribution of provisions during the war (our standing on line for perhaps thirty grams of *Wurst*), news of victories of our armies from all parts of the world where German troops were fighting, the breakdown of November 1918, the struggle against the new republican regime, interminable political arguments, battles in lecture halls, political terrorism, the economic difficulties during the inflation and deflation, and finally the death struggle between Marxism and middle class on the one hand, and the young revolutionary movement on the other—all will remain ineffaceable in the memory of the young German. The majority of the younger generation, whether it wanted to or not, had to take some position in regard to these events. In every instance, the standpoint was based on feelings conditioned by blood and race.

It was in March 1907 that I was born in the extreme northeastern part of Germany in Tilsit, a city that was enjoying prosperity as the center of trade with the neighboring country of Russia. Another factor contributing to its prosperity was that the region of the Memel River, in which three fourths of the districts was situated, provided a good market for the city. Through the "peace treaty" this purely German region was torn from its mother land; Tilsit became a border city. The economic prosperity of a progressive city was destroyed. Boundary duties and the narrow-minded attitude of the small border states created after the war did the rest. As a result many young people had to leave their places of work in order to find others in the "provinces" or in the *Reich*. I was among them.

Fate had not blessed me with riches. I was the son of a *Kleinbürger*. I received my education in a Tilsit public school. It depends only on one's teachers whether with the necessary diligence he can acquire in a German public school the general education required in life. I am proud of having had such teachers. By taking advantage of every opportunity, I was "promoted" and received satisfactory reports. Thus I had the necessary prerequisites for further theoretical instruction in business. I was able to apply for admission to the school of commerce in Tilsit. This state institution did much toward the broadening of my knowledge. After two years of study, I received a diploma corresponding to the so-called *"Einjährigen."*[1] I was exempted from the oral examination on the basis of the result of the written exercises. My will power and energy had been developed early. In life it is usually true that only through industry and perseverance can a maturing man win the position he deserves.

Hardly had I left school when I passed from theoretical to practical learning. One must bear in mind, however, that life itself is the best teacher, and thus all of life is an apprenticeship. The first continuation of my education was with a Tilsit wholesale merchant. It did not satisfy me, because I felt that in the customary education of apprentices in this field mental activity was badly neglected. In the very first months my employer realized this. He now used me for calculating and bookkeeping work. Fate however, determined things differently. Through the mediation of the head salesman I received a training position in a bank. This was my rightful place. In 1923, a mad tempo ruled the course of business of the German banks. They reckoned in millions, later billions, and finally even in trillions. Amounts which one day still had some value melted into nothing within twenty-four hours. The mushroom growth of prosperous banks was followed late in the fall of the same year by complete breakdown. The conversion of our currency from the paper mark to the gold mark occasioned a simplification of business everywhere. Further systematizing measures followed. Tens of thousands of bank employees lost their positions and had to seek new schooling in order to find employment in other branches of industry.

This second apprenticeship of mine satisfied me. A

---

[1] A high school diploma entitling the bearer to one year of service in the army.

hastened professional training quickly fitted me into a new position, for on the basis of my training my time of apprenticeship was decreased by half. After three quarters of a year I had an opportunity to demonstrate my broad knowledge of bookkeeping. But soon the business institution in which I had found employment was also closed, owing to economic depression. It was only through the recommendation of my chief that after a month I again found employment in Masuren, in the little town of Passenheim, in a branch of the same credit organization. However, I did not remain here long. The political battle which meanwhile had placed me quite in the foreground—about which I will speak later—demanded all my energies. Under these circumstances, it was no wonder that I soon became hated. The arguments about trifles became more frequent. After six months of work, I turned from this first scene of a real battle for National Socialism toward an uncertain future, going back to my home town, Tilsit. Naturally it was not easy for a "rebel" like me to find suitable employment. It is true, unfortunately, that the mass cannot endure sincere people. Therefore, in order to have any work at all, I had to take temporary jobs with city offices, gas works, and with the branch of the Memel Raiffeisenbank in Pogegen. As I was known as a National Socialist, in Pogegen I was daily threatened with expulsion by the Lithuanians as an "undesirable alien." It was natural that I wanted to get away from this uncertainty and was then "satisfied" to be employed in 1927 as a bookkeeper in the Vereinsbank Korschen. My references were good, but my last employer in Passenheim could not refrain from referring "incidentally" to my National Socialist activities. Despite many struggles, I succeeded in creating here the sounding-board which enabled me to help the National Socialists' idea to victory. In 1933 I became cashier, and soon thereafter, in October of the same year, I was chosen by the board of directors as vice-president of the bank.

Today, as a member of the old guard, with the member-

ship number 10,980, I am often asked for my reasons for joining the *N.S.D.A.P.* The world often does not understand and
is astonished that it was possible for the National Socialists to
conquer the state. They cannot see how we, the old fighters,
again and again worked up the courage and the energy to overcome all obstacles. Who knows the sacrifices and privations
of those years of battle, who knows the inner feeling of those
party comrades who sacrificed everything in constant faith
to the idea and to its first soldier, Adolf Hitler? Was that opportunism or chauvinism? As an old fighter, I maintain it
was neither. It was renunciation and sacrifice in a belief in
the great cause. It was, as I mentioned in the beginning, racial
feeling; it was the inner law that urged us to new action. In
order to be true to our own character, we gave up a quiet and
comfortable life to become political soldiers. I must go far
back to present the National Socialist aims and instructive
feelings as they first appeared in my development. In doing
this I only want to assert that National Socialism was not
learned by us old party members, but merely sprang from our
instincts. Thus it was a matter of course that the opinion of
the Leader was always also inherently our own before the
Leader made it public. In election campaigns this was best
expressed. We appeared as speakers before the people with
our own points of view and attitudes and afterwards ascertained that our words agreed with those of the Leader. Thus
in the National Socialist movement we find Leader and followers inseparably united. The attitude of the true National
Socialist is that of the German man. In the simplicity and
naturalness of our demands and the German's understanding
of them, lies the psychological foundation of the success of
the National Socialist movement.

The youth movement and *Wandervogel* were my personal
preparatory school for National Socialism. The German youth
movement was a training for personality in the best sense, for
it taught us independence of action. Blood and soil were the

two factors which played the largest part in this training. Love of the homeland and faith in the destiny and preservation of our nation were here for the first time experienced by maturing youths. They gave a meaning to life and turned us away from the superficial teachings of people who thought purely in terms of economics. We turned away from the skat-playing politicians of the beer table; we became rebels, revolutionaries, because we saw our nation in danger. We recognized the poisoning of the German soul in the form of superficial, shallow music, in the form of the trashy literature which could be bought cheaply at any newsstand. On the stage of the German theatre we heard words which were foreign to our nature and our spiritual attitude. Our mind's eye envisioned the breakdown of Rome, Babylon, Nineveh, and the other ancient states. Everywhere one turned one saw Jews. The press, theatre, motion pictures, literature, music—indeed art in every form—technical science, and education, were all decisively influenced by them. Was the degeneracy of the above-mentioned nations also to seize our people? Never! That must not be.

But the *Wandervogel* could not fulfill this mission of regeneration. The flood of bolshevism would have passed over it. Our youthful, vital forces, together with the other constructive forces of the nation had first to create a revolutionary movement and gain control of the state in order to accomplish reorganization of our entire national life. A man like Walter Rathenau, who, because he was a Jew, saw everything in a Jewish perspective, was insufferable to us, the youth who were consciously German. Therefore, the first determining factor of our movement was its anti-Semitism. The *"Deutschvölkischer Schutzbund"* was the vanguard of the movement which fought for our national Germany, until the government dissolved the organization and new ways had to be found to meet a new situation. Down in the south we heard of Adolf Hitler, the "Drummer" who was perceiving the same problem with the same emotions as so many other German fellow-country-men. Prussia was closed to him. In his spirit, which we recognized as right, we began our work in the years 1921 to 1923 in the *"Preussenbund,"* which was under the leadership of Captain Ammon, the "Chief," as we called him. From 1923 until 1924, I put my strength at the disposal of the "Schlageter [2] Memorial Association." Our present banner of war, the swastika, was even then our symbol of faith.

No sooner was it made known in 1925 that Adolf Hitler had decided to reorganize on a national scale the organization that had been prohibited and dissolved in 1923 than nothing could hold us back. In the extreme northeast, in March to April 1925, the first local group of the Party was formed. When the Leader then proposed the head of the general staff of the World War, Ludendorff, in the presidential election of 1925, we headed the ranks who fought for his candidacy. To be sure we were not understood. But we knew what we were doing. Half a hundred members were able to astonish the whole city: Ludendorff received a thousand votes. We were proud and prepared for further successes. The idea, its strengthening, and above all organization, were the problems that always had to be solved. The National Socialist press at that time was insignificant. The *Völkische Beobachter* in the beginning appeared with only four pages and only as a weekly. Because we were so far removed from its place of publication, Munich, the newspaper always reached our subscribers two days late, and even later, as a daily, it was always out of date. It did not have the needed staff of contributors. Therefore the newspaper offered our citizens nothing. Despite this, our will to build up the battling paper of our movement was stubborn and undaunted. At that time I succeeded in acquiring about a hundred subscribers for the party publica-

---

[2] Schlageter was shot by the French for subversive activities during the occupation of the Ruhr. He was made the object of hero-worship by German patriots.

tion. That was about 1925 or 1926. As a reward, I received from the party organization in Munich both volumes of *Mein Kampf,* with the signature of the Leader, and several photographs of our Leader likewise autographed. Today, after the victory, I look upon these proudly in memory of those hours.

Passenheim, 1926: Another field of action but the same work. New methods were discovered. The National Socialist press was enlarged by the addition of Goebbels' aggressive paper, *Der Angriff,* and the *National Sozialistische Briefe* published in Elberfield. These we utilized in our propaganda. We also sold several hundred copies of the first edition of the new picture magazine, the *Illustrierte Beobachter,* about the party congress in Weimar. We distributed handbills. One of these was confiscated by the police upon the instigation of the Jewish manufacturer Hirschweh. The handbill represented a Jew on a see-saw who was raising first the workman on his left and next the bourgeois on his right. It was undoubtedly brazen on my part to portray so rudely the powerful position of the Jewish group. The starting point for further activities was a meeting with the student Reiche from Frankfurt. Then in the summer of 1926 began the struggle to restore freedom of speech to Hitler. By means of written petitions the anger of the population at the entirely one-sided and unjustified prohibition was to be presented to the authorities in Prussia. With a few men I succeeded in securing about one thousand signatures. Only my old comrades know how much distrust and worry I experienced, what strength of character was necessary to go about this work. I like to recall those party comrades who shared joys and sorrows with me during that time of struggle, and I think especially of a young teacher, Herr Mascherrek, who was the only one among his colleagues to step forward and openly pledge himself to National Socialism. He never failed when I asked for his assistance, and many a time after a propaganda trip I enjoyed the hospitality of his home. When I think of Passenheim and the spread of National

Socialism in the districts of Ortelsburg and Allenstein, I can only say, "Only six months, but to me they are a history of many unforgettable hours."

Upon my return to Tilsit at the age of nineteen, I again found myself in a leading position, as secretary, treasurer and director of propaganda. Now local groups of the movement were being built up everywhere. After working hours the *S.A.* comrades took their bicycles, provided themselves with newspapers, and went out to sell them in order to obtain money for the continuation of the new work. One must keep in mind, too, that we received no outside help. Most of our expenses were paid by money contributed out of our own pockets. Germany and her future were at stake, the loss mattered not. Month after month of strenuous activity passed. Already 1927 was half gone. Fate gave me another field of activity. I came to Korschen, a railroad center in East Prussia with about 2400 inhabitants. Here was an entirely virgin field as far as National Socialism was concerned. Far and wide our movement was unknown. After having been here a few weeks I learned that a member of the Party from Karlsruhe had come to Gerdauen, a town in the adjoining county. Soon he organized an evening of lectures in order to establish a local group there out of the remains of the former *Deutschvölkische Freiheitspartei*.[3] I also joined in this and now began systematic recruiting in the districts of Rastenburg and Gerdauen. From these two districts the wave of propaganda spread over the whole province, the latter at that time completely untouched territory. There was no week-end and no Sunday that we did not travel more than a hundred kilometers on our bicycles. Sensburg, Rössel, Schippenbeil, Angerburg, Lötzen are names that played a significant part in our struggle. In consequence of the national point of view which prevailed among the people who lived in this province, we seldom made a trip in vain.

---

[3] A makeshift political party organized after the dissolution of the National Socialist party in 1924.

Our election campaigners in 1928 raised the hundred national-ist votes of the Korschen district to nearly 1100. One can evaluate this success only when one takes into consideration that on the same day the city of Rastenburg with its 14,000 inhabitants gave only forty votes for Adolf Hitler. If the day before, during a *Stahlhelm* district meeting, the party members of Korschen had not distributed handbills and newspapers on a large scale, the city would not have furnished even this number of votes. It must also be mentioned that the neighboring city of Gerdauen, although twice as large, and in spite of a district party meeting, gave only 100 votes for the National Socialists. Our young group was strong because of its constant activity in the neighborhood. Until we had gained eighteen members, we had to take part in the meetings of the local group of Gerdauen. This necessitated a bicycle ride of thirty-eight kilometres, so that each party member had to travel about eighty kilometres after work to take part in a meeting. To be sure, in the beginning they were always the same ones, but they were loyal and dependable. Otto Finkeisen, who then belonged to the Kobler Youth, was on the road with me many a night. His parents' warning to take care of his education and his health had no effect. In 1929 our group gained considerably in size; the local group was doubled. At the local council elections we secured three of the eighteen available seats; at the district elections we received one thousand votes in the district and one seat. Two-thirds of the votes came from the territory of the local group of Korschen. Our party member, the teacher Schulz of Wendehnen, was the first government employee of the district to be elected. The first great breach was effected in the enemy's front. We were able now to put our goals more effectively before the people and to secure the coöperation of local officials. To be sure, we were not interested in the council seats as such, for we were not parliamentarians and had no faith in numbers, but the election was a measuring rod of our progress.

Sooner or later it was our firm intention that the state made up of parties should be destroyed. A nation ruled by thirty-five parties would have to fall as a result of the friction between the different interests. Thus every mandate meant a position of power to us, and after each victory we girded ourselves for further battle.

Our indomitable will for national freedom was strengthened by the personal intervention of the district leader sent to East Prussia in 1928, Erich Koch of Elberfeld. The first district meeting in Gerdauen, attended by about three hundred members from all parts of the province, showed us that although we were still small in numbers we were all the stronger in individual idealism. The district leader that day, having just come from the Ruhr, expressed his devotion in ardent words to the Leader and to the idea for whose victory we were striving in East Prussia. If there were times when we wanted to give up, we looked to him, who made the greatest sacrifices. He had at his disposal for the support of the activities of the district, for travel and propaganda, and finally for his own maintenance, barely two hundred marks. How often did we see him beset by worries, but his iron will kept him going. This was especially true of the *Preussische Zeitung,* which we tried to publish at a time when the rest of the press was failing for economic reasons. Without means, depending on the spirit of self-sacrifice and the coöperation of the party members, we took a great risk. For us the press was a problem of honor that must be solved satisfactorily. Our fighting organ is today *the* newspaper of East Prussia, the strongest paper in the province.

The district leader was also most closely connected with Korschen in other ways, for he often stayed here as a guest in the hospitable home of the family Waldow, either in order to travel into the neighboring districts, or to speak here to his old guard. He was not, however, the only party member we were able to lodge at that time, for there were also other leading members, among them the present cabinet president Goering, the national leader of the *S.S.* Himmler, Ahlemann, and others. Thus Korschen became a center, in the best sense of the word, for the battles that were to follow.

The national party meeting of 1929 will remain ineffaceable in the memories of the old guard. Of the 125 participants from the province, there were ten from Korschen alone, ten from Insterburg, and over thirty from Königsberg. The other cities followed with smaller numbers. It could be seen that the poorest sons were the truest. Party members with a minimum income, part of them agricultural laborers, contributed travelling money from their own pockets. Many had literally starved themselves in order to come. In return they had the privilege of being allowed to take part with 60,000 other members from all parts of the nation in this third mighty review of the brown army. From this they gained the spirit which today excites the admiration of the whole world and with the help of which we were able to erect the gigantic organization of the totalitarian state.

With success, however, resistance also grew, as I soon noticed at my own place of business. The directors of the bank came from the group of the so-called satiated bourgeois, in the truest sense philistines, who lack any idealistic incentive. For them the only existing concepts were "peace and order"; everything else was undesirable. What, after all, did a young bank official have to do with workers and at political meetings? Among them the concepts of "classes" and "material gain" were supreme. At the first possible opportunity this opinion of the *"Bürger"* was presented to me. Defiant and stubborn, I could give only one answer, "I cannot act differently!" Now I often had to justify myself about trifles. These philistines were strengthened by the fact that the bank was approached by railroad employees, with suggestions that I should be discharged, else they would withdraw their membership and withdraw their savings accounts. I was given notice no less than four times. It was owing to my own conception of service and the sympathy I had won among the people that the notice was always withdrawn at the last moment. Petty chicanery was the order of the day. Let me mention only that all my incoming and outgoing phone calls were cut off, that I was no longer permitted to have my mail and newspapers brought to the bank. They even objected to my bicycle leaning against the side of thè house during working hours, because a National Socialist pennant was attached to it. Finally with the threat of being discharged, I was forbidden to speak at meetings, even at discussion evenings, and also forbidden to wear my uniform. This made it impossible for me to carry on any propaganda, and I had to turn the leadership of the local group over to another party member. My only pride was that the organization was standing and would continue to grow, for all the prerequisites were there.

At the instigation of the district organization leaders, I was entrusted with the cultivation of the local group of Rastenburg, which was still in a very poor state. The problem was to win a city of 14,000 inhabitants where the Communists were the strongest party. There were about eight party members, but new ones were not being added; for following our first appearance in January 1929, resulting in a battle in the lecture hall, they were terrorized by the Communists who construed the appearance of any Nazi as a "provocation." Therefore a hall could not be obtained, and we had to meet in very small rooms without any outsiders in order to discuss the tasks of organization and the strengthening of our idea. Difficulties arose because I lived twenty-four kilometres away, could make no train connections, and during the first months had to ride there after work on my bicycle. But difficulties are meant to be overcome. Today people will probably just begin to recognize the sacrifices that the old party members made everywhere.

After a while our circle grew. The elections of 1930 forced us to approach the solution of the problem of a meeting place. Master carpenter Thersky was the first Rastenburg citizen to find the courage at that time to put his furniture storeroom, holding a few hundred people, at the disposal of the Party, thereby assuring the success of the election. In return he was exposed to a boycott by the adherents of the left, and, indeed, even of the bourgeoisie. Often stones were thrown at his house, and demonstrations were a daily occurrence. The *S.A.* of the whole district acted as a guard for the hall at the first and second meetings. When we finally succeeded in carrying on the meetings in safety to the participants, the ground was cleared. The press printed half-way decent notices and we were able to hire a hall in the city. To be sure, we had to pay an excessive rent and besides be responsible for damages. You shall hear what that means. The three battles which took place in the hall cost us more than eight hundred marks in damages. The day following every meeting a collection had to be taken up. Contributions of a mark, really made with difficulty, sufficed in a few days to cover our bills. And we must never forget to thank our *S.A.* who beforehand distributed handbills and sold tickets for days and afterwards had to do the fighting. The *S.A.* of Korschen won everlasting laurels. Workmen, students, artisans, office employees, and unemployed formed the "mass" of the small but determined *S.A.* of that time. They gave their last pennies to pay for the trips scheduled for each day. The fighting was always severe and the Communists usually pursued us. I remember one ride after a battle in the hall, when we were able to reach Korschen only after making a detour of thirty kilometres. After a ride of one hour, one of our *S.A.* men still lay unconscious. The Red mob had struck down eight of our most loyal men. Where there was such a spirit of self-sacrifice, such faith, so much courage and renunciation, victory had to follow. The old guard was only hardened by tribulations. Party comrades who had been deprived of a livelihood fought all the harder for our goals, and those who fell by the wayside served as warnings to us never to rest in our battle. This courageous and heroic attitude certainly carried along many party comrades in the struggle. No prohibition of brown shirts and emblems long prevailed. Bit by bit the hostile fortresses were conquered; fellow-countryman after fellow-countryman was won over. In 1931 I left Rastenburg knowing that I had created a vital local group there. Besides the sub-groups of the Kobler Youth, there existed a local group of 125 party comrades. Two new local groups had been formed in the neighborhood, truly a satisfying result.

The time of the final decision was 1932. Our opponents defended themselves more bitterly, but our struggle, too, was more bitter. The lack of understanding of the middle class was shown when they refused to allow the Party to accept a compromise and to permit it to take over part of the responsibilities of government. The December elections brought us a loss of supporters because all too many of the mass of "adherents" could not understand the farsightedness of the Leader. We, on the other hand, held meetings and appeared as speakers in discussions sometimes as often as three times in an evening, just as formerly. The old fighter had not changed. It was he who made January 30, 1933, possible. The old guard had never failed. It was the staunch supporter of the movement and will remain so in the future, too.

I am particularly proud of having won over to our idea all my colleagues in my place of business, although they were constantly changing—all, that is, except for one who lives outside of our district and who has since also become a National Socialist. The designation of the bank as "Nazi fortress" during the years of battle will be the happiest reminder of my activities for our Leader and his idea.

What will come now? Is the revolution over? These questions are often asked in the press by reporters who simply cannot understand the unrivalled success of the Party and its supporters. Outwardly the revolution is finished. Germany is National Socialist. All important positions are filled by National Socialists, but some of the people have remained the same as before. In economic life and in the organizations the strength of the National Socialist revival makes itself felt. Only the younger generation, however, will surrender to the idea completely. It is the task of the old guard, after the governmental basis has been created, to deepen and intensify the spirit of Adolf Hitler and the idea of national life. We must keep in mind the dead comrades who were not permitted to experience National Socialist Germany. Let us think of what they called out to us so often: "Forward over graves!"

6. *The Story of a Farmer*

Exactly twenty years ago, when I was only five years old, I first saw field-grey-clad soldiers with sabers and guns, and my own father dressed the same way. My mother watched, serious and worried. War! I heard this word then for the first time, but I soon understood it. My father went to the front, my mother to a hospital in Königsberg. My great aunt, my little sister and I remained home alone on the 300 acre farm.

Soon the Russians came. Russian cavalry rode into the courtyard. With slack reins they let the splendid horses drink out of the watering place in front of the pump. The riders with their lances on their backs did not dismount. When they left the courtyard, we children followed them to the gate filled with curiosity. Here one Russian asked us the way to Berlin. We pointed to the south. Suddenly a Russian took his gun from his back and aimed at us. Another Russian, however, signed to him not to do anything, and so they rode away in the direction of Berlin. Later we heard the thunder of cannons and saw a great deal of fire. Villages were burning round about.

A small boy's heart soon feels what the Fatherland is. My childish soul, firmly rooted in the northern East Prussian homeland, felt the bitter injustice of the Russian incendiaries' conduct. Daily contact with the Russian prisoners of war who worked on my father's farm brought the realization that they were sons of another people, that they were different from father and his farm laborers. They were often sad and played and sang melancholy songs after their day's work. They spoke of home, of their families, of their native land. These Russian prisoners of war and I soon had one feeling in common: that the war was a bitter injustice, causing unspeakable misery on both sides.

If in the beginning the figures of the field-grey-clad soldiers were filled with strength and their eyes shining, in the last two years of the war the glance of the soldiers under their steel helmets seemed to me to be removed from this world. Their eyes had seen too much.

In the spring of 1918 I entered school in Tilsit. As the gymnasium was overcrowded, I attended high school until spring, 1919. In Tilsit food had become scarce. Among the poor there was a nervous tension.

Then came November 9.

The nine-year-old child, whose eyes had seen the armed enemy, burning villages, suffering and misery, who had even learned to know hunger, could not comprehend what was going on there. He would not and could not understand that treason, lies, destruction of weapons, disobedience, and licentiousness would introduce a glorious new era. In school I had read the saga of the Nibelungen. Siegfried was my ideal. Slowly but more and more strongly there grew up in me a hatred of this band of traitors and their followers. Soon the consequence of this betrayal of the nation became more and more evident. One day we children had to collect signatures for the retention of West Prussia and Danzig. We did it gladly. For the first time I realized that we children still thought just the same as our fathers did in 1914. We preserved our faith. One day it was rumored that East Prussia would also be lost. I cried bitterly in bed and prayed to the dear Lord that he should please let us remain Germans. Then the rumor became a fact; the region beyond the Memel River had to be relinquished, although only Germans lived there. Frenchmen occupied the country. Frenchmen on the Memel; We boys liked to go bathing on the other side of the Memel. One day after bathing I filled my pockets with stones and brought them over the present boundary. Triumphantly I poured them out onto the ground, filled with pride that I had brought back to the Fatherland a bit of earth even if only stones.

In the years of the inflation, when the suffering seemed to grow into infinity, the national conscience awakened here and there. Former officers, mindful of their common experience at the front, joined into associations with nationally minded persons, predominantly the youth of the country. During my school time I boarded in the home of the secondary school teacher and later assistant master, August Post. Post was a patriot, an old German. When my childish heart seemed about to break because of the calamitous circumstances, I found support in the unchanging German character of this unique man, who preserved his faith in Germany to his last breath. It was a moving sight to observe what a loving interest Post took in the teachers' widows and orphans suffering because of the inflation. If anyone followed the principle, "Common interest precedes selfish interest," it was my former foster-father. Unconsciously he was already a National Socialist at that time. Now he is covered by the green lawn; he did not live to enjoy the privilege of experiencing the reconstruction of the nation. And just as he thought and acted, so did his whole family.

From the days of the November revolution in 1918 I had often been brooding about one question. I wondered why in open contradiction to Prussian-German history, a nation should now be expected to become free and happy by catering to human traits which a well-bred child was taught to consider vicious. I saw the consequences of this immorality. I saw hunger and need in the poorest classes, but I also saw debauchery and carousing. People whose nature was foreign to me and who were called Jews, who had no manly character and no

moral discipline, had become rich and drank in restaurants and
laughed at the soldiers from the front.

The experiences of the war came back to my mind. I saw
the Cossacks ride through the fields, saw the skies reddened by
burning villages and thought of friends and relatives who had
fallen somewhere in the east and the west. They had been the
best men, and now a Jew who had never seen the terrors of the
war dared to desecrate a hero's death as well as all the virtues
of a German soldier. My inward aversion to these men of a
foreign race which had crucified the Savior and which now was
betraying our people increased until one day it grew into
hatred. The Jew was at fault for all the misery.

On the model of the older youths, we boys joined in a group.
Since Easter 1919 I had been attending the gymnasium. We
were twenty boys, of whom I was the leader. We proudly
called our association the "German Youth Batallion." We
marched erect like soldiers. Proudly we wore the swastika
and the black-white-and-red bow in our buttonholes. Soldiers'
songs were sung and stories of German history told. We held
our heads high and drew ourselves up proudly; we carried with
us our noble history into the future. We had become German
nationalists.

So the summer of 1923 passed. The national movement
grew from day to day. In Tilsit we already ruled the street.
The occupation of the Ruhr followed. The national conscience
was violently aroused. The nation was ready to oppose the
enemy. Expectantly we looked toward Berlin. Nothing however, happened. As a sign of mourning we covered the emblems on our caps with crepe. Prussia was put under martial
law. At the end of September and beginning of October 1923
our group went to participate in a rally of youth associations.
Proudly we unrolled our flag and marched into German Danzig singing, "Hindenburg and Ludendorff are not dead and
gone; they will bring us yet the dawn." The people of Danzig
watched us with enthusiasm. This old German Hanseatic city

made a deep impression on us. Everything we saw was German—the towers, the churches. Everything emanated glorious German history. It had been taken away from us. We returned home bearing these impressions.

Then came November 9, 1923.

Great and brilliant, the name of Adolf Hitler, which we heard not for the first time in these agitated days, appeared before us. We all were marching in step; we all had the same desire to wipe out the existing system which had come into power by betrayal of the people and the country. We did not know, however, what we should put in its place. We did not want pre-war conditions either. We wanted something that was to grow out of the common experience of the war and the front, that would know no estates and classes but only the German people. The word, Hitler, became for me a symbol of our future. Those who had fallen before the *Feldherrnhalle* in Munich became martyrs. I preserved the memory of this great event deep in my heart, even throughout the years when it seemed as though everything must drown in materialism and individualism. In Tilsit also everything seemed to go to ruin. The result of the inflation made by the Jews impoverished the nation. What wretchedness it caused me to know that old people, widows, and orphans were innocently suffering need and misery! Loans from foreign countries stimulated in the cities a prosperity which never existed. I myself never felt the blessings of the foreign loans. At Easter 1926 I left the gymnasium and went home to the farm. Here Dame Care was our guest. Scarcity of funds necessitated borrowing at usurious rates of interest. Since the loans could not be paid back the day they were due, they were added to the debts, so that these grew unbearable in a short time. Now in order to preserve the property, the soil had to be exploited to the limit as much as possible, and at the same time we had to curtail our expenditures for personal needs. It sometimes surpassed human power. Always the Jew was the obligingly smiling money-lender and

devilishly grinning collector of debts. Thus it went on until
1931. The greater our need became, the more deeply the farmer
attached himself to the soil. Everyone felt that if he had to
leave the soil his life would be destroyed, uprooted; he would
be rushing headlong to the end. Farmers' associations were
formed to take up the battle against the existing system, to
prevent bankrupt sales by force and to boycott tax collections.
Any method employed to defend the soil was for self-defense
and therefore appeared just. An attempt was made to form a
farmers' front in order to gain a majority in parliament. I have
always fought against this in my circle of acquaintances. My
idea was: first, it would be difficult to get the farmers together
into one camp; and, second, I was opposed to government of a
class. All classes of the people should have an equal share in
the blessings of a rational national policy. Was it strange,
therefore, that I again returned to the man for whose national
idea men of all classes, from the workman to the scholar, had
once gone to their death? No, I wanted no rule of the farmers,
because I knew that then the class struggle would really begin
in earnest. Besides, the farmers lacked leaders. I did not want
the work of conservatives, owners of large estates either, for
they rejected any kind of socialism. But in order to win the
laborer back to the people, one had to acknowledge socialism.
The landowners had in the past committed grave errors. The
workman was simply regarded as a tool who had to work for
money and had no higher claims, and that was the end of it.

In March 1931, after a short quarrel with my father, I left
my home and went out into the world. The reason for this step
was a difference of opinion about the management of the farm.
I had made the firm decision to mingle with the people, for a
while to be a workman among workmen. Through the employment bureau at Ragnit I was sent to Schillehnen on the
Memel to take the position of a coachman. I felt at home there
because I found that the people living there on the Lithuanian
border were true Germans.

If up to now I had been a National Socialist from the farmer's point of view, I now had the best opportunity to study the laborer's problem. In doing this, one thing became clear to me. The class prejudices of those in higher positions must first disappear from the nation before the back of the class struggle can be broken. I recognized the longing of the working people for acknowledgment of their achievements. Often I caught the most stubborn Marxist in an unconscious acknowledgment of his nation and homeland. It became clear to me that we must fight for the erring soul of the workman. Sons of farmers and agricultural laborers later became the best National Socialists. In political discussions I often took advantage of the opportunity to make recruits for National Socialism. In the course of this I made the discovery that the poorest brothers were often the best Germans, and on the other hand the wealthiest were often the greatest traitors to the people. My recognition of our true enemies caused in me an ardent love for the working people.

In the summer of 1931 I changed my position and went to Szillen. Here, too, hard work from morning to night helped me to find my way to the soul of the workman.

National Socialism had become my inner conviction and I was firmly rooted in it. . . . In July 1931 the treasurer of the local group at Szillen approached me with an invitation to join the party and I did so immediately. . . .

On November 1 I returned home to my parents. That same month I was determined to take an active part in the work of the Party. I wanted to help, to fight, and to suffer for the idea of our leader; I wanted to found a local group of the Party. I consulted the district leader, who advised me to organize a group in my home district. Filled with courage and confident of victory, I began my recruiting. I went from house to house, from farm to farm. What disappointment! Men who had always talked about themselves as if they were extremely ardent nationalists refused their aid. A few farmer's sons and young field laborers joined me. These first members are still our best. They grasped National Socialism not with their mind but with their emotions. They had not learned National Socialism from books. Their blood, their natural instincts drove them to the movement. Like myself, they sought the road to the people and, like myself, found it by ridding themself of class consciousness and seeing only the fellow-countryman in every good German. We gave something to the simple man: we strengthened his soul. Of a member of the socalled middle class, however, we made demands. We required that he step down from his assumed position of superiority and reach out his hand to the poorest of the nation and recognize him as a brother. The bourgeois who were so eager to use the word "nationalist" gave us the most trouble, but we recognized our true enemies. They were and still are not in the working class, but in the philistine middle class circles. Selfishness and ill will have always been their guiding stars. The middle class had the fate of the people on its conscience. Members of this class made possible the November revolution with its devastating consequences. Now that things were going badly with them they were constantly falling back upon the word "national." They inveighed against the taxes and the wages of the workmen; they wished again for the times when they were the lords. At the beer table they talked about the resurrection of the Fatherland, but they became quiet as mice when a Red entered the restaurant. If one called upon them to coöperate actively they usually did not have time. They were pleased when we fought against the Marxist and grumbled when we asked them to contribute to the battle fund. It was clear that in my district I should have to take up the struggle first of all against the philistine farmers, for they formed the reactionaries. The workman would find the way back to his people, without much urging.

Early in 1932 our home met with a serious affliction. The most valuable brood-mare, recognized as one of the best in

East Prussia, died of an internal hemorrhage five days after the birth of a colt. I myself had travelled with her from exhibition to exhibition. She had won first prizes in Berlin, Königsberg, Insterburg, and other cities. Now I had to watch her die, and what a death! The animal, still in her best years, reared up against her death; she did not want to die, but the hour came and with it pain for the entire family. We had loved the animal too much, indeed we adored it. My mother cried for days; even I was not ashamed to shed tears for my dear comrade. Then I took refuge in the movement. Even though the pain was great and the loss irremediable, yet in the service of the Party greater, mightier things were at stake. With doubled zeal I plunged into party work. March came. The presidential election was at hand. The deliberate lies told in the meetings of government supporters can hardly be repeated. We, however, carried on the battle openly and honestly. Hitler directed us and strengthened us. Courageous in our faith in the idea and our leader, we plunged into the combat. When I look back to the time, I am proud to think that never for a moment did I doubt our victory. Even the ban on the *S.A.* could not curb us. They could dissolve our *S.A.* ten times, but they could not forbid the *S.A.* men to live on this earth; they could not prevent him from voluntarily submitting to the Leader.

The Leader wanted to gain power by legal means. Therefore we also fought legally. Powerless, our opponents had to see that they could charge us with nothing. Then Bruening and Groener fell and with them went the ban on the *S.A.* and the wearing of uniforms. The movement grew rapidly. Even in my province people gradually began to take the movement seriously. The Babbits were pleased with us. After all they hoped that we would now give a death blow to the hated regime. They hoped then that they would get higher prices for their produce and would have to pay lower wages. The common people would have to learn to obey again. Those were approximately the thoughts and the hopes that they pinned on the assumption of power by the Nazis! In the course of this vigorous and joyful struggle, I often left my home for days and thereby aroused my father's displeasure, for he needed me as a farmhand. However, I did not take his moral sermons seriously any more. I was convinced that all our work and daily toil was in vain if we did not destroy the prevailing order and erect a new Third Reich on its ruins.

How miserable and petty were the election speeches, from Marxists to conservatives! One shouted, "Proletarians of all countries, unite!" The other saw the salvation of the nation in economic planning; the third granted the right to exist only to the farmer; the fourth even saw fit to suggest the founding a new party on the issue of revaluating the inflation currency. They fought "bravely and courageously" for Reichstag and Landtag seats and wondered why the people wanted to have no more to do with them. All these parties promised a great deal but kept none of their promises. We, however, promised nothing and caused much to be expected. Just the lie could be read in the faces of those representatives of vested interests. We stuck to the truth, and thus the Party was able to overcome victoriously all obstacles and crises, in contrast to the parties of the regime, which suffocated in the web of their own lies.

In July the Leader came to Tilsit. I saw him for the first time. About 40,000 people from near and far had gathered to greet him. I wore the brown shirt for the first time. Those hours are never to be forgotten. The Leader spoke. For the first time I heard his voice. His words went straight to the heart. From now on my life and efforts were dedicated to the Leader. I wanted to be a true follower. The Leader spoke of the threatened ruin of the nation and of the resurrection under the Third Reich. What matter personal interests, and social status? How insignificant had all parties become to my eyes!

How despicable was Communism, whose champions attempted to interrupt this meeting and had to be driven away by force.

A few days later we were in Königsberg. Truck after truck filled with brown shirts. In the streets flag after flag. And flowers! A review of the East Prussia *S.A.* by the Leader. I was able to get a place near the Leader; the review lasted for hours. What an enormous effort for the Leader to hold up his hand constantly. In his face one could see clearly the play of his muscles. I admired the energy with which he fought against weariness. This energy was almost uncanny. It was the same energy that directed a movement involving millions and brought it closer to its final victory. It was the same energy that suppressed the wish to strike out when the legal way seemed momentarily to be closed. We all gained something of this energy. We spoke more urgently when people did not wish to believe us. We remained firm when everything wavered about us. It was clear that we were bound to win if we kept control of our nerves. Another thing the Leader gave us was faith in the German people. If we won, Germany was saved; if we were defeated, a gate would open up in the east and Moscow's Red hordes would swarm in and plunge Europe into night and misery. We had to conquer for the sake of the world, for the sake of Europe. Germany's fate, however, was most important to us. Without the Leader I could not conceive how we could have carried on this enormous struggle. His name was too closely interwoven with everything that happened. He had created the movement; he had led it upward; he was now knocking on the gates of power. The confidence of all of us was boundless.

The thirteenth of August, when the Leader said "No!" [the reference is to Hitler's refusal to accept the position of Vice-Chancellor] brought the first test of the movement, which was millions strong. The Marxists rejoiced: Now it's over with the Nazis. The bourgeois shook their heads thoughtfully. Why did not Hitler grab the opportunity? Vice-

Chancellor is a fine position, too. To become Chancellor is asking a bit too much. After all, Hitler is only a simple man of the people. Chancellor? No, for he must be a highly educated man. And the Nazis altogether are wanting in leaders. Brains? They belong to the conservatives. They are old, experienced men, one of whom said quite correctly, *"Vox populi, vox Rindvieh."* (The voice of the people is the voice of cattle.) Yes, the Nazis have the numbers, but we have the heads. The Nazis should be modest again; they should recognize the conservatives as leaders. They should drop their socialism. And then, with such a common platform, we could win Marxism; we would show it to the workmen!

The hardest battle began. It was clear that they wanted to put us on the defensive. There was, however, one thing which pleased me immeasurably: in the battle with the reaction we could prove to the workmen that we wanted to deal honestly with them. They saw that we were protecting them from the ambitions of the reactionaries. We were loyal to them. The November election brought what we had expected, a small decrease in votes. Those who had voted half-heartedly for us in July had left us and now had lost interest completely. My greatest pride is that in the November election of 1932 I did not lose a single vote in my district.

While our Leader was preparing for the decisive blow in the state of Lippe, I employed my time in enlarging and strengthening the local group. Then came January 30. The gates of power were opened; we entered with iron discipline. We might have avenged ourselves bitterly, but we disdained to do so. Our love for our nation was so great that petty plans for revenge had no room. Day and night we sacrificed ourselves for the reconstruction of the nation. Our quick tempo drew along the diffident ones. Then came the longed-for hour when the web of lies of miserable seducers of the people was torn apart. The workman in the office or behind the plow, the one behind an anvil and in the mines, the government employee, the farmer, the artisan—all had their faith in Germany restored.

We, however, swore faith and obedience to our Leader, an oath which I shall keep to the death.

APPENDICES

Appendix I

Chronology of the Hitler Movement

February 24 First mass meeting of the National Socialist party in Munich, at the Hofbrauhaus. Hitler proclaims the 25 theses of the National Socialist program.

March 13-17 Kapp *Putsch*. Hitler flies with Eckart to Berlin to take part in it, but arrives too late.

December 17 Purchase of the first National Socialist newspaper, *Völkische Beobachter,* Herrmann Esser, first editor. (Alfred Rosenberg, editor since March 1923.)

1921

January 21 Annual National Socialist meeting. Anton Drechsler elected chairman. Reported membership about 3,000. During the past year 42 mass meetings were held by the Party.

February 3 First mass meeting in the largest hall in Munich, the "Zirkus Krone." Hitler speaks to about 6,500 listeners on "Future or Destruction."

May-June Hitler visits Berlin to establish contact with the North German Nationalists.

July 29 First incident of internal dissention in the Party. Hitler enforces acceptance on his conditions, becomes chairman in place of Drechsler, and is given special powers to reorganize the Party and substitute the principle of personal responsibility for majority decisions.

August 3   Organization of the Storm Troops (*S.A.*).

October 11   Organization of the first local group outside of Bavaria, in Zwickau.

November 4   First large-scale battle at a mass meeting, between members of the Social Democratic party and the recently organized Storm Troops.

1922

January 29   Reported membership about 6,000. (During the past year 81 mass meetings had been held by the Party.)

June 24-
July 27   First imprisonment of Hitler for breach of peace.

August 16   The National Socialist party, together with other nationalist organizations, participates in a mass demonstration against the "Decree for the Protection of the Republic," which was enacted after the assassination of Rathenau.

December 10 Ten mass meetings of the Party in Munich in one day. Subject: "Jewish International Marxism and Freemasonry as Germany's Grave Diggers."

1923

January 26   Twelve mass meetings on one day in protest against the occupation of the Ruhr.

June 16   Annual meeting of the National Socialist party, together with patriotic organizations to honor the memory of Leo Schlageter, executed by the French in the Ruhr.

September 25 Hitler becomes political leader of the German *Kampfbund,* a union of all nationalistic societies in Bavaria. The *S.A.* became part of the military organizations of the *Kampfbund* early in February.

November 8-9 Hitler proclaims a national revolution and dictatorship. Suppression of the *Putsch* by the Bavarian police who shot at the marching National Socialists before the *Feldherrnhalle* in Munich. Fourteen party members killed, many wounded. Hitler flees.

November 11 Arrest of Hitler, also of General Ludendorff and a score of other leaders of the *Putsch.* Dissolution of the Nazi party. (At the time it had 55,787 enlisted members.)

1924

February 24	Beginning of the trial of Hitler and his co-defendents. Hitler sentenced to 5 years' imprisonment in a fortress.
May 4	Nationalists obtain nearly two million votes in Reichstag election.
December 7	Nationalists, who opposed the signing of the Dawes pact, secure only 900,000 votes in new Reichstag election.
December 20	Freed, Hitler leaves the fortress of Lansberg where he was held prisoner.

1925

February 24	First mass meeting after Hitler's return to Munich. Reorganization of the National Socialist party.
March 9	Bavaria, Saxony, Prussia, etc., issue a decree barring public appearances of Hitler. (Ban lifted September 1928.)
July 18	Publication of the first volume of *Mein Kampf*.

1926

February 20	Organization of the "National Socialist Union of University Students."
July 3-4	Second National assembly of the Party in Weimar. (The first was held in Munich January 1923.) Organization of the "Hitler Youth."
November 1	Dr. Joseph Goebbels takes over the leadership of the Party in the district Berlin-Brandenburg.
December 11	Publication of the second volume of *Mein Kampf*.

1927

February 11	First great battle at a meeting in Berlin in the *Pharushalle*.
May 5	The Nazi Party banned in Berlin. (Ban lifted March 31, 1928.)
July 4	First appearance of Goebbels's newspaper *Der Angriff*.
August 19-23	Third National Assembly of the National Socialist party in Nuremberg.

1928

May 20 — Reichstags election. The Party obtains 809,000 votes (2.6 per cent of total).

October 11 — Organization of the "National Socialist Union of Lawyers."

November 16 — Hitler's first appearance in Berlin in the Sport Palace, scene of his greatest oratorical triumphs.

1929

June 23 — The Party obtains for the first time an absolute majority in a city election (Koburg).

August 1-4 — Fourth National Assembly of the Party in Nuremberg. Organization of the "National Socialist Union of Physicians."

December 8 — First significant electoral victory of the Party in a provincial election in Thuringia (11.3 per cent of the total votes).

1930

January 23 — First appointment of a National Socialist to the post of minister (Dr. Frick in Thuringia).

February 23 — Death of Horst Wessel, creator of the anthem of the movement. Mass demonstration at the cemetery.

June 1 — Darré entrusted with the organization of the German peasants.

July 5 — The Brown House in Munich becomes general headquarters of the Party.

September 2 — Hitler takes over supreme command of the *S.A.* and *S.S.* (100,000 members).

September 14 — Reichstag election. The Party obtains 6,406,000 votes (18.3 per cent of the total electoral vote). Next to the Social Democratic party, the National Socialist party the strongest parliamentary group in the Reichstag.

December 6 — Beginning of a concerted campaign led by the National Socialist party against the Bruening government in the Reichstag. The number of unemployed reported to have passed the four million mark.

1931

January 15 — Beginning of the organization of Nazi units in industrial establishments.

March 28 First "emergency measure" of the Bruening government directed against the National Socialist party.

April 1 Second incident of dissention in the Party. Revolt of Stennes against Hitler. (Revolt suppressed by April 12.)

May 1 Goering sent by Hitler to confer with Mussolini.

May 17 In the provincial election at Oldenburg, the National Socialist party obtains 37.2 per cent of the total vote, and becomes for the first time the strongest political group in a provincial diet.

July 9 First conference between Hitler and Hugenberg, the leader of the conservative German-National party, aiming at the organization of a concerted national opposition against the republican regime.

July 17 Second "emergency measure" of Bruening, restricting the freedom of the press.

September 12 First large-scale anti-Semitic outbreak, initiated by the *S.A.* against Jews in the streets of Berlin.

October 1 Organization of the "Union of National Socialist Women," under Elisabeth Fander.

October 6 Third "emergency measure" of Bruening, enpowering the police to close Nazi meeting places and *S.A.* houses.

October 11 Creation of the "Harzburg Front," the national opposition against the government under the leadership of Hitler, Hugenberg, Schacht, and Seldte (head of the *Stahlhelm* organization of veterans).

October 17 General assembly of the Storm Troops in Brunswick, 104,000 *S.A.* and *S.S.* march in a six-hour parade before Hitler.

December 8 Fourth "emergency measure" of Bruening forbidding the wearing of uniforms and party insignia. The number of unemployed has passed the five million mark.

1932

February 25 Hitler announces his candidacy for President of the Reich.

March 13 First presidential election. Hitler obtains 11.33 million votes (Hindenburg, 18.65 million, the Communist candidate Thaelmann 4.98 million).

April 5 Minister of Interior Groener orders dissolution of the *S.A.* and *S.S.* (Decree enacted April 13.)

April 10   Second presidential election. Hindenburg elected President with 19.35 million votes, against Hitler's 13.41 million and Thaelmann's 3.7 million.

April 24   In all elections to provincial diets (except in Bavaria) the National Socialist party emerges strongest.

May 29   First visit of Hitler to Hindenburg after the organization of the Bruening government. Papen appointed Chancellor.

July 13   Election to the Reichstag. The National Socialist party obtains 36.9 per cent of the total electoral vote.

July 17   "Bloody Sunday." Communists and National Socialists fight pitched battles in many cities.

August 13   Second conference between Hindenburg and Hitler. Hitler refuses position of Vice-Chancellor.

November 6   Election to the Reichstag. The National Socialist party obtains 33.1 per cent of the total vote, losing 2 million votes from the July election total.

November 19   Third conference between Hitler and Hindenburg after the resignation of the Papen cabinet. Hindenburg rejects Hitler's conditions for participation in a new cabinet. General Schleicher appointed Chancellor.

December 8   Third incident of dissention in the Nazi party. Revolt lead by George Strasser against Hitler. Strasser, former leader of the National Socialist faction in the Reichstag, leaves the Party. Number of unemployed nearly six million.

1933

January 15   In the provincial elections in Lippe the National Socialist party regains the prestige lost in the November 1932 election by polling 39.6 per cent of the total vote (as against 34.7 per cent National Socialist vote of Lippe in the last Reichstag election).

January 28   Resignation of the Schleicher cabinet.

January 30   Hitler appointed Chancellor of the Reich by Hindenburg.

Appendix II

Statistics

A. *The Growth of the Movement*

1. *Number of members in the National Socialist party*

1920 (January)	64
1921 (January) about	3,000
1922 (January) about	6,000
1923 (November)	55,787
1924 (Party dissolved)	
1925 (December)	27,117
1926	49,523
1927	72,590
1928	108,717
1929	176,426
1930	389,000
1931	806,294
1932 (April) about	1,000,000

2. *Number of supporters in elections*

Reichstag election	May 20, 1928	810,000
Reichstag election	September 14, 1930	6,406,400
Presidential election	March 13, 1932	11,341,400
Presidential election	April 10, 1932	13,418,000
Reichstag election	July 31, 1932	13,745,781
Reichstag election	November 6, 1932	11,737,386
Reichstag election	March 5, 1933	17,277,180

B. *General Statistical Data*

In the introduction on pp. 4-5 are some data on the age, occupation, and class membership of our contributors, as well as information on the year in which they joined the Party. The following summary provides additional information on the six hundred authors of the life histories.

1. *Geographical distribution*

TABLE V

Place of Birth	No.	Per cent
Not given	13	2
Northern Germany	222	37
Central Germany	174	29
Southern Germany	177	30
Outside of Germany	14	2
	600	100

TABLE VI

Residence	No.	Per Cent
Rural	98	16
Town	303	51
City	199	33
	600	100

2. *Education*

TABLE VII

School	No.	Per Cent
Not given	67	11
Public school	329	55
Professional school	50	8
High school	123	21
University	31	5
	600	100

TABLE VIII

Home Influence	No.	Per Cent
Not given	401	67
Nationalistic	165	27
Social Democratic and Communistic	34	6
	600	100

3. Religion and marital status

TABLE IX

Religious Denominations	No.	Per Cent
Not reported	373	62
Catholic	59	10
Protestant	168	28
	600	100

TABLE X

Marital Status	No.	Per Cent
Married	290	48
Not reported	310	52
	600	100

4. History of employment (1919-32)

TABLE XI

Changed	Occupation		Job		Residence	
Never	521	87%	376	63%	474	79%
Once	66	11	65	11	33	5
Twice	11	2	81	13	43	7
Thrice	1		31	5	21	4
Four times ..	1		13	2	8	1
Five times ...			34	6	21	4
	600	100	600	100	600	100

TABLE XII

Were Unemployed	No.	Per Cent
Never	479	80
Once	90	15
Twice	27	4
Thrice	3	1
Four times	0	
Five times	1	
	600	100

5. Military activities

TABLE XIII

Participation in World War	No.	Per Cent
None	293	49
Volunteer	76	13
Conscript	231	38
	600	100

TABLE XIV

Participation in Military Activities After War	No.	Per Cent
Yes	109	18
No	491	82
	600	100

6. *Membership in organizations before joining the National Socialist party*

TABLE XV

Political Parties	No.	Per Cent
None	407	68
Nationalist	139	23
Democratic	12	2
Socialist and Communist	42	7
	600	100

TABLE XVI

Semi-Military Organizations	No.	Per Cent
None	414	69
Veterans' organizations	75	12
National youth organizations	101	17
Socialist and Communist youth organizations	10	2
	600	100

7. *Miscellaneous data*

TABLE XVII

First Contacts with National Socialist Party	No.	Per Cent
Not given	106	18
Friend	96	16
Co-worker	32	5
Meetings	199	33
Family influence	18	3
Printed material	149	25
	600	100

TABLE XVIII

Economic Status at Time of Joining National Socialist Party	*No.*	*Per Cent*
Not reported	39	6
Unemployed	47	8
In economic difficulties	36	6
Economically secure	478	80
	600	100

TABLE XIX

Economic Status as Result of Joining National Socialist Party	*No.*	*Per Cent*
Not reported	42	7
Lost employment	32	5
Got into economic difficulties	40	7
No change	480	80
Improved position	6	1
	600	100

INDEX

Index

A

Abel, Theodore, 186n
Aggressiveness as a factor, 177
Ahrand, 163
Anti-Semitism, 8, 60, 154ff.
  opposition to, 163-164
Army, attitude of:
  in 1918, 20-21
  in 1933, 110
Artamane movement, 51
Authority, 147n, 150
Autobiographies:
  clues in, 23, 39, 69, 99, 135, 148,
    153, 176, 193-194
  omissions in, 8
  reliability of, 7
  statistical data, 44, 51, 65, 80-81,
    89, 100, 121-122, 164n, 170n

B

Bismarck, 17
Black Reichswehr, 22, 41-44
Blockade, 32
Bolshevism, 110 (*see also* Communists)
Bothmer, Count v., 55
Brady, R. E., 199-200
Bruening, 94, 198

C

Capistrano, 161
Catholic Church, opposition to Hitlerism, 97
Causes of the Hitler movement, summary of, 184-185
Chamberlain, H. S., 162
Charismatic Leadership:
  basis of, 151ff.
  clues to, 182
  defined, 67
  function of, 180ff.
Clark, R. T., 1n
Class system, opposition to, 139ff.
Communists, 16, 19, 30, 74, 99,
  105, 132ff., 173-174, 185
Councils, Workers' and Soldiers',
  19, 20, 21, 27
Confidence, role of, 176
Conflict, 88, 89ff.

D

Dawes Plan, 75
Der Angriff, 116
Deutsch Nationale Volkspartei, 52,
  128-130
Dictatorship, 68-73
Discontent:
  basis of, 121ff.
  nature of, 168-169

Explanation of Number Symbols

Each quotation from the life histories is preceded by three numbers. The purpose of the numbering is to give to the reader information in each case on the age and occupation of the informant and the duration of his membership in the National Socialist party. The first number gives the age group to which the informant belongs. The second number refers to the respective occupational group. The third number states the period in which the informant joined the Party. For example: A notation [2.3.4.] means that the person from whose life history the quotation is taken belongs to age group 2 (was 27-33 years old in 1934), that he was employed in industry, and that he joined the Party in 1930-31.

Age Groups

		Age in 1934
1. Post-war generation	....	20—26
2. War generation	....	27—33
3. War volunteers	....	34—40
4. War conscripts	....	41—59
5. Old generation	....	60 and over

Occupational Groups

0. Not reported.
1. Mining.
2. Agriculture.
3. Industry.
4. Trade.
5. Personal service.
6. Professional.
7. Clerical occupations.
8. Government service.

Year of Joining National Socialist Party

0. Not reported.
1. 1920-24
2. 1925-27
3. 1928-29
4. 1930-31
5. 1932-33